The public employment service in a changing labour market

D1427387

5405600050450

The public employment service in a changing labour market

Phan Thuy,
Ellen Hansen
and David Price

INTERNATIONAL LABOUR OFFICE • GENEVA

Phan, T; Hansen, E; Price, D.

The public employment service in a changing labour market
Geneva, International Labour Office, 2001

Employment service, job placement, developed country, developing country. 13.02.4

ISBN 92-2-111388-4

ILO Cataloguing-in-Publication Data

Printed and bound in Great Britain by Biddles Ltd, *www.biddles.co.uk*

PREFACE

Over the last two decades, economic liberalization and globalization have altered the world economy and as a result, market forces have been playing a more dominant role in both capital and labour markets. At the same time, expectations for government services have become more demanding while resources have often been constrained. These changes have had a significant impact on the public employment service (PES).

The 1990s have seen numerous reforming initiatives in the PES intended to improve operational efficiency and service quality, particularly in developed countries. These initiatives represent a substantial shift away from the traditional bureaucratic PES towards a PES that is both more customer oriented and more closely integrated into other areas of government activity such as social security administration and economic and social development. Although these reforms clearly offer a number of benefits to the PES, they have also contributed to an environment of turmoil and to growing tensions between competing values and goals.

At the beginning of the new millennium, the challenges facing the PES are considerable. External problems affecting the PES are numerous: structural unemployment; social exclusion; the vulnerability of many workers because of a shortage of decent work; less stability in employment and careers; an increasing demand for lifelong learning; public concern about the escalating costs of social security; the ending of the PES monopoly in many countries; and a multiplicity of public and private labour market actors. Factors affecting the PES as an organization include pressures to reduce resources and the tendency to introduce more competition in the delivery of public services.

International Labour Organization (ILO) support for the PES goes back to the inaugural labour conference in Washington, DC, 1919, when through the Unemployment Convention (No. 2), the establishment of a public employment service in member States was recommended. In 1948, the International Labour

Conference adopted the Employment Service Convention (No. 88) concerning the organization of the employment service. In most countries, the PES started as a national job-broking organization, often with a monopoly in placement as stipulated by the Fee-Charging Employment Agencies Convention, 1933 (No. 34) and the Fee-Charging Employment Agencies Convention (Revised), 1949 (No. 96). Over the last two decades, however, the PES monopoly in placement has been challenged by the liberalization and deregulation of placement services and by the exponential growth of private employment agencies (PREAs). These changes have led to the revision of Convention No. 96. The Private Employment Agencies Convention (No. 181) adopted in June 1997, recognizes the contribution of PREAs in the functioning of the labour market and in the protection of temporary workers; it also advocates cooperation between the PES and PREAs. It is therefore appropriate that in the turmoil of a changing labour market, the ILO should review the recent developments regarding the PES and suggest guidelines for the future.

This publication is the first major ILO publication on the PES since Sergio Ricca's book *Les services de l'emploi: leur nature, leur mandat et leurs fonctions* was published in 1982. It has been written for those in government who are concerned with employment policies affecting the PES and also for PES managers who themselves face these challenges every day. This publication examines the *why, what* and *how* of recent reforms undertaken by the PES in various countries. After first describing the history and current labour market context of the PES, it describes the overall role and four major functions of the PES and how these are evolving. There follows a review of the management and partnership challenges that are critical to the success of the modern PES. Finally, there is an exploration of how present reforms might evolve in the future. It is argued that if the present drive towards reform is to be beneficial, a balance will need to be struck both between competing values and goals on the one hand, and between stability (which allows continuous gradual improvement) and radical change (which results from an uncertain and constantly changing environment) on the other. Furthermore, no matter how efficient the PES may be, its effectiveness depends in part on the coherence of the employment policy of the government it serves.

This publication was prepared by the Employment Services Unit as part of the 1998–99 work programme of the Labour Administration Branch in the former Industrial Relations and Labour Administration Department of the ILO. It is based on twelve country studies prepared by national experts on Argentina, Canada, France, Japan, the Netherlands, Norway, Poland, Spain, Tunisia, the United Kingdom, the United States and Hong Kong, China. In addition, it uses information and comments collected from meetings and workshops organized by the Organisation for Economic Co-operation and Development (OECD), the European Commission (EC) and the World Association of Public Employment Services (WAPES). We are grateful for the quality of the work that was done and for all the help we have received from PES managers and experts in many countries.

It should be noted that the information provided in this publication is based on policies and practices that were in operation in 1998 and 1999 and these are subject to change. In order to allow readers to find more current information or to explore topics in detail, an annex of relevant web sites has been included. It should also be noted that the strategies needed to combat the marginalization of various special groups such as women, workers with disabilities, displaced workers and unemployed young people are not dealt with in depth, as they are covered by other ILO publications. This publication, however, does review the contribution of the PES to the administration of these programmes. Finally, it should be recognized that resource and time constraints made it impossible to undertake an in-depth study of the different issues faced by the PES in many developing countries, though some general thoughts are presented about these issues in the conclusion.

I wish to thank Jean Courdouan, Chief of the former Labour Administration Branch, and his colleagues Bjorn Dolvik, Yves Malépart, Junko Nakayama and Gregor Schulz; the two experts Ralph Cantrell and Vincent Merle for their valuable contributions (particularly Ralph Cantrell who prepared the first draft of Chapter 8). My thanks also go to Ruby Correya, Sol Dobberstein and Jane Trotter for their administrative and secretarial support.

H.T. Perret-Nguyên
International Institute for Labour Studies
(Former Director, Industrial Relations and
Labour Administration Department)

CONTENTS

Preface   v

Executive summary xv

1   Origins and historical evolution   1
    Introduction   1
    Origins   1
    Between the Wars   3
    1945 to the mid-1970s   4
    Trends since the mid-1970s   5
    Conclusion   8

2   The changing labour market   9
    Introduction   9
    Demographic and social trends   9
    Global forces for change 11
    The public sector 13
    Occupational change 14
    The flexible labour market 14
    Unemployment 16
    Inequality and social exclusion 17
    Conclusion 18

3   Role, functions and resources of the public employment service 21
    Introduction 21
    Rationale, role and mandate 21
    Legal status and institutional character 23
    Mission and strategy 24

The PES in the European Union 25
The PES in North America 26
The PES in South-East Asia 26
Functions 27
Resources 29
Current evolution of the PES 34
Current trends in developed countries 35
Current trends in transition countries 36
Current trends in developing countries 36
Issues facing the PES at the turn of millennium 37

4   **Job-broking** 41
Introduction 41
General aspects of job-broking 42
Registering jobseekers and vacancies 43
Marketing PES services 45
Job-matching and information display methods 45
Innovations and good practices by the PES 48
Self-help services and enhanced personalized services 50
Measuring the impact of job-broking 52
Conclusion 53

5   **Labour market information** 57
Introduction 57
PES roles in labour market information 58
LMI as a by-product of PES functions 58
The PES as a producer of primary labour market statistics 60
Synthesizing, interpreting and distributing labour market information 61
Trends in service delivery 65
Increasing demand for information 65
Alternative labour market information service providers 65
Innovations in labour market information analysis 66
Innovations in LMI dissemination/self-service LMI 67
Conclusion 67

6   **Administration of labour market adjustment programmes** 71
Introduction 71
Governments and labour market adjustment programmes 72
The PES and labour market adjustment programmes 73
Kinds of adjustment programmes 73

Job-search assistance 74
Training and education programmes 81
Direct job creation programmes 83
Innovations and good practices in integrated market adjustment programmes . . . 86
    Vocational rehabilitation programmes 86
    Mass lay-off programmes 87
    Welfare-to-work programmes 88
Effectiveness of labour market adjustment policies 90
    What works? 91
Conclusion 92

7   **Unemployment benefits and the public employment service** 97
Introduction 97
The main forms of unemployment benefit 97
Unemployment benefits: General policy issues 99
The PES role in unemployment benefit 101
    Job-search assistance or re-employment services 101
Continuing eligibility and job-search verification 105
Overall unemployment benefit programme administration 106
Conclusion: Trends and issues 107

8   **Organizing and managing the service** 111
Introduction 111
Governmental framework and accountability 112
    Stakeholders 112
    Strategic and operational planning 113
    Performance management 115
    Evaluation of programmes 119
Organizational issues 119
    Decentralization 119
    Integration of services 121
    Competitive service delivery 126
Management strategies and tools 129
    Quality management 129
    The use of information and communications technology 135
    Facilities planning and management 137
    Internal communications 138
    Staff training and development 139
Conclusion 142

9   **The PES and other organizations** 145
     Introduction 145
     Relationships with the social partners 146
     Relationships with governmental institutions and other national bodies 147
     Relationships with local partners 148
     Relationships with PREAs 151
     Networking among public employment services 155
     Conclusion 156

10   **Conclusions** 159
     Introduction 159
     General conclusions 159
     Responsiveness to the external environment 160
     Relations with government 160
     Integrated service delivery 161
     A new kind of service enterprise 162
     Special factors affecting the PES in developing countries 163
     Dilemmas facing the public employment service 165

ANNEXES

I   Glossary of terms 171
II   Main functions and tasks of the PES 175
III Public expenditure in labour market programmes as a percentage
     of GDP in 26 OECD countries, 1997 178
IV   Examples of PES innovations and good practices 181
     IV.1 Canada: Setting up computerized kiosks 181
     IV.2 France: Computerized operational repertory of occupations
           and jobs (ROME) 182
     IV.3 Japan: Overall employment information system (OEIS) 185
     IV.4 Mexico: National employment information service system 186
     IV.5 Slovenia: Use of internet technology 188
     IV.6 Sweden: Customer self-service systems on the Internet 190
     IV.7 United Kingdom: Employment Service Direct: A telephone
           jobs hotline 194
     IV.8 United States: America's Career Kit (ACK) – Internet employment
           services system 194
     IV.9 France: *Fichier historique* (FH) – A history file of jobseekers
           registered at the ANPE 197
     IV.10 The Netherlands: The *Kansmeter* – A new instrument for the
           administrative intake of jobseekers 198

IV.11 France: New tools and services for job-search assistance 200

IV.12 United States: Integrated menu of employer services – The case
of the Racine County Workforce Development Centre (WDC)
in Wisconsin 203

IV.13 United States: Successful state practices in job-broking -
An assessment study 204

IV.14 Sweden: Customer workstations – Self-service for jobseekers 208

IV.15 Denmark: Local labour market monitoring 210

IV.16 Canada: Local labour market information 211

IV.17 Finland:Activation and improvement of individual employment
service processes (job-search assistance) as part of a comprehensive
labour market policy reform 212

IV.18 France: The notion of guidance in the context of the extended
range of ANPE services 215

IV.19 United Kingdom: The New Deal 219

IV.20 United States: The Welfare Reform – Temporary Assistance
for Needy Families (TANF) programme 221

IV.21 United States: Unemployment insurance administration –
Telephone claims service 224

IV.22 France: *Espaces Cadres* – Placement centres for managerial
and technical staff 225

IV.23 Hong Kong, China: The Employment Information and
Promotion Programme (EIPP) 227

IV.24 Sweden: The Idea Bank 229

IV.25 Canada: The PES comprehensive staff development commitment 230

IV.26 Relations with PREAs: Some examples of innovation 231

A. Belgium 231

B. France 232

C. United Kingdom 233

V   Involvement of the PES in training and education programmes:
Some examples 235

      VI   List of web site addresses 243

      VI.1 A. National public employment services 243

            B. International organizations 247

      VI.2 Selected specialized PES web sites 247

Bibliography 251

Tables

3.1 PES staff distribution by level in selected countries 30

3.2 Unemployed people per staff member in PES, 1988 31

3.3 Number of unemployed people per staff member in certain
     European countries, 1996 32
5.1 Data sources for LMI products in Alberta, Canada 63
7.1 Unemployment insurance, unemployment assistance and social
     benefits in the 12 countries covered by ILO country studies, 1998 100

Figure

8.1 State of Wisconsin: Partnership for full employment 125

EXECUTIVE SUMMARY

1.   The public employment service (PES) emerged in industrialized countries around the end of the nineteenth century as a result of concerns about the social and economic impact of unemployment. The early labour exchanges were mainly concerned with job-broking, that is with the process of arranging for jobseekers to obtain jobs and employers to fill vacancies, but some also became involved in new systems of unemployment insurance. In 1919, the newly formed International Labour Organization (ILO) recommended the establishment of the PES to member States through the Unemployment Convention (No. 2). For many years, the ILO sought through other Conventions such as the Fee-Charging Employment Agencies Convention, 1933 (No. 34) and the Fee-Charging Employment Agencies Convention (Revised), 1949 (No. 96) to secure a monopoly position for the PES and the abolition of private employment agencies (PREAs).

2.   In the 25 years following the Second World War, the PES developed in many countries, normally combining job-broking and unemployment benefit work. Since the economic dislocation of the 1970s and the growth in unemployment in many countries, the PES has increasingly been used as an instrument for government employment policies or labour market adjustment programmes designed to tackle unemployment problems. In the 1990s, in a climate of economic liberalism and globalization, the ILO abandoned the notion of the PES monopoly and recognized that PREAs with appropriate regulation could contribute positively to the functioning of the labour market.

3.   The PES now operates in a rapidly changing labour market. Powerful demographic forces are working to create an ageing labour force in developed countries while continued population growth in most developing countries is creating problems of youth unemployment. Even more formidable in their impact on the labour market are the forces of global competition and

information technology. One of the results of this revolution has been a decline in manufacturing employment in the developed world. Although some transference of manufacturing jobs to developing countries is occurring, technological change will continue to cause a general decline in manufacturing employment in the long term. Service jobs are taking the place of manufacturing jobs but the transition is proving difficult, particularly for men displaced from production industries. The PES will continue to be heavily involved in assisting people who are vulnerable in these conditions.

4.   While some of the new service jobs are low-skilled and low-waged, others require a wide range of constantly changing skills. Many observers believe that a new "knowledge economy" is emerging which places a premium on education and modern communications skills. In developed countries, there are large numbers of highly educated people who form a new kind of market for information about jobs and the labour market. The PES can serve this market through attractive self-service provision. At the same time, given the speed of change, people constantly need to update their education and skills if they are to compete in the labour market. There is thus a need for "lifelong learning". The PES is potentially well placed to act as a gateway for lifelong learning.

5.   The labour market is becoming more flexible, with the duration of both jobs and careers less than before. This trend is accompanied by a growth in self-employment, part-time and temporary employment and also a greater variation in working hours. This is increasing both the diversity and the amount of recruitment activity. If the PES is to retain its position in the labour market and thus be able to help its more vulnerable clients, it must adapt to servicing these new kinds of jobs.

6.   The rationale for the PES role is that on the one hand it improves labour market transparency and on the other hand it offers special help to those who might otherwise be disadvantaged in the labour market. Institutionally, the PES may either be part of a government department or be autonomous, in the latter case often with the social partners (employer and trade union representatives) as part of its supervisory board. However, Australia has replaced its PES with a job network selected on the basis of a competitive market. In general, PES strategies and resources are highly variable but in some countries, the PES faces very tight resource constraints. There is no correct level for PES resourcing, but resources do need to match strategies being pursued. In countries with heavy expenditure on unemployment benefits, cuts in PES expenditure may prove to be false economies. On the other hand, some charging of employers may be helpful provided it is restricted to enhanced services which extend beyond the basic services listed in the Employment Service Convention 1948 (No. 88).

Overall, the PES in many countries faces difficult problems and dilemmas and this is particularly true in developing and transition countries.

7. Four main functions can be associated with the PES:

- Job-broking
- Providing labour market information
- Administering labour market adjustment programmes
- Administering unemployment benefits

8. Job-broking operates in a highly competitive labour market in which most vacancies are filled through other channels. The function was transformed in the 1970s with the introduction of self-service vacancy displays and is now being transformed again as the PES in several countries makes vacancy files and sometimes jobseeker files available on the Internet. Such developments offer much improvement in transparency and might at first sight seem to cast doubt upon the continuing need for the PES local office infrastructure. But despite the high potential for internet services in the home, direct interaction between staff and the public will still be needed, particularly for those who are disadvantaged in the labour market. The deployment of information technology gives rise to a number of policy issues for the PES. Firstly, it needs to strike a proper balance between providing computerized self-help services and providing more in-depth help to vulnerable customers. Secondly, the PES must decide whether in its expanding internet business it should offer screening services to employers, perhaps on a fee-paying basis. Thirdly, the PES must decide how best to measure the success of its job-broking activities in an environment where it simply provides the technological infrastructure and leaves employers and jobseekers to get on with job-matching themselves.

9. The PES role in labour market information is both as a producer of labour market information (often as a by-product of its day-to-day operations) and as a user and interpreter of labour market information. With the greater sophistication of many employers and jobseekers and mounting information needs among education and training institutions and vocational guidance specialists, there is a growing market for the kind of labour market information which the PES can supply. Certain countries such as Canada, the United States and Denmark have made a deliberate investment in this function; in Canada and the United States, this has meant the provision of labour market information on the Internet. Effective labour market information delivery requires specialist staff resources and may not be a realistic option for the PES in developing countries where resources are constrained and statistical coverage is limited for all but the informal sector.

10. The administration of labour market adjustment programmes has been a major growth area for the PES in recent decades. Governments and international organizations such as the Organisation for Economic Co-operation and Development (OECD) and the European Union (EU) have sought to shift the balance from passive labour market policies (which provide income support to unemployed people) towards more active policies (which improve the employability of unemployed people). While the PES has no automatic right to deliver these programmes, in practice it has become both the gateway and the gatekeeper for them in many countries. There are three main types of programme involved: job-search assistance programmes; training and education programmes; direct job creation programmes.

Job-search assistance programmes include self-help provision, group activities (in the form of job clubs, job fairs and workshops), and individual assistance (in the form of vocational guidance and intensive counselling programmes). The PES often plays a direct delivery role in these programmes. Training and education programmes are an important way in which unemployed people can become more employable in an age when lifelong learning is becoming a way of life. The PES role here is to at least refer participants to these programmes, but it may also involve the administration of courses outsourced to other providers and in a few remaining cases, even extend to running training centres directly. Direct job creation programmes are sometimes intended to increase demand in the economy or to provide work experience with a view to improving employability, or to achieving both these objectives. They include public sector work programmes, assistance to self-employed businesses, wage subsidies and work trials. As is the case with training programmes, the PES role may simply involve referring participants or it may extend to organizing and sponsoring programmes.

11. The current trend in countries such as the United Kingdom and the United States is to combine some of these functions in large-scale and varied packages in order to reduce welfare dependency. This has the advantage of drawing on the strengths of the different approaches and offering a range of options to unemployed people. In some countries, there is a proliferation of schemes which need streamlining on the basis of evaluation findings. Evaluation suggests that job-search assistance can be highly cost-effective. For the PES to play an effective role in labour market adjustment, it needs both to be prepared to work in partnership with others and to build up its expertise in programme management.

12. The fourth of the PES functions, the administration of unemployment benefits, includes administering contribution-based unemployment insurance and state-funded income support. In some countries, the PES directly

administers these schemes. Even where this is not the case, the PES is normally heavily involved because of its provision of job-search assistance to unemployed claimants and because it registers claimants and checks their continuing eligibility and fulfillment of job-search obligations. This sometimes gives rise to awkward tensions between the policing role which the PES plays in relation to unemployment benefit and PES job-broking work, which aims to maximize employer and jobseeker satisfaction. PES managers cannot simply separate themselves from benefit issues, as the PES has a key role to play in encouraging people to move off welfare into work. But they need to monitor the impact of this work on the PES culture and be ready to take remedial action where necessary.

13. In the turbulent environment within which the PES now operates, organizing and managing the service has become an increasingly complex and difficult task. The first priority for PES senior managers is to establish good relationships with their stakeholders who range from their Minister to jobseeker and employer customers. PES activity needs to be set within a strategic plan which takes account of the changing political, social and economic environment. PES accountability is likely to be built around a performance management system which also monitors the performance of different units within the organization. To minimize the risks involved in such systems, performance measures must reflect underlying programme aims. In addition, periodic evaluation is needed for all major programmes if cost-effectiveness is to be maintained.

14. Three important trends are affecting the organization of the service. Firstly, there is the decentralization of authority and responsibility which is needed in order both to tap the energy of local managers and staff and to adapt services more closely to local needs. Secondly, there is the integration of services by which the delivery of the various PES functions is being closely integrated. This integration is being achieved through one-stop shops at local level and through tiered service delivery which systematically differentiates the service provided to different clients according to their needs. Thirdly, there is competitive service delivery. This is an important trend in the public services and leads to elements of the PES having to compete in the market or as is now the case in Australia, virtually the whole operation having to compete. This needs skilful management both to ensure cost-effective results and to deal with problems of staff morale.

15. PES senior managers are pursuing several management strategies in order to achieve success. Five strategies can be distinguished in this regard. First,

quality management principles including customer-based planning and work process reform are being introduced. Second, the use of information and communications technology is being extended both to improve internal management and to provide services directly to the customer. Third, facilities planning and management is being improved. Fourth, a high priority is being attached to internal communications and to creating two-way flows of information between local office staff and central office. Finally, staff training and development programmes are being overhauled both in the light of changes in the objectives and techniques of the service and in the light of the environment in which it operates.

16. The success of PES programmes depends as never before on the relationship between the PES and other organizations. The handling of these relationships requires a great deal of skill. A variety of relationships and correspondents can be distinguished. First, there is the relationship with social partners; this can arise through the supervisory board of an autonomous PES or in more informal arrangements. Support from the social partners can greatly ease PES work in areas such as labour market adjustment programmes. Second, labour market programmes are now increasingly organized on the basis of partnerships between a wide range of governmental and non-governmental organizations; the importance of partnership strategies has been emphasized by PES directors in the EU and the PES is well placed to play a central role in such partnerships. Third, local partnerships designed to deliver programmes adapted to local needs or to provide services through a one-stop shop are particularly significant. Fourth, there is the relationship with PREAs. With the end of the PES monopoly, this relationship can be one of cooperation, complementarity or competition and all three play their part. It is notable that when it comes to programme delivery, cooperation is playing an increasing role. Finally, PES senior managers can gain from international dialogue with other PES practitioners through the World Association of Public Employment Services (WAPES) or through information exchange at member level in the EU or at state level in the United States.

17. The following can be considered to be the key imperatives for the PES. First, the PES must be ready to constantly change and adapt its services in the light of changes in its external environment while striking a balance between change and stability. Second, the PES must recognize its position as an instrument of government policy, win the confidence of government and influence employment policies. Third, the PES must try and integrate the four functions identified in this study as much as possible. Fourth, the PES must try and work closely with as wide a range of partners as possible and where

necessary, to exercise a leadership role. Finally, the PES must try to become a new kind of service enterprise with a new profile for managers and staff and must strive for continual improvement in effectiveness and quality.

18. It has not been possible to investigate in depth the special problems of the PES in developing countries. On the basis of what information we gathered, we recommend that developing countries should begin by seeking political commitment to the PES role. They should avoid simply introducing practices from specific developed countries but carry out a broad analysis of labour market requirements in the context of their overall approach to economic development; this should determine what PES services are appropriate. Where a large informal economy in particular exists, they should look critically at the case for job-broking services. We recommend that further research should be carried out into the role of the PES in developing countries.

19. Finally, we identify the following unresolved dilemmas facing the PES. First, there is the tension between a universal self-help service and enhanced personalized service. Second, there is the tension between providing customer-oriented services and policing unemployment benefits. Third, there is the future role of the PES in lifelong learning and vocational guidance. Finally, there are organizational issues such as private ownership and decentralization.

ORIGINS AND HISTORICAL EVOLUTION   1

*Each Member which ratifies this Convention shall establish a system of free public
employment agencies under the control of a central authority.[1]*

Introduction

The public employment service (PES) has been recognized by many authorities
as one of the vital institutions of the modern State. As early as 1910, a rising
British Cabinet minister named Winston Churchill opened the first national
network of labour exchanges in Britain by claiming that the exchanges were "a
piece of social mechanism, absolutely essential to a well-ordered society".[2]
One of the very first actions of the ILO after its formation in 1919 was to
encourage member States to establish a PES and in 1970, the OECD said that
the service was the single most important tool for ensuring the proper
functioning of the labour market.[3] More recent still, in 1996 the EU Council of
Ministers described the PES as a key instrument in addressing the structural
problems of the labour market.[4] But despite such high-level endorsements of its
activities, the PES has had a somewhat chequered history. This chapter outlines
the origins and historical evolution of the PES.

Origins

The idea of linking people with jobs has had a long history, but it was not until
the development of widespread industrialization that the emergence of labour
exchanges happened on a significant scale. However, public institutions for
helping jobseekers find employment did not appear rapidly. For one thing, a
distinct proletariat did not emerge quickly in large mechanized companies (in
1830 these workers comprised only one-in-fifteen workers in France). For
another, traditional guilds or corporations of trades often retained control over

finding employment. Under these conditions, intermediary institutions (which we would call private employment agencies) specializing in matching those offering and requiring labour were concentrated in particular areas like domestic work and the butcher's trade. Furthermore, the prevailing philosophy of laissez-faire in countries such as the United Kingdom and the United States stood in the way of public intervention in the labour market.

By the middle of the nineteenth century, some writers saw the potential of public employment services as a way of introducing real transparency and increased mobility into the labour market. Gustave de Molinari designed projects for labour exchanges modelled on stock markets with the aim of redistributing excess labour as rapidly as possible according to the needs of industry.[5] Others went further and saw labour exchanges as a means of organizing the supply of jobs and rationalizing the labour market. Few institutions, however, were established in response to these ambitions.

As industrialization progressed, both trade unions and employers increasingly set up organizations to act as recruitment intermediaries in the labour market. But in conditions of industrial struggle, there could be problems of mistrust if the intermediary was seen to represent one particular interest. Unions were concerned that labour exchanges funded by employers could be used for strike-breaking. Employers were uneasy about having a union dominated recruitment system which could lead to a closed shop. This mistrust was one factor leading to public intervention in the labour market.

A second factor which led to public intervention in the labour market between 1880 and 1910 was the growing realization that unemployment was a source of poverty and of popular unrest. Social reformers analysed unemployment and pointed out that while some was linked to the economic cycle, there was also an element of frictional unemployment which could be reduced if there were better mechanisms for matching the supply and demand for labour. Moreover, where unemployment was due to the structural decline of an industry, a labour exchange system could help settle people in other industries or locations.

Thus labour exchanges of various kinds emerged in a number of European countries including Austria, Belgium, France, Germany, Norway, Switzerland and the United Kingdom, and also in certain cities and states in the United States. Labour exchanges managed by workers existed briefly in France in the 1880s but quickly disappeared because employers opposed them as a barrier to labour mobility. The greatest early development was in Germany where not only employers and unions developed exchanges, but where also municipal or public exchanges emerged. The German trade unions were less hostile to economic liberalism than their French counterparts and could see advantages in separating employment services from the social struggle by planting them on neutral ground. By 1907 when the young British economist William Beveridge visited the German exchanges, he found 400 public labour exchanges functioning beside 3,500 others run by trade unions, employers or guilds. Altogether, these various institutions filled over a million and a quarter vacancies a year, but the public exchanges were already the most important and were filling nearly half of these jobs.[6] It was this which helped to inspire Beveridge and others in the United Kingdom to launch a major new development.

At the same time, there was growing interest in the provision of unemployment insurance as a means of protecting workers and their families from the poverty caused by unemployment. Trade unions played a pioneering role and certain public authorities such as those of Ghent supported the unions with subsidies from public funds. In 1910–12, Winston Churchill and William Beveridge introduced in the United Kingdom both a national network of labour exchanges and a state-run unemployment insurance scheme (initially covering 17 per cent of the workforce and extended to nearly all in 1920). In the United Kingdom and elsewhere, it was recognized that the provision of unemployment insurance depended on labour exchanges to apply work tests to benefit recipients. The first International Conference on Unemployment was held in Paris in 1910. It discussed statistics of unemployment, labour registries and insurance and led to the formation of an international society to study all phases of the problem.[7]

Between the Wars

The creation of the ILO in 1919 gave renewed impetus to the movement for labour exchanges. The inaugural Washington Conference adopted the Unemployment Convention (No. 2) which advocated "a system of free, public employment agencies under the control of a central authority", with advisory committees being drawn from both sides of industry. On the principle that labour was not a commodity and that private employment agencies were potentially exploitative, the majority of ILO member States favoured giving the PES a monopoly and prohibiting the establishment of private employment agencies (Unemployment Recommendation, 1919, No. 1). In 1933, the Fee-Charging Employment Agencies Convention (No. 34) provided for the abolition of all private agencies within three years, subject to some exceptions.

The development of labour exchanges and of unemployment insurance in the inter-war years was gradual and piecemeal, carried out against a background of high unemployment and economic insecurity. In 1922, a federal exchange service was set up in Germany and in 1927, this was placed under a federal institute for unemployment insurance and labour placement – a structure which in some ways survives to this day. In North America, the PES was first established in Canada in 1918. The United States developed an effective PES during the First World War but this fell into decline after the war through lack of congressional support. It was not until 1933, in the context of Roosevelt's New Deal, that an effective peacetime PES was established in the United States under the Wagner-Peyser Act; unemployment insurance then followed in 1935. In 1930, the Netherlands established a PES with a monopoly.

1945 to the mid-1970s

At the end of the Second World War, governments committed themselves to the achievement of full employment. In the context of this, the ILO agreed in 1948 to new standards for the PES through the Employment Service Convention (No. 88) and the Employment Service Recommendation (No. 83). Employment services were to help ensure the best possible organization of the employment market for the achievement of full employment and the development and use of productive resources. Convention No. 88 proposed a network of conveniently located local offices that provided such services as assistance to workers and employers, placement, labour market information and which also facilitated occupational and geographical mobility. In 1949, the ILO softened its stance on private employment agencies through Convention No. 96 on Fee-Charging Employment Agencies (Revised). This gave member States a choice between abolition and regulation. One commentator on the standards set in 1948–49 claimed:

> Most of the principles they set forth remain valid: non-paying services, voluntary recourse to them by employers and jobseekers, decentralized structure, tripartite participation in the management of the institution, and the competence, independence and integrity of its agents. Nevertheless, the 1948 and 1949 instruments need to be updated on several points.[8]

The notion of the PES monopoly, still evident in Convention No. 96, gradually became obsolete over the next 50 years. Moreover, these standards could not anticipate the development of other labour market institutions besides the PES, the ending of full employment or the extensive involvement of the PES in labour market adjustment programmes.

In the two decades immediately following these Conventions, there was a period of unparalleled economic growth, in which the PES in many countries faced more problems of labour shortage than of unemployment. The PES continued to be seen as a useful instrument for tackling particular employment problems and as an adjunct to unemployment insurance schemes, but in many countries it was in a state of relative decline. In the 1960s, however, there was a revival of interest in the PES in developed countries as a key instrument in the development of manpower policies for economic growth. The OECD was a strong advocate of the PES role. The most influential model was Sweden, where a labour market board of the social partners combined the running of the PES with responsibility for training and other active labour market measures, their aim being to facilitate economic change while avoiding inflation and unemployment. In France, the Ortoli report called for institutional change to promote occupational mobility, leading in 1967 to the creation of the *Agence Nationale Pour l'Emploi* (ANPE). In contrast to the more unified Swedish and German models, France maintained separate institutions for training (AFPA) and for unemployment insurance (UNEDIC).[9]

There were other important changes in the 1960s and early 1970s. The idea of the self-service vacancy display was introduced first in Sweden and the United Kingdom and was then adopted by other countries. Self-service vacancy displays reflected a consumer oriented self-help approach that drew on modern marketing ideas. Employment exchanges were redesigned to be attractive to the public and in the United Kingdom and several other countries, were renamed "Jobcentres". In several countries, the PES started to use computers to carry out operations and to improve productivity. In some countries such as Canada and the United Kingdom, the modernization of the exchanges included a separation from unemployment insurance which was believed to give the service an unhappy "dole" image and prevented it from building up its market share.

Trends since the mid-1970s

In the 1970s, the period of post-war full employment came to an end and with the oil price rises of 1974 and 1979 came severe inflation and increased global competition. In the 1980s, unemployment soared in many countries to levels that had not been seen since the 1930s. Given the high rate of inflation and the revival in economic liberalism, Keynesian macroeconomic measures to revive employment were generally ruled out. The PES became involved in special employment measures to alleviate unemployment often on a much larger scale to their traditional job-broking activities. Remedies for unemployment were increasingly sought in the supply side of the economy. The continuing high levels of unemployment were attributed in part to rigidities in the labour market and there was a belief that over-generous and indefinite systems of unemployment compensation were creating a problem of "benefit dependency". Renewed emphasis was given to the role of the PES in applying work tests to those drawing unemployment benefits. In Canada (1976) and in the United Kingdom (1987), placement and unemployment benefit were again placed under common management.[10] In countries such as the Netherlands and the United Kingdom, the PES has focused its efforts in recent years on the difficult-to-place and the long-term unemployed. In France, there has been an attempt both to increase overall market share and to bring down long-term unemployment.

The new supply-side approach was summed up in the OECD *Jobs study* of 1994.[11] The study noted that 35 million people were unemployed in OECD countries, comprising 8.5 per cent of the OECD labour force. The principal cause of this was a growing gap between the need for OECD economies to adapt and innovate and their capacity or even their will to do so. The study stressed the need to shift the focus of labour market policies from the passive provision of income support to more active measures which assist redeployment – an approach also advocated by the EU. The study suggested that places should be guaranteed on Active Labour Market Programmes (ALMPs) as a substitute for passive income support (a policy long practised in Sweden).

The OECD placed considerable emphasis on the role of the PES. In the first place, it argued that the functioning of the PES needed to be enhanced by integrating three basic functions under the PES, namely, the placement and counselling services, the payment of unemployment benefits, and the management of labour market programmes. Moreover, the report advocated that the PES should give greater attention to the inflow, processing and dissemination of information on vacancies. Secondly, the report argued that the PES should ensure that claimants remain in regular contact with it and that the claimants maintain job-search efforts. Thirdly, the report argued for the elimination of the PES monopoly position and advocated a complementary role for private placement agencies and temporary work agencies. This process would require the PES to compete in the market for short-term placements in order to increase the flow of vacancies. In addition to these measures, the study also urged a revision of unemployment benefit systems to reduce disincentive effects.

The importance of the PES has also been stressed in the policy statements of the EU formulated in response to high unemployment. Thus in December 1996, the European Council called for stronger employment services:

Recognizing that the costs involved can be more than offset through the successful integration of the unemployed into the labour market, public employment services (PES) should be given a capacity for early action, based on a clear identification of individuals and groups at risk, sufficient means to provide active counselling and other services for job seekers and employers alike, and a stronger role as a mechanism to provide a sustainable transition from training or temporary support measures into employment.[12]

The implementation of the 1997 Luxembourg guidelines on employment policies (offering a new start to unemployed young people and to the long-term unemployed) similarly emphasized the need for upgrading the capacity of the employment services.[13]

The ILO has consistently emphasized the importance of the PES as it has promoted policies designed to maximize employment and decent work. But it has also recognized that the notion of the PES monopoly is obsolete in the modern world. In 1997, the Private Employment Agencies Convention (No. 181) recognized the role which private employment agencies could play in a well-functioning labour market and while still envisaging regulation to prevent malpractices, the Convention advocated cooperation between public and private employment agencies.

The demise of the communist regimes in the former Soviet bloc around 1990 has also had implications for the PES. The countries involved previously had virtually no unemployment though their industries were often heavily over-manned. The introduction of a market economy to these countries in the early 1990s quickly led to unemployment. For instance, in Poland unemployment rose from zero in 1988 to 15 per cent in 1993. This gave rise to an urgent need both for the establishment of a modern PES and for the provision of unemployment compensation systems. The World Bank, the ILO, the EU and other bodies helped in the establishment of these new institutions, using experts from many countries. It was a notable achievement that by 1997 in Poland, the newly formed PES with a staff of 20,000 was already providing many services including job-broking, vocational counselling, job clubs, training programmes and services for people with disabilities. Moreover, they were recording a 57 per cent placement rate in permanent jobs.

Until the mid-1990s, South-East Asian countries seemed immune from the high unemployment that had been plaguing so many other parts of the world. But the sharp downturn in their economies from 1997 onwards presented the PES in those countries with new and unaccustomed problems to which they could not easily respond. Nonetheless, there was a response in certain countries. In Hong Kong, China for instance, the PES strengthened the systematic job-matching programme which had already been introduced to help people from declining sectors to move into expanding sectors. In addition, a large marketing campaign was launched to attract new vacancies. In Japan, some new programmes were introduced in 1998 such as the measure to support the re-entry into employment of middle-aged white-collar employees who had been made redundant.

Conclusion

It is now 80 years since the ILO first recommended the PES to its member States. The progress that has been made across the world since then has been patchy and uneven. At the same time, the PES in many countries has proved resilient and dynamic in the turbulent conditions of the last quarter of a century and has demonstrated a capacity to adjust to rapidly changing situations. In the century to come, the PES will continue to face the challenge of complex labour market conditions that will be constantly changing. It is to these that we turn next.

Notes

[1] ILO: *Unemployment Convention* No 2 , Art. 2, para. 1.

[2] Interview in the *Daily Telegraph* quoted in R.S. Churchill: *Young statesman: Winston Churchill 1901–14* (London, Minerva, 1991), p. 313.

[3] OECD: *Manpower policy in the United Kingdom* (Paris, OECD, 1970), p 173.

[4] European Commission: *The way forward: The European employment strategy – Contributions to and outcome of the Dublin European Council, 13 and 14 December 1996* (Luxembourg, Office for the Official Publications of the European Communities, 1997), p 25.

[5] Molinari (1819–1912) was a Belgian liberal economist who spent most of his career in France. Among other things, he advocated international labour exchanges (similar to their commodity counterparts) to improve employment information and labour mobility.

[6] W. Beveridge: "Public labour exchanges in Germany", in *Economic Journal*, Vol. XIII, 1908, p. 2.

[7] Article on unemployment in *Encyclopaedia Britannica* (Cambridge, University Press, 11th ed., 1911), Vol. 27, p. 580.

[8] S. Ricca: "The changing role of public employment services", in *International Labour Review*, Vol. 127, No. 1, 1988, p. 30.

[9] AFPA stands for *Association Nationale pour la Formation Professionnelle des Adultes* (National Association for the Vocational Training of Adults). UNEDIC stands for *Union Nationale pour l'Emploi dans l'Industrie et le Commerce* (National Union for Employment in Trade and Industry). UNEDIC is organized as a federation of the ASSEDIC agencies (*Associations pour l'Emploi dans l'Industrie et le Commerce*). These are private, non-profit associations run by the social partners which administer the employment insurance system and pay out on behalf of government, unemployment insurance and early retirement benefits.

[10] The background to this change of policy in the United Kingdom is set out in D. Price: *Office of hope: A history of the public employment service in Great Britain, 1910–97* (London, Policy Studies Institute, 2000).

[11] OECD: *Jobs study: Facts, analysis, strategies* (Paris, OECD, 1994), p 41; p. 47.

[12] European Commission: op. cit., p. 25.

[13] European Commission: *Employment policies in the EU and in member States: Joint report* (Luxembourg, Office for the Official Publications of the European Communities, 1997).

THE CHANGING LABOUR MARKET 2

The world is rushing headlong into greater integration, driven mostly by a philosophy of market profitability and economic efficiency. We must bring human development and social protection into the equation.[1]

Introduction

We live in an age in which change in the world economy is occurring faster than ever before. The impact of such change on the labour market can bring great benefits and numerous problems. The PES has the potential to play a vital role in developments, poised as it is between the public and private sectors and involved both in the everyday dynamics of the labour market and government interventions to address failures in the market. As a labour market instrument, its effectiveness depends on how far its services can make the labour market function more effectively in the interests of jobseekers, employers, the economy and society. To achieve this, PES practitioners need to understand what is happening in the labour market. This is the theme of this chapter. We first look at demographic and social trends and the global forces for change. We then go on to discuss the public sector, occupational change, the flexible labour market and unemployment. Before drawing conclusions, we examine inequality and social exclusion in the labour market.

Demographic and social trends

Population trends have an important underlying impact on the labour market. The world population recently reached 6 billion and is still increasing. One of the most significant features of current population trends is occurring in the age structure of the world population: the twenty-first century will be known as an era of population ageing. In 1950, 8 per cent of the total world population

(200 million) was aged 60 or over and these were evenly distributed between developed and developing nations. By the year 2025 their numbers are projected to increase sixfold and to reach 1.2 billion or about 14 per cent of the total population. Of these, 72 per cent will be living in developing countries.[2] Even though there are markedly different population trends in different countries, in terms of current demographic structures the world can still be divided in two: the ageing populations of developed countries and the youthful populations of the developing countries.

In most of the developed world, family size has declined and labour forces will become significantly older over the next several decades.[3] A recent ILO paper stated:

> Reduced inflows of younger workers and increased life expectancy of the older ones will alter the age structure on the labour markets. The proportion of older workers will increase, while those of younger workers will decline. Also the old age dependency rate will increase dramatically. While ageing on the labour market needs specific responses in terms of training and changes in work organization, the increase of dependency rates points to the problem of financing the retirement systems.[4]

The reduced inflows of younger workers can be observed in countries such as the United States. There, the current tight labour market can be attributed in part to the much slower labour force growth, particularly among young labour force entrants, which followed the absorption of both the baby-boom generation and new female labour force entrants in the 1970s and 1980s. Shortages of workers, in particular those with information society skills, are expected to increase.

The ageing population makes the recent trend towards early retirement appear perverse and paradoxical and there is already discussion about the need to raise the age of retirement in developed countries. The success of such a policy depends on various conditions. First, it depends on whether there are enough good jobs for older workers. Second, it depends on whether employers are willing to retain and recruit older workers. Third, it depends on the extent to which older workers are themselves willing and able to update their skills, since lifelong learning will be a prerequisite for the continuing employment of older workers.

The first of these conditions depends mainly on overall economic and employment policies. The second and third conditions require active intervention in the labour market both to influence employers and to provide counselling and guidance for older workers. In many countries, the PES is the organization best placed to play such a facilitating role. This is already happening in Japan, where concern about the ageing of society has led the PES to set up special work programmes and to support greater regular employment for older people. It seems likely that the PES in other developed countries will also begin to introduce programmes of this kind.

In contrast to the trends in developed countries, populations are still growing in developing countries. For example, an ILO country study on the PES showed a projected 26 per cent increase in population between 1989 and 2001 in Tunisia.[5] Population growth at this pace is almost certain to lead to a massive problem of youth unemployment, which is likely to be a priority area for PES activity. However, in the developing world the increase in the numbers of young people goes hand in hand with an increase in the numbers of older people. Indeed, the current growth rate of the elderly population is double that of the world population as a whole. This trend disproportionately affects women, because in most countries women live much longer than men. Since the problem of ageing is shifting to the developing countries, it is women in these countries who will be most affected.[6]

The most important social trend affecting the labour market in recent decades, particularly in developed countries, has been the increased participation of women. Between 1973 and 1993, the female participation rate rose from 51 per cent to 69 per cent in the United States, and from 45 per cent to 55 per cent in the countries of the former European Community.[7] Women's share of employment is continuing to increase while men's share has been declining.

Global forces for change

Apart from demographic and social trends, the two principal forces causing rapid change in the labour market are global competition and information technology. With a relatively unregulated world economy, global competition and capital flows from global financial markets can generate both rapid industrial development and sudden economic crisis, as was the case in South-East Asia in recent years. The direction of economic change is often set by multinational companies whose resources may exceed those of many countries and whose agendas are not necessarily tied to the interests of any one nation. New business ventures often take the form of complex international partnerships between these multinationals and smaller companies. Indeed, it is a world environment in which small new specialist companies can establish themselves very quickly if they have professional leadership, well-targeted business ideas and good connections with the financial markets.

Technology, particularly information and communications technology, is no less a potent force for change. During the twentieth century, the pace of change has quickened astonishingly. As one writer commented:

It took 38 years for radio to reach 50 million users in the USA. It took 16 years before the same number of Americans used personal computers. The Internet reached 50 million Americans within four years of being available to ordinary consumers.[8]

Already the number of internet users is 150 million worldwide and this figure is expected to exceed 700 million by 2001.[9]

One of the outstanding trends of recent years has been the decline in manufacturing employment in developed countries due to a combination of global competition, improvements in productivity and shifts in production to lower cost countries. Technological change has transformed the methods of work in many industries, causing major reductions in the workforce. The transfer of work to developing countries has greatly reduced employment in the developed world in certain manufacturing industries such as textiles. This decline in employment has not been confined to long-established industrial countries like the United States and the United Kingdom. Between 1984 and 1998, Hong Kong, China lost more than half of its manufacturing jobs. The PES there was able to help former manufacturing workers to shift to jobs in services. (See "Mass lay-off programmes" in Chapter 6.) Although there have been big increases in employment in the manufacturing sector in some developing countries in recent years, the long-term global trend must be for manufacturing employment to decline as technology makes possible ever greater productivity improvements.

The hectic pace of change has not had an entirely adverse effect on jobs. Fortunately, in modern economies such as the United States, the United Kingdom, Hong Kong, China and many of the smaller EU member States, there have been large compensatory increases in service jobs, swelling the total numbers in employment to record levels. Competition and technology are stimulating the creation of new products and businesses all the time. But the transition from the old to the new is by no means easy. Redundant miners and steel workers do not readily move into less well-paid service jobs and may withdraw from the workforce into early retirement.

Various commentators have described the new emerging economy as the "knowledge economy".[10] Rapid economic development depends on companies taking advantage of knowledge of science and technology and of markets and finance. More scientists are at work today than in the rest of human history. The speed with which their research can be turned into marketable products is unprecedented. Knowledge is more accessible than ever before and now even the most remote village can tap a global bank of knowledge in ways that would have been beyond the dreams of anyone living a century ago. They can also do this more quickly and cheaply than anyone could have imagined even a few decades ago.[11]

The World Bank argues that knowledge is decisive for development. It quotes the comparative examples of the Republic of Korea and Ghana both of which had the same per capita income 40 years ago. By the early 1990s, however, the per capita income in the Republic of Korea was six times that of Ghana and some reckon that half of this change is due to the success of Koreans in acquiring and using knowledge.[12] The development of high levels of skill and knowledge in the population are critical in the new kind of economy which in turn raises questions about access to education and training. We believe the PES may have an important role to play as a gateway for this learning and training. (See "Training and education programmes" in Chapter 6.)

The knowledge economy offers great opportunities for development and advancement, but there are serious risks that these opportunities will be taken up in a very unequal way. The example of remote villages and their access to the Internet illustrates this point. Most villages in the developing world lack the access to a modern communications infrastructure which would enable them to use the Internet. The developed world, with only 15 per cent of the world's population, has 88 per cent of all internet users, while south Asia, with one-fifth of the world's population, has less than 1 per cent of all internet users.[13] Even within developed countries, the same inequality in usage is occurring with the new technology. The risks of greater divisiveness and polarization in the twenty-first century because of this are discussed later in this chapter.

The term "knowledge economy" can be an over-simplification. In addition to the new knowledge-based jobs can be found large numbers of new service jobs which are relatively low-skilled and low-paid. These jobs provide an ever increasing range of consumer services to the rest of the community.

The public sector

One sector that has been reducing in size in the modern economy is the public sector. In the early post-Second World War period, the public sector in many countries tended to absorb a growing proportion of the workforce. The most extreme case of this was the communist economies of the former Soviet Union and its allies, where the public sector was co-terminous with the economy.

In general, two conflicting tendencies are noticeable with regard to the public service in recent years. On the one hand, some governments like those in Austria, Denmark and France have created public-sector jobs as a response to high unemployment. On the other hand, there has been a more powerful trend towards public-sector downsizing in other countries reflecting both a strong political pressure to cut public expenditure and a belief that a large public sector is a constraint on economic dynamism and enterprise. In transition economies, governments have embarked on the difficult process of dismantling the huge public sector. According to the World Bank, authorities throughout the developing world have been turning to downsizing in an effort to reduce budget deficits and address the inefficiencies engendered by state-led development strategies which left a legacy of a bloated bureaucracy and overstaffed public enterprises.[14] In the developed world, the public sector is relatively efficient but there still have been pressures to reduce costs and to further increase efficiency by the introduction of competition and privatization.

Occupational change

Changes in the world of work affect the pattern of occupations. As the ILO has argued elsewhere,[15] globalization, information technology and changes in the organization of work have combined to increase the demand for professionals, technicians and highly skilled labour. Workers with the knowledge and skills to exploit new technologies can command high rewards in the international market place. The demand for less skilled production workers is likely to decline though as we pointed out earlier, there has been a countervailing rise in demand for service workers. Some old occupations will disappear while new ones will arise, making it necessary to frequently update the occupational classifications used by the PES. In new-style companies, people will need to be more and more polyvalent or multi-skilled. They will have broadly drawn job descriptions and work in multidisciplinary teams.[16] Certain common skills, such as communication skills, will become more critical. All this has profound implications for vocational guidance experts within the PES. (See under "Individual or intensive assistance" in Chapter 6, p.78.) One example of a large occupational area that could be at risk due to information technology is clerical employment. The ILO has recently commented that:

> Though employment for clerical workers has not shown any consistent pattern across countries, a study on the changing role of clerical workers between 1990 and 2000 has forecast that their employment will fall dramatically as computers do more routine office work.[17]

The flexible labour market

Economic liberalism and global competition have led to greater flexibility in the labour market. Flexibility takes many forms. It can affect working patterns (hours worked), wages (up and down), numbers of employees, functions (willingness of workers to switch between tasks), skills and geographical mobility. Some governments have taken measures to promote flexibility in the labour market, for instance by permitting private employment agencies to operate, by removing restrictions on the discharge of workers (which can inhibit firms from recruiting people in the first place) and by reducing disincentives within the social security system for taking up jobs. In many countries, the flexible elements within the labour market (self-employment, part-time work and temporary work) have increased. In France for instance, 40 per cent of all initial recruitment is now into temporary or fixed-term employment.[18] In the Netherlands there is a remarkable abundance of part-time work, so much so that by 1998, part-time workers comprised 38 per cent of the total Dutch workforce.[19] Indeed, the proportions of the workforce in flexible employment arrangements are significant enough to question the use of such terms as "non-standard" or "atypical" to describe them.

Flexibility within an organization is also important and work may increasingly look like a form of self-employment in which the individual moves from project to project as demands evolve. One study from the United Kingdom forecasts further rapid changes in the direction of greater flexibility:

> The world of work in 20 years time will look very different. It will be a world where there are few fixed boundaries between public, private and voluntary sector; we will no longer make assumptions about what belongs to a sector or place. Most people will be working but fewer will have jobs; the days of the job-shaped job and the job-based career are numbered. Over their working lives, many people will work for different kinds of organization; many more will work for themselves rather than for someone else...[20]

In the developing world, these trends are reflected in what the ILO has called "pervasive informalization" or a growth in the informal sector where workers are most vulnerable and social protection the least.[21]

The extent of the trend towards greater flexibility is debatable. In 1996, the ILO pointed out that there was no clear and universal trend towards reduced periods of job tenure (the duration of employment with a single employer).[22] Moreover, the pace of change in different countries is highly variable. Some highly dynamic economies such as Hong Kong, China have very few self-employed or part-time workers. But in those countries where the trend towards greater flexibility takes hold, the challenge for the PES is to move with the labour market and not get trapped in declining sectors of employment. Provided the PES is flexible and innovative, it can play a valuable role in guiding and supporting vulnerable people through the flexible labour market.

Unemployment

In Chapter 1, it was observed that since the 1970s, the role of the PES in many countries has been dominated by high levels of unemployment. Global ILO estimates suggest that out of a world labour force of 3 billion, 25–30 per cent are seriously underemployed and 150 million people are fully unemployed. Even in developed countries, unemployment figures do not necessarily give a full picture of the problem, as people may withdraw from the labour market altogether when there is a shortage of jobs.[23] High unemployment not only increases the numbers drawing unemployment benefits; it also increases the numbers of those dependent upon other benefits which do not carry job-search obligations. This may partially explain the fact that since the 1970s, the employment rate (total employment as a percentage of the population aged 15–64) in EU member States has fallen from 64 per cent to 60.5 per cent and one of the EU's objectives is to push this up again.[24]

The impact of high unemployment tends to fall particularly on vulnerable groups, such as the young, older people, the less skilled, people with disabilities and those belonging to ethnic minorities. Youth unemployment is particularly worrying, with an estimated 60 million people aged 15 to 24 unemployed across the world.[25] A "gender gap" can also arise whereby the impact of the jobs crisis falls more heavily on one sex; in most countries this is women. Moreover, prospects for re-employment diminish with duration of unemployment. As a result, high unemployment creates a large group of long-term unemployed whose prospects of returning to work are slim without state intervention. Hence, the importance of labour market adjustment measures, which are often delivered through the PES.

Another characteristic of high unemployment is that it tends to become endemic: once unemployment reaches a high level, it becomes very difficult to bring it down. Thus, despite agreement in both the OECD and the EU about strategies to reduce unemployment during the 1990s (see "Trends since the mid-1970s" in Chapter 1), levels of unemployment in the year 2000 are likely to be higher both in OECD and EU member States than they were in 1990. (In the EU, this is due to continuing high unemployment in France, Germany, Italy and Spain.) This does not mean that the strategies were misconceived but rather that structural reform of the kind proposed by both bodies is a long-term and difficult process.

The outstanding recent example of a country which has both increased employment and cut unemployment is the United States. Fifteen million jobs have been created there since the early 1990s and unemployment has come down from a recession peak of 7.8 per cent in the early 1990s to around 4 per cent today. It is debatable how far this can be attributed to a consistently favourable macroeconomic climate of low interest rates, or how much it is due to the relatively unregulated and flexible labour market in the United States. It seems unlikely that the activities of the PES made a huge contribution given that PES resources were constrained during this period. On the other hand, active measures taken by the PES probably did contribute to the reduction of unemployment in the United Kingdom from around 10 per cent in 1992–93 to around 6 per cent in 1999 (see Chapter 6). Similarly, the PES may have contributed to recovery from the recession in Norway which began in 1988. During the recession, PES staffing was doubled and thus the PES was able to support active labour market measures.

Inequality and social exclusion

One worrying trend in recent years has been the growing polarization between rich and poor, both between countries and within countries. In part this is caused by higher unemployment which can, as we have seen, trap people for long periods in conditions of social exclusion and poverty. But problems of poverty can also apply to those in work. Since the 1980s, wage differentials between skilled and less skilled workers in OECD countries have increased.[26] In the United States for example, the remarkable growth in new jobs has been accompanied by a striking deterioration in the relative position of lower paid workers in the labour force.[27] This led Robert Reich, former Secretary for Labor in the United States to observe:

> Rapid globalization and massive technological change have made the bottom third of advanced workforces less valuable. Their old jobs, often involving manufacturing, can now be done more cheaply elsewhere around the world, or by computers or robots.[28]

The position in developing and transition economies is even more disturbing. While the shifting of manufacturing jobs from developed to developing countries brings undoubted benefits to the latter, these benefits may be short-lived. Technology is always moving ahead creating a new wave of redundancies in its wake. Moreover, as we noted earlier, the advantages offered by the knowledge economy may be much more readily seized by developed countries than by developing countries. The World Bank has observed:

> …with these opportunities come tremendous risks. The globalization of trade, finance and information flows is intensifying competition, raising the danger that the poorest countries and communities will fall behind more rapidly than ever before.[29]

The recent ILO report, *Decent work*, calls for a specific focus on the "working poor" in development policies,[30] which implies a drive to halt and reverse the trend towards greater inequality within and between countries. It remains to be seen how far this problem will be tackled in the twenty-first century. But in any effort to improve the opportunities available to the disadvantaged, the PES is potentially an important instrument.

Conclusion

What features of the current, unstable and rapidly changing labour market environment have the greatest implications for the PES?

First, the growing pace of economic change and the increasing flexibility of the labour market mean that duration of employment will be shorter and that workers will face more frequent changes in jobs and occupations. This in turn means that the amount of recruitment activity in the labour market will increase, creating more job-broking opportunities for labour market agencies such as the PES. (This topic is discussed in more detail in Chapter 4.)

Second, patterns of employment are likely to be more diverse, with more self-employment, part-time and temporary work and with greater variety in working hours. Moreover, there is an increasing multiplicity of labour market agents competing in the recruitment market. If the PES is to continue to be an important player in the labour market and be able to compete effectively with other agents, it has to adapt its services to handle new kinds of employment situations. (This topic is discussed further in Chapters 4 and 9.)

Third, many people are vulnerable in a situation of rapid economic changes. The PES plays an important role in handling redundancy situations (see "Mass lay-off programmes" in Chapter 6) and is normally involved in some way or other in the provision of unemployment benefits (see Chapter 7). Active policies are required to ensure the future employability of those who have been displaced from their employment. Provided governments are willing to make the necessary resources available, the PES is well placed to give additional support to these vulnerable people by providing job-search assistance and providing access to training, education and job creation or work experience projects. (These measures are discussed further in Chapter 6.)

Fourth, more vulnerable jobseekers must now compete with many jobseekers who are more highly educated than ever before, better able to use new technology, more self-reliant in their job-search and wanting not just job information, but more sophisticated information on such topics as labour market developments. These jobseekers are demanding and present a different kind of challenge to the PES. If the PES is to assist them, it needs to develop self-service instruments that are attractive, modern, fast and responsive, and which use the latest technology. These more self-reliant jobseekers may still need access to in-depth services on occasion. (This is discussed further in Chapters 4 and 5.)

Finally, the advent of the knowledge economy requires a policy of lifelong learning, since existing knowledge can become quickly dated. Lifelong learning is also necessary because demographic trends make it desirable that older workers should remain active in the workforce for longer. Although the development of lifelong learning goes beyond the role of the PES, the PES still has the potential to become a resource centre, effectively acting as a gateway for lifelong learning. (This is discussed further in Chapter 6.)

Notes

[1] R. Jolly, Coordinator of the UN *Human Development Report 1999*, quoted in *The Guardian*, London, 12 July 1999, p. 1.

[2] A. Samorodov: *Ageing and labour markets for older workers*, ILO Employment and Training Paper No. 33 (Geneva, ILO, 1999), pp. 2–3.

[3] OECD: *Employment Outlook 1998* (Paris, OECD, 1998), p 145.

[4] P. Auer and M. Fortuny: *Ageing of the labour force in OECD countries: Economic and social consequences*, ILO Employment Paper 2000/2 (Geneva, ILO, 2000), p. 41.

[5] ILO: *Les services de l'emploi: Tunisie* (Geneva, ILO, 1998; mimeographed), section 317.

[6] It is expected that 70 per cent of all older people will be living in the developing world by 2025. See Samorodov, op. cit., Sect. 1.1.

[7] ILO: *World Employment Report 1996/97* (Geneva, ILO, 1997), p 19. The EC countries exclude the *Länder* of the former German Democratic Republic.

[8] C. Leadbeater: *Living on thin air: The new economy* (Viking, London, 1999), p. 20.

[9] United Nations: *Human Development Report* (New York, Cambridge University Press, 10th ed, 1999), p. 58.

[10] Leadbeater: op. cit., passim. See also R. Reich: *The work of nations* (London, Simon and Schuster, 1991), passim.

[11] World Bank: *World Development Report 1998/1999: Knowledge for development* (Washington, DC, Oxford University Press, 1998/99), p iii.

[12] Ibid., p. 20.

[13] United Nations, op. cit., p.62.

[14] M. Rama: "Public sector downsizing: An introduction", in *World Bank Economic Review*, Vol. 13, No. 1, 1999, p. 1.

[15] ILO: *World Employment Report 1998/99* (Geneva, IlO, 1998), p 33.

[16] Ibid., pp. 41–43.

[17] ILO: *World Employment Report 1998/99* (Geneva, ILO, 1999), p 47.

[18] ILO: *Les services publics de l'emploi: Le cas de la France* (Geneva, ILO, 1998; mimeographed), p 11.

[19] ILO: *The public employment service in the Netherlands* (Geneva, ILO, 1998; mimeographed), p 9.

[20] V. Bayliss: *Redefining work* (Royal Society of Arts, London, 1998), p. 7.

[21] ILO: *Decent work*, Report of the Director-General at the 87th Session of the International Labour Conference, (Geneva, ILO, 1999), p 9.

[22] ILO: *World Employment Report 1996/97*, op. cit., pp. 24–37.

[23] ILO: *World Employment Report 1998/99*, op. cit., p. 9.

[24] Employment rates are highly variable across the EU, with rates well above average in Austria, Denmark, the Netherlands, Portugal, Sweden and the United Kingdom See European Union: *Employment Rates Report 1998: Employment performance in the European Union*, (Luxembourg, Office for the Official Publications of the European Communities, 1998), pp. 11–12.

[25] ILO: *World Employment Report 1998/99*, op. cit., p. 1.

[26] Ibid., p. 49.

[27] OECD: *The public employment service in the United States* (Paris, OECD, 1999), p 25.

[28] Quoted in *The Guardian*, London, 14 July 1997.

[29] World Bank: *World Development Report 1998/1999: Knowledge for development*, op. cit., p. iii.

[30] ILO: *Decent work*, Report of the Director-General, International Labour Conference, 87th Session, 1999 (Geneva, ILO 1999), pp 8–9.

ROLE, FUNCTIONS AND RESOURCES   3
OF THE PUBLIC EMPLOYMENT SERVICE

The employment service is a key instrument in addressing the structural problems
of the labour market. Member States are encouraged to proceed with a rapid
modernization and empowerment of the employment service.[1]

Introduction

Chapter 1 showed how the PES has evolved in recent decades to become a
key instrument in government employment policy. Chapter 2 explained the
challenging labour market environment within which the PES operates. This
chapter looks at the modern PES and discusses what kind of organization or
group of organizations the PES has become. It looks at the mission, strategy and
functions the PES is expected to pursue and how strong it is in terms of resources
and other assets. In the chapter we first look at the rationale, role and mandate
of the PES and we discuss its legal status, its institutional character and its
mission and strategy. We then go on to discuss the various functions of the PES,
how these functions can be integrated, and discuss the resourcing of the PES.
Before drawing conclusions about the issues facing the PES, there is a review
of current trends in developed, transition and developing countries respectively.

Rationale, role and mandate

The rationale for government intervention in the labour market through a public
employment service relates both to the importance of human resources in a
nation's economic development and to the need to improve social welfare. Several
good arguments for a public employment service can be put forward. In the first
place, a public employment service can increase efficiency in labour market
functioning and increase transparency in labour market information
– all for the public good. Second, a public employment service is a useful means

of promoting equity in access to the labour market and of protecting the position of those who might otherwise be disadvantaged. Third, a public employment service serves to counterbalance the negative impact of structural adjustment on labour demand. Fourth, in countries with unemployment benefit systems, a public employment service can be used to provide measures for ensuring that benefit recipients return to work as quickly as possible. There is room for much debate as to how far such interventions in labour markets should extend, but it will become clear in the course of this chapter that one or more of these broad principles underlies the various forms of PES interventions described in this study.

The Employment Service Convention, 1948 (No. 88) defines the role and scope of the PES, its organizational structure and its relationship with other bodies. Article 1 of the Convention stipulates the core mandate of public employment services as follows:

> 1. Each Member of the International Labour Organization for which this Convention is in force shall maintain or ensure the maintenance of a free public employment service.
> 2. The essential duty of the employment service shall be to ensure, in cooperation where necessary with other public and private bodies concerned, the best possible organization of the employment market as an integral part of the national programme for the achievement and maintenance of full employment and the development and use of productive resources.

The main emphasis of this article is that the PES is central to the best possible organization of the employment market, not just as a direct provider of placement services and labour market information, but also as partner, facilitator and catalyst in the achievement of full employment and in the development of productive resources. This always was an ambitious remit and looks even more so today when the goal of full employment seems less achievable than it did in 1949. Moreover, the central place of the PES is in many ways less well-assured today than it was in the past.

But Convention No. 88 did provide a broad framework within which many countries have established the PES by law and specified its role and mandate in appropriate legislation. The roles and mandates of the PES differ according to the political and socio-economic situation in which it operates. For instance, the extent to which the PES has played a regulatory role in the labour market varies according to national traditions. But as was indicated in Chapter 1, the role of the PES in developed countries in recent decades has shifted from that of traditional job-broker or labour exchange to that of the executor of employment policy and labour market programmes. In the main, this has been due to much higher levels of unemployment, for example among EU member States, Canada and the United States.

Some developed countries such as Austria, Canada, Finland, France, Germany, the Netherlands and the United States introduced legislative amendments to the legal role and mandate of the PES in the 1990s which reflect the changes in the effective role of PES in the labour market. At the same time, some transition and emerging-market economy countries such as Argentina, Bulgaria, Greece, Hungary, Poland, Tunisia and Ukraine have stipulated an enlarged role for the PES through legislation. However, the existence of a legal mandate for an enlarged role for the PES in a country provides no indication of how effective this enlarged role actually may be. Later in this chapter we consider how strong the PES really is as an institution.

Legal status and institutional character

Another factor which affects the organizational status of the PES is its legal status, in other words, how it is legally defined as an institution. Broadly speaking, the PES is likely to fall into one of three legal categories:

1. An integral part of the Ministry of Labour (or whatever department has the relevant responsibilities).[2] Historically, this is how the PES was set up in most countries. Decisions concerning the running of the PES are taken in the exercise of the normal powers of the State. However, this status can take two different forms:

   a. A fully integrated part of a government department. The minister and the senior officials of the department are in charge and may intervene on a day-to-day basis. Staff members have the same status as other officials in the public service with regard to recruitment, promotion, transfer, conditions of service, social protection, trade union rights and so forth.

   b. An executive agency within a government department. In this model, the functions of the PES have been hived off to a separate organization within a government department. The organization is led by a director-general or chief executive who is directly accountable to the relevant minister under an agreement on aims, objectives, resources and performance. In this model, the minister's role is less hands-on and the staffing regime less like that of the civil service. This is the case at present for instance in the United Kingdom.

2. Autonomous administration under a commission or council representing the social partners. The status of such a body is established by legislation which usually defines the general mandate of the PES, its method of financing and also the main forms of management and control. In addition, this body defines the organization's relations with ministers and with

employers' and workers' organizations. The priorities, orientations and action plans are generally established by a tripartite management council or board. Executive management rests with a director-general or chief executive appointed by the management council/board or on its proposal. Staff may be granted a status different from that of officials in the public service. The Federal Institute in Germany is a classic example of this model.

3. Privatized organizations. This is a new model, recently introduced in Australia, where the public employment services have been replaced by the "job network", a fully competitive market in which private, community and public sector agencies are contracted to place unemployed people in jobs. The privatized PES is established as an enterprise/corporation under a corporation act. (This important development is discussed further in Chapter 8.)

The PES in developing and transition countries is most commonly a department or division of a Ministry of Labour while the PES in developed countries, particularly those in the EU such as Austria, Belgium, France, Germany, Greece, Ireland, the Netherlands and Spain has been transformed into an administrative autonomous institution. Only in Australia is it a privatized service.

Each of the models has its advantages and disadvantages. Direct ministerial control as in model 1(a) has the advantage that the PES is more likely to be "owned" by ministers, when they have direct control over it. The main disadvantages of this model is that when the PES is too closely integrated into a government department, it may lack clear unified leadership and suffer instead from arbitrary political intervention. This can lead to the organization being unable to make decisions on sound business grounds, for example on the location of local offices and so forth. Secondly, the civil service staffing regime may cause undue bureaucracy and get in the way of the running of a business that must be responsive to its customers. Model 1(b) overcomes these problems, but its success clearly depends on having a good working relationship between the minister and chief executive. Model 2 is a very popular model, but again its success ultimately depends on mutual understanding between ministers, social partners and the PES leadership. (These issues are discussed further in Chapter 9.) A further complication in all the models is that different PES functions are organized in different ways in different countries. This is discussed later in this chapter.

Mission and strategy

The PES mission and strategy varies from country to country, influenced by such factors as political forces, labour market conditions and initiatives taken by the PES leadership.

The PES in the European Union

Considerations of space preclude the description of the PES in every EU member State so we will concern ourselves here with the overall framework set out in the policy guidelines developed by the EU. These have been supplemented by further guidelines for the development of PES services to support the policy guidelines. The guidelines were built on four priorities or pillars:[3] employability; development of entrepreneurship; adaptability of firms; and equal opportunity.

With more than 5,000 local employment offices and about 160,000 employees, the PES is vital to the delivery of the EU's employability pillar. The main responsibility of the PES is to identify at an early stage those people at risk from long-term unemployment and to establish individual action plans for unemployed jobseekers. In addition, it has to deliver counselling, guidance and training services and implement job subsidy schemes: in general, it has to deliver most of the measures for re-integrating workers into the labour market. The Commission calls for among other things, the systematic case management of all registered unemployed people – a formidable task. In addition, the PES often plays a role in the implementation of the other three pillars of the employment guidelines.

Taking account of the EU employment guidelines, the PES in EU member States have agreed on a joint development strategy. The strategy can be summed up in the following eight points.[4]

1. The PES will develop features of a service enterprise, in other words seek to be centrally placed in the market and try to be sensitive to the changing needs of jobseekers and enterprises.
2. The PES will make full use of modern information and communication technology to improve client services.
3. The PES case management of the unemployed will focus on early action and a planned sequence of services tuned to individual needs.
4. The planning and delivery of employment services will benefit from a continuous monitoring and an in-depth analysis of labour market conditions and trends.
5. The PES will seek to strengthen coordination between the various PES functions.
6. The PES will build upon a partnership strategy involving other actors in the labour market.
7. A comprehensive package of employment services that responds fully to market needs requires various active partnerships between the PES, the

social partners, institutions in the field of education and training, municipalities, benefit agencies and private employment agencies.

8. Cooperation between the PES at the European level will be strengthened.

Progress of the strategy is regularly monitored by means of a national action plan prepared by each member State.

The PES in North America

There is no common or coordinated employment strategy among countries of the North American Free Trade Association (NAFTA) such as Canada, Mexico and the United States. The new vision of the Canadian PES is based on enabling Canadians to participate fully in the workplace and the community while its strategy focuses on partnership with provinces and territories. (Canada's integrated policy approach is described later in this chapter.) In the United States, strategic development has been hampered by a continued funding crisis. But in the mid-1990s, various leaders from state employment security administrations, the business community, the United States Department of Labor and other organizations came together to develop a workplan to revitalize the PES in order to ensure that it survived the funding crisis and met employer and jobseeker needs in the new global economy. The integrated programme is described later in this chapter, but the following statement sums its long-term vision for the PES:

> To be the nation's leader in providing services to its customers and serving as a universal gateway to workforce development resources by professional, empowered staff. Its strategy focuses on quality improvements in service to customers and new ways of doing business and serving customers.[5]

The PES in South-East Asia

Like the NAFTA countries, the countries of the Association of South-East Asian Nations (ASEAN) have no common regional employment strategy but certain States do have a national employment policy, for example China, Japan and the Republic of Korea. In Japan, the mission of the PES is to adjust labour supply and demand by referring jobseekers to the most appropriate jobs and by referring employers to the most qualified workers. Its strategy is to try and attain employment security by strengthening the PES functions of providing employment exchange services and employment information. In addition, it tries to strengthen the role of the PES as a provider of comprehensive services. The mission of the of Hong Kong, China Labour Department is to improve the utilization of human resources by providing a range of employment services to meet the changes and needs in the labour market. Its strategy is to highlight professional excellence, proactiveness, premier customer service, partnership and staff participation.

Functions

Although the PES is now generally well established in developed and transition countries, its mission, strategy and organization vary from country to country and depend largely on the economic, social and industrial relations background and on the employment policies pursued by governments. Nevertheless, there is considerable common ground in the kind of functions which the PES carries out. The general tasks of employment services are defined in Convention No. 88 as being: the recruitment and placement of workers; facilitating occupational and geographical mobility; collecting and analysing data on the labour market; cooperating in the administration of unemployment insurance; and assisting in social and economic planning. There are different ways of categorizing these general tasks,[6] but in this study, the major tasks or activities of the PES are grouped into four main functions, each of which is discussed in one of the four following chapters: job-broking (Chapter 4); development of labour market information systems (Chapter 5); administration of labour market adjustment programmes (Chapter 6); administration of unemployment benefits (Chapter 7).[7]

To these four main PES functions a fifth can be added: the administration of regulatory activities. PES regulatory activities are usually limited in developed countries, but they still play an important role in developing countries.[8] In general, the PES may carry out regulatory activities in several areas: the employment of foreign workers; the trans-border placement of national workers; the regulation of the activities of PREAs; the coordination of employer/worker plant closing activities; and the monitoring of adherence to statutes regulating the hiring of special groups of workers. In this regulatory role, the PES usually has to prepare the groundwork for decisions to grant or refuse permits or licences, issue permits and monitor the application of regulations. This regulatory role can conflict with other PES roles. For instance in the United States, the PES has to ensure that farmers meet certain standards when recruiting workers but farmers resent these regulations and their enforcement. In general, PES managers need to look carefully at the possible adverse impacts of regulatory responsibilities on job-broking and try to mitigate these as far as possible. As this study is concerned with the role of the PES in improving the functioning of the labour market, these regulatory activities are not discussed further.

While the five PES functions we have outlined are often treated as separate and distinct programmes, in reality there are several policy and operational linkages between them. The importance of these linkages is increasingly being recognized and the integration of services has become a major trend in the PES in many developed countries. Service integration can be carried out in several ways, for example through institutional integration, through customer-focused integration or one-stop centres, or through tiered service delivery. (Approaches are discussed further in "Integration of services" in Chapter 8.) No matter what institutional arrangements a particular PES may have, it is desirable that policy in relation to these functions is closely integrated. This is a theme of the OECD, which emphasizes the building up of active labour market policies rather than passive policies. The same emphasis is evident in the EU policy guidelines described earlier.

It is interesting to look at two recent examples where this integrated approach has been expressed in legislation. In 1996, Canada comprehensively reformed its active and passive labour market programmes to complement each other better. Parliament adopted an Employment Insurance Act and the shift in policy towards a more active employment policy was clearly signalled in the use of "Employment Insurance" rather than "Unemployment Insurance". The new Act built on reforms introduced in the 1980s and early 1990s. These were intended to streamline programme benefits and to ensure that income benefits and employment programmes supported each other in the pursuit of a more efficient and equitable labour market. Under the new Act, income benefit recipients, recent recipients and those who have recently received maternity or parental leave benefits are eligible to receive a new package of services. These services include employment benefits that specifically target wage subsidies, earnings supplements, self-employment assistance, job-creation partnerships and skills loans and grants. In addition, support measures such as employment assistance services, labour market partnerships and research and innovation assistance are included. This comprehensive package of services was based mainly upon the evaluation of what had worked best in previous programmes.

In the United States, the main objective of the 1998 Workforce Investment Act was to achieve a better integration of the American workforce development system. It sought to do this by realigning the patchwork of federal job-workforce development programmes that had developed over 60 years into a more rational, customer-oriented and result-driven system. The reforms were based upon the principles of streamlined services, individual empowerment, universal access, increased accountability, a strong local and private sector policy role, and state and local flexibility. There were several other features worth noting in the Act. First, there was the emphasis placed on the role of labour market information in the planning and management of the other programmes. Second, job-search assistance activities, in support of other labour market adjustment programme measures, were restructured into a graduated or tiered delivery system, making more people eligible for core universal services. In this context there was also an emphasis on improved planning for intensive services. Third, job-broking services were to be integrated into the one-stop career centres that had been piloted over the last decade. There is clearly an important trend across the developed world towards closer integration of the various functions in which the PES can become involved. (The implications of this are discussed further in Chapter 8: see "Integration of services".)

Resources

Few issues in the world of the PES are more contentious than the question of resources. At national level they are often the subject of acrimonious negotiation between senior PES officials and government while at local level, managers are always in need of more resources. There are several reasons why resources are such a contentious issue. As a job-broker, the PES remit is essentially open-ended. This means that the more resources the PES has available to it, the more of an impact it can have. In addition, relatively high unemployment creates pressures on the PES from government, benefit authorities and jobseekers themselves to help unemployed people into jobs. But this conflicts with strong political pressures in many countries to cut public expenditure. From every point of view, resources are a crucial issue and inadequate resourcing is bound to restrict the effectiveness of the PES.

It is not at all easy to make comparisons between PES resourcing at an international level. This is mainly because of the subtle differences between countries in terms of PES functions themselves and also in the way these functions are distributed between organizations. For instance, Table 3.1 gives staffing information about the organization which is most commonly regarded as the "public employment service" in a number of countries. However, the functions carried out by such bodies vary greatly from country to country. For example in countries such as the United States, the PES administers unemployment benefit whereas in France and the United Kingdom, it does not. Moreover, countries vary in size and for proper comparative validity this factor needs to be taken into account in any comparison.

The OECD has gone some way towards addressing the problems in the regular comparisons it has made of overall PES expenditure as a percentage of GDP in a variety of organizations for each country. Recent OECD figures can

Table 3.1   PES staff distribution by level in selected countries

| Country | Total number of PES offices[1] | PES staff distribution by level | | | National total | | | |
| | | National head-quarters | Regional offices | Local offices | Total staff | Staff profile (%) | | |
						Managers	Profes-sionals	Adminis-trative support
Canada (1998–99)	n.a.	1 758	1 042	12 203	15 003	0.83	52.04[2]	47.12
France (1997)	736[3]	638	1 804	14 579	17 021	7.70	80.66	11.64
Japan (1991)	479	239[4]	2 242[5]	12 843[6]	15 324	n.a.	n.a.	n.a.
Netherlands (1999)	147	650	5 742[7]		6 392	n.a.	n.a.	n.a.
Norway (1999)	120	263	418	2 809	3 490	13.70	77.05	9.25
United Kingdom (1999)	1 100	2 063	4 616	29 313[8]	35 992	3.12[9]	96.88	
United States (1997)	2 260	632[10]	70 050[11]		70 682	n.a.	n.a.	n.a.

[1] OECD: *Labour market policies in Switzerland* (Paris, OECD, 1996), table 2.1, p. 64; OECD: *The public employment service in the United States* (Paris, OECD, 1999), table 2.12, p. 42.   [2] Including administrative and foreign services which have 7,521 staff, i.e. 50 per cent of national total staff.   [3] 1997 figure. See ILO: *Atlas* @ http://ilo.org/english/dialogue/govlab/admitra/atlas/france/.   [4] Staff of employment security bureau at the national level.   [5] Staff of divisions in charge of employment security (namely employment security division and employment insurance division) at prefectural levels.   [6] Staff of public employment security offices (479 main offices; 120 branch offices; and 32 local offices).   [7] Employment offices and regional staff.   [8] This figure includes staff of district offices (1,291) and local offices (28,022).   [9] It comprises heads of division (19), regional directors (9), assistant regional directors (12), district managers (135) and business managers (947).   [10] Estimated federal PES staff for fiscal year 1997: Wagner-Peyser Act staff (154); one-stop staff (43); unemployment insurance staff (208); job training partnership act (JTPA) staff (227).   [11] Estimated state and local staff for fiscal year 1996 of which 38,900 are unemployment insurance staff and 31,150 are employment services and related staff (including JTPA).

Source: ILO: *Additional information to the ILO country studies* (Geneva, ILO, 1999; mimeographed).

be found in Annex III. When interpreting these figures, it is important to realize that the column headed PES and administration is quite broadly defined, including as it does job-broking, job-search assistance and all the administrative costs of labour market agencies such as unemployment benefit agencies (even when separate institutions) and the administrative costs of other labour market

Table 3.2   Unemployed people[1] per staff member in PES, 1988

Country	Employment offices	Employment offices plus network and programme management	Employment services including unemployment benefit administration	Unemployment rate (%) [2]
Sweden	14	10	9	1.6
United Kingdom [3]	53	36	36	6.9
Norway [3]	68	47	46	4.9
Germany	86	57	39	6.2
Australia	109	58	44	7.2
Netherlands	152	131	42	9.2
Canada	213	82	49	7.7
France	271	122	78	10.0
Spain	713	...	...	19.1

[1] Standardized unemployment data, mostly based on labour force surveys.   [2] Standardized unemployment rates.
[3] 1989.

Source: OECD: *Employment Outlook 1991* (Paris, OECD, 1991), p. 213.

programmes. In other words, this heading includes the great mass of the operational costs of the PES. The figures presented suggest extraordinary disparities in resource levels, with countries such as the Netherlands allocating more than ten times as much of GDP to the PES as Japan and seven times as much as the United States. It should be noted that the very low percentages quoted for Japan and Poland seem out of line with information in ILO country studies.[9] Despite this, the comparisons do have a general validity when showing for instance that the Netherlands, Sweden and Germany spend a great deal more on the PES than do the United States or Japan.

In 1988, the OECD tried out an alternative measurement approach by comparing PES staffing with the numbers of unemployed they served. Table 3.2 shows the results for some of the countries listed in table 3.1.

Again, wide discrepancies can be seen. The first column in table 3.2 confirms the picture in Annex III that, in 1998 Sweden had one of the best resourced services with only 14 unemployed people per staff member compared with over 700 in Spain. The third column, which includes benefit administration, shows a greater convergence. Most countries had around 35–50 unemployed people per staff member, with Sweden well below the average and France well above. It is significant that the countries with the highest levels of unemployment at the time had the highest ratios of unemployed people per staff member. This may have reflected difficulties in securing extra staff to cope with an unemployment crisis.

Table 3.3   Number of unemployed people per staff member in certain
             European countries, 1996

Country	Number of unemployed per staff member	Number of long-term unemployed per staff member
France	239	141
Germany	133	87
Sweden	58	27
United Kingdom	95	55

Source: Unpublished study carried out by consultants Bernard Brunhes for the French Minister of Labour and quoted in *Le Monde*, 31 October 1998.

More recent calculations of this kind relating to 1996 confirm that the ANPE in France is less well staffed than its equivalents in Germany, Sweden and the United Kingdom. The number of unemployed per staff member is shown in table 3.3.

Some further work on cross-nation PES resource comparisons would be useful despite the inherent difficulties in making such comparisons. Unemployed/staff ratios as a method seems to produce more credible results than analysing shares of GDP, but it must be remembered that it does not take productivity differences into account. To address this point, at least partially, comparisons of investment in information technology could also be made.

The relatively low showing of the United States in Annex III reflects the serious funding crisis that has occurred over recent years in the United States to which we have already referred. Core funding has been reduced to the extent that the number of staff working on mainstream employment work under the Wagner-Peyser Act provisions has fallen from 30,000 in 1984 to 15,000 in 1998. Total staffing, including staff funded by individual states and under other provisions, is much higher than this. In 1996, it stood at 70,000, of whom 39,000 were engaged in unemployment insurance work. One of the results of the funding cuts has been a severe squeeze in job-broking operations. The PES response to this has in part been to introduce extensive computerization (see Chapter 4) and to devise the one-stop approach to delivery (see Chapter 9). Counselling has been reduced, so that only about 35 per cent of worker profile and re-employment service claimants who are identified as being likely to exhaust benefits each year are referred to the employment services.[10]

Canada is another country with very tight resources despite its relatively good showing in table 3.1. According to an ILO country study,[11] the number of staff engaged in placement work fell from 3,330 in 1987 to below 2,000 in

1997. Like the United States, Canada has responded with the introduction of extensive computerization. In addition, it has abandoned registration and is unique in its exclusive reliance on self-service for job-broking.

As the above tables suggest, there has been a greater willingness in Europe to enhance resources to meet new pressures, particularly those arising from high unemployment. For instance, the rapid growth in unemployment in Norway from 1988 onwards led to a doubling of the number of staff in the PES from 2,049 in 1988 to 4,234 in 1995. This may well have contributed to the fall in unemployment which has allowed recent reductions in staffing. The United Kingdom also makes an interesting case study in relation to resource levels. Between 1979 and 1986, the Thatcher Administration cut PES staffing levels by one-third. During the same time, unemployment rose to 3 million (1982) at which level it became stuck and long-term unemployment (over a year) rose to 1 million. It is arguable that with more staff and a different strategy, the PES might have reduced these figures. The change in strategy did not come until 1986 when a new Minister, Lord Young, secured extra resources for "Restart", a new large-scale counselling programme for the unemployed, which incorporated a range of employment and training opportunities. From 1987 to 1990, unemployment and long-term unemployment fell considerably. Economic commentators attributed much of this fall to Restart. Learning from this lesson, the United Kingdom Government has maintained relatively high levels of PES staffing since then with further enhancements when unemployment has increased. Current PES staffing in the United Kingdom is around 36,000.

Given the current resource pressures on the PES in many countries, it may be time to reconsider the question of fee-charging. Convention No. 88 calls for a free public employment service and for most purposes, this remains a sound principle. Charging jobseekers would obviously be undesirable and charging employers for job-broking services could lead to a service biased in favour of employers. This was clearly demonstrated when the United Kingdom, having denounced Convention No. 88 in 1971, started charging employers for its professional and executive recruitment service (PER) from 1972 to 1988 (when the service was privatized). There is no doubt that the PER became an employer-oriented service.

However, the situation is now more complex. In more and more countries, the PES is introducing additional or enhanced services for employers that extend beyond mainstream job-broking. Countries such as Canada, Norway and the United States now offer sophisticated labour market information to employers. In the Netherlands, recent legislation allows charging and the PES has started entering into partnerships with private agencies. It is also planning to offer full recruitment services including assessment, consultancy on personnel management issues and outplacement services for organizations facing redundancies. In Denmark, employment offices can now offer services such as personnel management consultancy on a commercial basis. Belgium also charges a fee for intensive screening and outplacement. In all these cases, a fee-charging system can help the overall financial position of the PES and enable it to deliver quality services to employers thereby enhancing its reputation. The ILO position is that Article 6 of Convention No. 88 prohibits all charging of workers. It also prohibits charging employers for the basic services provided by the PES. However, it is legitimate for the PES to charge employers for enhanced or special services provided there is no damage to the basic services and provided that consultation and cooperation is sought from representatives of employers' and workers' organizations.

In relation to resourcing, four conclusions can be drawn. First, there is no correct level of resourcing for the PES: resources need to be matched to strategy. If for instance, a strategy of systematic case management for all registered jobseekers is adopted as is the case in the EU, then the considerable resource implications involved need to be recognized. Second, strategy needs to take a broad rather than a narrow view of the implications of PES activities. In countries with costly unemployment benefit systems, savings in PES counselling and job-broking facilities may be false economies if they lead to higher welfare expenditure because people remain unemployed for longer. Third, the PES needs to give constant attention to value for money and evaluation and make sure that the cost of all its activities are justified. Finally, some charging of employers may be helpful if it is restricted to enhanced services which extend beyond the basic employment services described in Convention No. 88.

Current evolution of the PES

How strong is the PES across the world as we enter the third millennium? We have not carried out a comprehensive survey but one indicator is that 81 ILO member States (out of a total of 180) have ratified Convention No. 88, suggesting that nearly half the countries of the world have committed themselves to a PES corresponding to the broad principles set out by the ILO in 1948. In addition, there are those countries which have a PES but which like China, Indonesia, Poland, Senegal and the United States, have not yet ratified the Convention or which like Italy and the United Kingdom, have denounced it. However, the fact that the PES exists in a country does not tell us how effective it is. Clearly conditions vary greatly among developed, developing and transition countries. We look at each in turn.

Current trends in developed countries

This chapter has already drawn attention to the enormous discrepancies found by the OECD in 1988 in terms of numbers of unemployed per staff member in OECD countries. The same survey also showed that the PES in many OECD countries faced serious difficulties in job-broking because of an acute shortage of vacancies in relation to the huge numbers of unemployed:

> It seems likely that, at least in many EC countries, many people becoming un-employed during the 1980s were not contacted with any proposal to apply for a specific job during their first year in unemployment.[12]

One response to this situation has been to shift the balance of effort in the PES towards greater involvement in labour market adjustment measures. It is unlikely that this point of weakness in job-broking identified by the OECD in 1988 has fundamentally changed since then. Another factor that has affected the service in recent years has been outsourcing. The transfer to the private sector of significant elements of the employment service has been under debate in Australia, New Zealand and Switzerland. In the United States, it has been discussed in Massachusetts, Texas and Michigan. Only Australia has carried this to the point where in effect it no longer has a public employment service. (See "Competitive service delivery" in Chapter 8.)

In addition to these, four more evolutionary trends in relation to the PES in the developed world can be distinguished. Firstly, the PES role has been extended beyond job-broking as a result of a shift in employment policy away from passive labour market policies towards active market policies. In some cases, the PES has taken a central role as an agent of far-reaching and costly government programmes that have sometimes involved sweeping welfare reform. Secondly, and linked to these active policies, is a trend towards a PES role which emphasizes the individual's responsibility for job-search as a condition of receiving unemployment benefits, the aim being a reduction in social security costs. Thirdly, there is a greater differentiation in services offered to jobseekers and employers alike based on needs. Instead of services of the "one-size-fits-all" type, services are increasingly being integrated and customized to address the unique labour market needs of individuals, with gradations and tiers of service being provided on the basis of these needs. Finally, changes in information technology, which are altering the character of PES operations in every function, are changing the way in which the PES interacts with the public through computerized self-service provision. In countries such as United States and Canada, this trend has to some extent been mitigated by a decline in staffing resources.

Current trends in transition countries

As was suggested in Chapter 1, one of the encouraging developments in relation to the PES in recent years has been the considerable efforts made to set up public employment services in many of the countries of the former Soviet bloc. This was a very necessary response to the unemployment that arose as previous state-controlled systems were dismantled. In Poland for example, a carefully planned and substantial PES has been created in a short time. Nonetheless, there have been difficulties in a number of countries in establishing a viable PES because of a shortage of resources. For instance in Ukraine, the ILO employment policy review mission found several obstacles to effectiveness in the working of the state employment service which was established in 1991. These included low staffing in relation to the high number of unemployed people in need of assistance, lack of incentives to motivate staff for such demanding work, a low level of computerization in labour offices and poor physical working conditions in many local employment offices.

There are acute problems of priorities for economic development in many of the transition economies. But creating an effective PES deserves serious attention, particularly in those countries where an unemployment benefit system is introduced. Whatever its wider advantages, an effective PES can be seen as essential in helping benefit recipients back to work as quickly as possible. Without it, considerable wasted expenditure could arise.

Current trends in developing countries

There is enormous variety in the condition of the PES across the developing world. In this study we have been unable to investigate the situation in depth and here can offer little more than a few snapshots. In particular, we draw on some recent studies of English-speaking Africa and of Papua New Guinea. An ILO study of the PES in English-speaking Africa showed how the economic turbulence affecting many developing countries has had an adverse impact on the PES. The study commented:

> Many of the PES...have always been operating on a very low level of human and financial resources. Structural Adjustment Programmes have additionally reduced the resources, often to a level below the very basic needs to keep up a minimum service of core functions.[13]

As a result, the PES in most of these countries was unable to react in a flexible manner to labour market developments and thus escape from a vicious circle of poor performance and budget cuts.

The need to refocus the role of the PES in developing countries is further highlighted in a study of the labour market in Papua New Guinea by Fraser.[14] The author argues for abolishing the PES as a placement agency per se and replacing it with a much more broadly conceived national employment options service, albeit with a placement function among the range of options it might offer. He argues that the current PES model has never fitted the labour market needs in Papua New Guinea, based as it was upon an Australian full-employment model of the 1960s. Consequently, he suggests a new PES which should provide the following services: basic information and advice; referral to other bodies and agencies with specialized knowledge or services; job placement only where it becomes possible; placement in existing training courses; organization and provision of short courses which are otherwise not available or accessible (including skill formation needs in sectors other than the formal wage-earning sector); and assistance in job-search skills (including the enabling of jobseekers to develop their own jobs).

In many developing countries, the PES faces severe unemployment and under-employment problems plus the threat of serious budget cuts and retrenchments. In addition, there has been the exponential growth of the informal sector and severe skill shortages for long-term economic development. Despite these unfavourable circumstances, the PES in many developing countries still maintains the traditional role of manpower placement though sometimes with only limited success. In countries such as Indonesia, the Philippines and Sri Lanka, the PES faces a further problem in that it has geared the bulk of its efforts to the administration of overseas placement.

The idea of changing the focus of the PES in developing countries is not new and was already mentioned by Richter in 1975 when he argued for a re-orientation of existing activities of employment services in developing countries from the more traditional placement and registration of the unemployed, to an information-seeking and provisory role.[15] A case may also be made for focusing on promoting self-employment and implementing short-term employment creation programmes. (These issues are discussed further in Chapter 10.)

Issues facing the PES at the turn of millennium

We conclude this chapter by identifying some of the current issues which affect the future of the PES and which are discussed in greater depth later in this study. As we move into the third millennium, the PES in many developed countries has seen its mandate extended beyond the traditional functions of job-broking and administration of unemployment insurance to include the provision of extensive labour market information, the management of labour market adjustment programmes and the provision of specialized services for certain target groups. The PES plays many roles: it acts as service provider, labour market information provider, job-broker, facilitator, mobilizer, coordinator, commissioner, partner, and catalyst in the implementation of labour market adjustment programmes. Moreover, it is expected to be innovative, efficient, responsive and accountable to a wider and diversified public that comprises its customers. It faces the challenge of increasingly pressing social and economic conditions and high expectations – all of this with limited human and financial resources.

The PES in many developed countries is continually adjusting its role, trying to find a balance between many conflicting demands:

• between equity and efficiency in service delivery (see Chapter 4);
• between the placement of the long-term unemployed and labour market penetration (see Chapter 4);
• between resource allocations directed at self-help facilities and providing intensive services to disadvantaged groups (see Chapter 4);
• between centralization (for a coherent national labour market policy) as opposed to decentralization and devolution (for a more effective management of operational activities and greater impact) (see Chapter 8);
• between providing direct services as opposed to outsourcing them (see Chapter 8);
• between competing and cooperating with private agencies (see Chapter 9); and
• between being a service enterprise and being a delivery agency for public policies (see Chapter 10).

The trade-offs involved in these conflicting demands are discussed in the subsequent chapters.

The impact of the information society upon PES operations is profound and is providing new ways to carry out all the PES functions. Not only are the possibilities for PES service delivery being transformed, but the expectations of PES customers and citizens for access to information are generating radical changes in public services in general. As a result, the trade-offs just mentioned are being substantially redefined. For example, the analysis in Chapter 4 suggests that there is no inherent contradiction between a universal self-help service and personalized service because new technology gives the PES the opportunity to run relatively low-cost self-service systems alongside enhanced personalized services. Open self-service systems can radically improve labour market transparency while at the same time releasing staff for labour intensive work with disadvantaged jobseekers or for employers with specific recruitment problems.

The biggest challenge for the PES on the path of modernization is to answer the following questions: How great is its capability? How best can it fulfil its enlarged role? Can it match its role to its capability? The strategic choices arising out of these will have an impact on the programmes that the PES undertakes and on PES management, organization, staff capacity and relations with other organizations. The chapters that follow show how the PES in various countries implements its enlarged role.

Notes

[1] European Commission: *The way forward: The European employment strategy – Contributions to and outcome of the Dublin European Council, 13 and 14 December 1996* (Luxembourg, Office for the Official Publications of the European Communities, 1997), p. 25.

[2] In a number of countries, there is no longer a Ministry of Labour as such so government management of the PES may rest with a ministry concerned with education and employment (as in the United Kingdom and Canada) or with trade and industry (as in Ireland).

[3] European Commission: *The modernisation of public employment services in Europe: Three key elements* (Luxembourg, Office for the Official Publications of the European Communities, 1999), pp. 26–27.

[4] Ibid.

[5] ILO: *The United States public employment service country study* (Geneva, ILO, 1998; mimeographed).

[6] S. Ricca made a distinction between traditional functions (e.g. unemployment insurance management; placement; vocational information and guidance; mobility assistance; employment of foreign workers; trans-border placement of national workers; and production of labour market information) and new functions (e.g. specialized forms of placement; self-placement; assistance to jobseekers; vocational guidance; job training; advisory services to enterprises; occupational redeployment measures; special employment promotion measures; and management of employment funds). See S. Ricca: *Introduction to public employment services – A workers' education manual* (Geneva, ILO, 1994), Chs. 2 & 3. The OECD in its series of country reviews on the PES has classified the main functions of the PES under three categories: placement, the management of unemployment benefits, and the application of active labour market measures.

[7] The functions of the PES and the major tasks associated with it are also listed in summary form in Annex II. Not all these functions and tasks are provided by every PES. Indeed, the PES in some cases only provides a minority of the services. Nevertheless we thought it useful to set out the main potential services which could be offered by PES.

[8] In Indonesia for example, a significant amount of PES effort is devoted to the placement of migrant workers, interregional placement and the regulation of private employment agencies.

[9] The Japan country study reported 13,000 staff working in PES offices in 1991. See ILO: *The public employment service in Japan* (Geneva, ILO, 1998; mimeographed), p. 43. The Poland study reported 20,500 staff in labour offices in Poland at the end of 1997, an increase of 7,324 over 1996. See ILO: *The public employment service in Poland*, (Geneva, ILO, 1998; mimeographed), p. 43.

[10] ILO: *The public employment service in the United States* (Geneva, ILO, 1998; mimeographed); Additional information, 1999.

[11] ILO: *The public employment service in Canada* (Geneva, ILO, 1998; mimeographed), p. 78.

[12] OECD: *Employment Outlook 1991* (Paris, OECD, 1991), p. 213; p. 217.

[13] G. Schultz and B. Klemmer: *Public employment services in English-speaking Africa: Proposals for reorganization* (ILO, Harare, 1998), p. 1.

[14] D. Fraser: *Managing the Papua New Guinean labour market for the 21st century*, SEAPAT Working Party Paper No. 2 (Manila, ILO, 1998), passim.

[15] L. Richter: *Present and potential role of employment services in developing countries* (Geneva, ILO, 1975), p.29.

JOB-BROKING   4

The increasing use of self-service systems will gradually make it possible to relieve
staff of information service duties and make it possible to devote more staff time to
tasks where personal contact is necessary. In the long run, new ways of organizing
the PES must be developed.[1]

Introduction

It was suggested in Chapter 1 that job-broking was the starting point for most
of the PES. Job-broking remains a fundamental but controversial function of
the PES today, not just because of changing labour market conditions and
employment policies, but also because of the problems that have arisen in
relation to private employment agencies following the ending of the PES
monopoly in many countries. It is also the area where new methods and new
technology are causing the most profound changes.

For the purposes of this study the term "job-broking" is used to describe the
classic labour exchange function of the PES. It can be defined as: the processes
through which the PES or PREAs arrange for jobseekers to find jobs and for
employers to fill vacancies. The rationale for job-broking is that since neither
employers nor jobseekers have full information about vacant jobs and
candidates, there is a need for a service which can help make the links between
the two sides. Without such a service, jobs take longer to fill and people stay
unemployed for longer periods than is necessary. The PES tries to fill this lack
of information and put employers and jobseekers in touch with each other.

The PES is not the only channel for filling job vacancies. Other channels
include personal contacts, newspaper advertisements, notice boards and
PREAs. According to a survey undertaken across seven EU member States,
newspaper advertisements, professional networks and personal contacts are the
most frequently used recruitment tools.[2] National studies on the same questions

also confirm that the majority of vacancies are not filled through the PES, but mostly through newspaper advertisements and informal contacts.[3] There is no guarantee, however, that other methods of filling jobs look after the interests of the most disadvantaged in the labour market. In addition to the mainly economic arguments for public intervention therefore, most countries also see the PES as having a particular responsibility for helping more disadvantaged jobseekers.

This chapter first examines the general approach to the job-broking process in terms of how jobseekers and vacancies are registered, how the PES markets itself to target audiences and how information is displayed and jobseekers matched with jobs. It then details instances of good practice and innovation and discusses the merits of a personalized service in comparison to a universal self-help system. Before drawing conclusions, the issues involved in measuring the impact of job-broking are discussed. (Further discussion of the latter topic can be found in Chapter 8 while the relationship between the PES and PREAs is discussed further in Chapter 9.)

General aspects of job-broking

The general principles underlying the job-broking function of the PES can be summarized as follows.[4]

- Labour exchange services should be available on a voluntary basis and put at the disposal of all workers and employers.
- Labour exchange services should be provided free of charge to enable all to use them irrespective of their economic situation.
- Confidentiality and privacy of information should be maintained in relation to jobseekers.
- The job-broking process should be impartial and avoid unfair discrimination towards employers or workers.[5]
- The PES must remain neutral in disputes between employers and workers.

While the latter may well be the case in theory, in practice the emphasis varies according to the labour market situation and national employment policies.

The basic function of the PES is therefore to match jobseekers with vacancies in accordance with the above principles. However, because of the persistence of unemployment, especially long-term unemployment, and the systematic difficulties facing certain disadvantaged groups, the PES has been given the additional task of assisting disadvantaged jobseekers in ways other than just providing a job-broking service. These groups of disadvantaged workers include people with disabilities, retrenched workers, young people, lone parents and the long-term unemployed. (The special services provided for these groups are discussed in "Job-search assistance" in Chapter 6.)

The traditional job-broking process consists of listing job vacancies from employers and obtaining information from individual jobseekers, then matching the two. This involves the following major tasks:

* interviewing jobseekers and registering information about them;
* job canvassing;
* registering and advertising job vacancies on display boards, computer screens, newspapers, radio, TV and the Internet;
* appraising job vacancies and jobseekers and matching them;
* liaising between employers and jobseekers; and
* providing job-search assistance (see Chapter 6) for those jobseekers who need it in order to successfully compete in the labour market

Registering jobseekers and vacancies

Where PES staff undertake the matching of jobseekers and vacancies, they need to have a register of vacant jobs and a register of jobseekers. These registers can vary in sophistication according to the complexity of the labour market involved. The most basic kind may consist of a list of vacant jobs with the names and addresses of relevant employers plus a list with the names and addresses of jobseekers. However, most employers require more specific skills and experience and the labour force tends to be comprised of people with a variety of skills and experiences. Therefore, the PES needs more sophisticated registers which differentiate vacancies and jobseekers by occupation and this in turn requires an occupational classification system. An International Standard Classification of Occupations (Revised 1988), known as ISCO-88 was established by the ILO to assist countries in building up their own occupational classification system.[6]

Registers may be manual or computerized. Computerized systems have several advantages over manual systems, especially for circulation, statistics and matching. A computer network that links job centres can make vacancies available in a number of local offices simultaneously and can produce aggregated labour market statistics based on the information collected from employers and jobseekers. Job-matching is facilitated by being able to search for specific requirements through the jobseeker and vacancy register. A computerized system involves extra equipment costs and requires skilled staff, but it can free up staff time for customer services. (See "The use of information and communications technology" in Chapter 8.)

Jobseekers who wish to be referred to a job by the PES are normally registered in the jobseeker register. Traditionally, the register has been the basic tool that has enabled the PES to refer jobseekers to a job vacancy. The information compiled has to be relevant and accurate since the information should make it possible for a PES officer to assess which candidates have the aptitude for filling a notified job. The information system has to be regularly updated to ensure that people registered as unemployed are still in fact unemployed. The register should contain all necessary information about the jobseeker such as name, address, age, education, skills, work experience (coded by an occupational classification system) and job wishes. Some countries ban the inclusion of information which might be used as a basis for unfair discrimination such as ethnicity, but others deliberately include such information to provide a statistical check on whether discrimination is taking place. Information should, where appropriate, be verified.

Several developed countries and many developing and transition countries have a statutory notification requirement for employers but this law is often not enforced. In practice, only employers who want assistance in filling vacancies notify the PES who then enter the vacancy in the vacancy register. The Norwegian PES includes in its vacancy file not only those vacancies about which it has been directly notified, but also vacancies advertised in newspapers and magazines – the latter being responsible for 7 per cent of all placements in 1997. When giving notification of vacancies, the employer should provide all necessary details about them to facilitate the PES search for appropriate candidates. The information should include items such as name and address of employer, description of tasks, skills required and conditions of employment (e.g. short time, fixed term or permanent contract, wages, hours of work and so forth). Jobs are generally coded according to an occupational classification system such as the ISCO-88.

As part of the vacancy registration process, the PES may assist employers in clarifying the requirements for the job. Furthermore, the PES may provide advice to the employer about the prospect of finding candidates that match their requirements. For example, where employers pitch a salary at an unrealistically low level, a PES officer might advise the employer about potential recruitment problems and the employer may then either increase the salary offered or reduce the job requirements. Often during this process, the PES officer provides additional labour market information to give the employer a broader picture of the labour market. Vacancy registers tend to be extremely volatile and it is vital for their credibility that the status of vacancies is regularly checked and that vacancies that are filled are promptly cancelled throughout the system.

Marketing PES services

The majority of employers do not notify vacancies to the PES. However, if the PES wants to assist the jobseekers on its registers to find jobs, it needs vacancies. Therefore it is important for the PES to attract as many vacancies as possible which match the qualifications of jobseekers. The PES uses a variety of strategies to canvas for job vacancies.

Regular contact with employers and the provision of useful services for them can help to improve employers' perception of, and confidence in, the PES and thereby increase the vacancies notified to the PES. In an increasing number of countries including Belgium, France, China, Japan, Spain, the United Kingdom and Hong Kong, China, the PES has established active and extensive contacts with employers by undertaking regular visits to enterprises either for consultation on hires and/or for providing information on employment services and assistance on problems of employment management. In the United Kingdom, the PES has been appointing specific officers as account managers to manage the PES relationship with particular firms. In Austria, Germany and Sweden, every employer has one counsellor as a fixed contact person at the PES. Each counsellor has an average list of personal contacts consisting of jobseekers, employers and other unemployed. The numbers of these vary: Austria has 250, Germany 300 and Sweden 150 (limited to large or medium enterprises). Counsellors are expected to spend 15 to 20 per cent of their time visiting employers. In Belgium, the vocational training an employment service of the Walloon and German-speaking community (FOREM)[7] has established enterprise relations units for developing a systematic plan for proactive vacancy searches. The plan includes the type of enterprise to be targeted, the method used for approaching it, numeric goals of vacancies to be collected and guidelines for evaluation of the operation.

Job-matching and information display methods

In the 50 years following the ILO's original commendation of the PES in 1919, matching was normally carried out as a closed system by PES staff on behalf of their clients. However, in the 1970s, there was a self-service revolution which meant that vacancies were placed on display enabling jobseekers to match themselves against them with only limited, if any, intervention by PES staff. The degree of involvement of the PES in the job-broking process thus varies according to how information on jobseekers and job vacancies is made available. The PES can present information as "closed", "semi-open" or "open".

In the closed system, information about vacancies and jobseekers is restricted to PES staff. Both employers and jobseekers then have to rely on the assistance of PES staff. The PES fully controls the referrals of jobseekers to employers. Employers welcome a service which screens applicants carefully so that they only need to interview a shortlist of well-qualified applicants. Such a system also offers the PES opportunities to press the claims of hard-to-place and less qualified jobseekers in order to increase their chances of receiving a job. However, too much emphasis on social objectives can sometimes undermine employers' confidence in the service and thereby reduce their use of the PES in comparison to other recruitment methods. In a closed system therefore, the PES has to strike a balance between its responsibilities to the disadvantaged and its need to maintain credibility with employers.

The advent of self-service systems led the PES in most countries to introduce a semi-open system in which information about vacancies was made available to jobseekers without publishing the name and address of the employer. This enables jobseekers to carry out their own job-search and when they find a suitable job, they have to obtain the name and address of the employer from PES staff. The PES officer then plays a screening role, which could on the one hand simply entail checking that the individual is not unsuitable or on the other, could involve a thorough check against the employers' requirements. Subject to this screening, the PES office then contacts the employer to arrange an interview.

In the third option, the open system, the PES presents information directly to both sides of the market and lets the two sides make contact with each other without further intervention from the PES. On the vacancy side, an open system means that the vacancies on display include details of the name, address and phone number of the relevant employer. This enables jobseekers to contact employers directly, without screening by PES staff. Open access to jobseekers' particulars is more unusual, since this can raise difficult issues of personal privacy. However, the Internet has opened up the possibility for jobseekers to place themselves if they wish in an open jobseeker file.

There is now a variety of methods available for displaying vacancies in an open or semi-open system that ensure easy access for jobseekers. The simplest way is to display vacancy cards on boards in PES offices or to publish vacancy bulletins which jobseekers can consult. In many countries these methods are still the only method of publicizing vacancies. However, new technology such as telephone databanks, computer kiosks, teletext and the Internet allows more sophisticated ways of accessing vacancies.

Open systems present a number of potential problems. In the first place, employers may object to the loss of screening by the PES of jobseekers approaching them for a post. This can in conditions of labour surplus lead to employers either receiving more applicants than they wish or receiving candidates who do not match the requirements of the job. (Possible PES responses to this are discussed later in this chapter.) The second potential problem of the open system is that the PES is less likely to know if a vacancy has been filled and so may be slower to remove it from circulation. Furthermore, the PES needs an effective system to check the status of current vacancies. Finally, open systems make it difficult, if not impossible, to find out whether a vacancy has been filled as a result of PES action; thus, where PES performance has previously been measured on placements, a shift to open systems means a fundamental reappraisal of performance management.

These three different ways of handling vacancies have advantages and disadvantages, and therefore many countries use a combination of all three. The method of handling vacancies affects the degree of involvement for PES staff in job-broking with heavy staff input for closed vacancies, modest staff input for semi-open vacancies and little or no staff input for open vacancies. Thus, an open system has the potential advantage of saving staff time. Jobseekers who are capable of managing their own job-search do not need assistance from the PES. The PES can thus focus on candidates who have more severe problems in finding jobs.

In many developed countries, the pattern of job-broking has been affected by rising unemployment, staffing pressures and changing technology. ILO and OECD country studies on the PES have led to the adoption of several principles by the PES towards the handling of jobseekers, employers and job-broking. When dealing with jobseekers, countries such as the United Kingdom (where registration takes place within systems closely integrated with unemployment benefits) still use the traditional system of administrative registration. The same is true for developing countries where regulatory activities on placement and employment still play an important role. In other countries such as Belgium and France, the administrative registration is handled by benefit offices while PES registration is restricted to jobseeker profiling and to determining competencies for placement purposes. In Canada, where resources are tight, registration has been abandoned and the PES relies solely on self-service broking.

In every country, the PES does its best to provide general jobseekers with information on job vacancies through contact with staff and/or through self-service facilities such as billboards, automated telephone systems, computer terminals and the Internet. In addition to providing vacancy information and matching jobseekers with job vacancies, the PES in most developed countries also offers more intensive and personalized services to special groups of jobseekers such as women, the long-term unemployed, young people and people with disabilities. (Job-search assistance is discussed further in Chapter 6.)

With regard to employers, the PES still tends to receive vacancy notifications from employers in traditional ways such as by telephone, mail and fax.

However, countries that use advanced information technology such as Canada, the Netherlands, the United States and the Scandinavian countries also encourage employers to register their vacancies directly, thus enabling job-seekers to scan what is available. The PES in many developed countries also reach out to employers through regular visits to enterprises. This is done mainly to better understand employers' staffing problems and needs and also to market PES services and canvass for job vacancies. In some countries, the PES extends its job canvassing visits to provide advice on human resource planning (Canada), to provide employment management problems (Japan), and to provide labour market information and analysis (the United States). They also organize job fairs, employer workshops and seminars.

In relation to the handling of job vacancies and job-broking, the development of information technology has contributed to PES efficiency in registering jobseekers and job vacancies and in listing job orders and applicants: in short, it has facilitated self-service and automatic broking. The PES in many developed and transition countries such as Canada, Hungary, Norway, Poland, Slovenia, the United States and the EU member States have their own web sites in which they present general information concerning their role, functions, activities, publications and the labour market. (For a list of these sites, see Annex VI.1.) Many of these also maintain a job vacancy database on the Internet to enable jobseekers to look for vacancies. But only a few have so far introduced a jobseekers' database on the Internet which can enable employers to search for suitable job applicants: these include Canada, Finland, Slovenia, Sweden and the United States. In the United States, America's Talent Bank (ATB) enables jobseekers to submit their resumés via the Internet. This information can then be directly accessed by employers or through the PES.

Although most countries have self-service facilities of one kind or another, only Canada relies almost entirely on open self-service broking without any attempt to pre-screen workers. Because of considerations such as employer expectations, problems of performance measurement and the social objectives of the PES, the PES in other countries maintain closed or semi-open systems for filling most of their vacancies, even if they also use open systems to some extent. In most countries, unfortunately, the PES does not have a clear view of the right balance between self-service and active broking.

Innovations and good practices by the PES

To improve operations, the PES in various countries have introduced technological innovations and developed new ways of handling employers and jobseekers and of putting both in touch with each other. Examples of these technological innovations can be found in Annexes IV.1 to IV.8. Briefly, these innovations include:

- computerized kiosks and internet employment services in Canada (see Annex IV.1);
- a computerized operational repertory of occupations and jobs called ROME in France (see Annex IV.2);
- an overall employment information system called OEIS in Japan (see Annex IV.3);
- a national employment system information service called SISNE in Mexico (see Annex IV.4);
- internet employment services in Slovenia (see Annex IV.5);
- internet self-service systems in Sweden (see Annex IV.6);
- a jobs hotline in the United Kingdom (see Annex IV.7); and
- internet employment services in the United States (see Annex IV.8).

Of these developments, the one with potentially the most profound implications for the PES is the use of internet technology. This is still undergoing intensive development and refinement and so far no thorough evaluation of its effectiveness as a vehicle for delivering PES services has been made available. Nonetheless it is already extensively used in countries such as Sweden and the United States. In November 1998, 6 million job searches were carried out on America's Job Bank (AJB). Similarly in September 1998, Sweden's Job Bank registered about 250,000 unique visitors and this figure excludes jobseekers accessing the site from PES customer workstations. The figure amounted to 6 per cent of the total Swedish workforce. In both Sweden and the United States, internet services comprise not only a vacancy bank but also a jobseeker bank designed to be compatible with the vacancy bank. In addition, other services such as career information are also being made available via the Internet.

In France and the Netherlands, new practices for registering jobseekers have been introduced and developed but for different purposes. In 1993, France introduced a *Fichier historique* or "History file" (FH) of jobseekers registered at the ANPE (see Annex IV.9). This file helps the agency to evaluate the impact of its employment measures and changes in services including the benefits provided to participants and benefit recipients respectively. In this way, it helps to ensure that ANPE services are planned to match the characteristics of jobseekers. In addition to this, France introduced new quality services in 1998 for dealing with jobseekers (see Annex IV.11).

The Netherlands has developed an instrument called *Kansmeter* (see Annex IV.10) which is used to assess the "remove" or "distance" of a jobseeker from the labour market in an effort to develop a realistic method of appraising the scope for re-integrating jobseekers into the market. With this method, jobseekers are placed in one of four categories or phases. Those with a good record are assigned to Phase 1 and the PES only nominates these clients for vacancies. Phase 2 clients are deemed to need limited re-integration services, while Phase 3 clients need more extended services, such as training or work experience. Phase 4 clients are at the greatest remove from the labour market and are assigned first to the services of social assistance institutions, though they may later move back into Phases 3 or 2.

For dealing with employers, the Workforce Development Centre (WDC) of Wisconsin has provided an example of the renewed importance placed on employer services through an integrated menu of services developed in consultation with an employer advisory board. It is notable that this service does not generally provide job-broking assistance directly to employers, but rather gives them access to the database. In response to an employer request, the WDC can screen potential applicants using objective criteria but this option is not commonly used (see Annex IV.12).

Self-help services and enhanced personalized services

At the beginning of this chapter, it was argued that there were two main justifications for a PES role in the labour market: an economic-based argument for promoting greater labour market transparency; a social-based argument for supporting those at a disadvantage in the labour market. The character and emphasis of the PES depends on which of these rationales is given priority at any given time. This in turn is normally a function of national employment policy.

In recent years, national employment policies have placed emphasis on active policies as a means of getting disadvantaged unemployed people back to work and as a means of preventing unemployed people from sinking into long-term unemployment. (See "Governments and labour market adjustment programmes" in Chapter 6.) The PES job-broking role is clearly critical to these policies. At the same time, new technology is opening up previously unheard-of opportunities for improving overall labour market transparency. Thus a major issue under consideration in a number of countries is achieving a balance between a universal labour exchange that strives for the broadest possible penetration of the labour market, and the desire to focus limited public resources on serving the most disadvantaged jobseekers.

We have seen that the self-service revolution of the 1970s made job-broking much more transparent, enabling jobseekers to conduct their own job-search without having to rely so much on PES staff. Information technology facilitated this first by assisting and speeding up the display of vacancies and second, by making vacancies accessible to the public either through computer screens in PES offices, through electronic kiosks in public places, through automatic telephone facilities or most recently, through the Internet. Internet access arguably represents a revolution as profound as the previous self-service revolution, since it provides a powerful means of round-the-clock delivery in the home without using the offices of the PES. This would seem to further reduce the intermediary role of the PES. Both jobseekers and employers can now immediately provide and retrieve the information they need without asking an intermediary for assistance. For basic information on job vacancies and candidates, the automated self-service approach is replacing the service assisted approach provided by PES staff.

It is significant that in the United States, the changes in core job-broking activities as a result of dramatic changes in technology have not been uniform across states. An assessment study was undertaken in 1997 to help states tailor public job-broking to meet their own needs. This study identified options available in the major areas of the job-broking process, the advantages and disadvantages of choosing each option and the criteria for evaluating the options. (The study is described in Annex IV.13.)

The full implications of the internet revolution on the PES will take some years to become apparent. Meanwhile, it must be expected that the PES in the more developed countries will want to take advantage of what the Internet offers. After all, the PES risks losing its position as the provider of the leading national vacancy bank to the private sector if it fails to exploit the potential of the new technology. However, in this context it is important that certain important issues are addressed and debated by PES managers in relation to the use of the Internet.

The first of these concerns the level of service on offer: will all jobseeker customers receive the same universal self-help level of service, or will some customers be offered an enhanced level of service? Does the brave new world of the PES simply imply the provision of computerized broking conducted in the home with no further need for local offices and a minimal need for staff? Such a vision of the future seems highly implausible. In practice, it seems unavoidable that the PES must continue to provide personalized assistance to those who are more disadvantaged or vulnerable in the labour market. Often these will not have access to the Internet in their homes. Excessive reliance on the Internet could thus increase social exclusion. To avoid this, the PES must continue to provide self-help access to vacancies in local offices or other public places and they need to make these as user-friendly as possible. Even then, some of their unemployed clients will still lack the skills to take advantage of these facilities and PES staff will need to coach them, as was suggested in the ILO country study conducted on the PES in the United States.[8] Moreover, many clients who are fully competent to use the Internet are still likely to need staff assistance. This applies to those who have been made redundant after a long spell in work and who may be unfamiliar with job-search or to those who may need to discuss alternative career choices.

Human contact will continue to be required for a significant proportion of jobseekers for all sorts of reasons, but we can expect technology to change PES offices profoundly. For instance in Sweden, computer workstations have been installed at PES offices (for details, see Annex IV.14). These function as resource centres in a system in which the public use the computer but also rely on PES staff for both technical assistance and for assistance on those matters for which the computer is no help. We are entering a phase of very uncertain development in which the critical issue will be achieving the correct balance between the provision of readily accessible services for the full range of qualified jobseekers and the provision of enhanced services for certain disadvantaged jobseekers. (See also "Job-search assistance" in Chapter 6.)

The second issue arising out of the introduction of the Internet concerns relationships with employers. As the trend towards use of the Internet and other computerized self-help mechanisms gathers pace, the question as to whether vacancies should be displayed in an open or a semi-open form needs to be addressed. In other words, should internet users be given enough information to contact employers directly or should they be made to contact the PES first? One attractive option would be to leave the choice up to employers, in other words a PES screening service would be available if preferred. But if PES resources are further reduced, as they have already been in some cases (see "Resources" in Chapter 3), would the PES be then able to afford to offer such a screening service? This introduces the issue of charging employers for an enhanced service and thus making the PES more like a PREA. Another option would be to reach an understanding with an employer that the PES would provide a selective service and in return the employer would give serious consideration to disadvantaged jobseekers. The United Kingdom used to run a programme like this called the "job interview guarantee" scheme.

Measuring the impact of job-broking

The final issue that needs to be addressed here is PES performance and labour market penetration: in short, how can the success of PES job-broking operations be measured? One approach is to judge the PES by its labour-market penetration or market share, for example the proportion of jobseekers registering with the PES, the proportion of total vacancies notified to the PES and the proportion of total engagements in the labour market achieved by the PES. All these statistics on market shares are derived from ratios of absolute figures on stock and flows of jobseekers plus vacancies and placements. These can create a number of data definition and calculation problems and must be interpreted with caution.[9] Neither is this kind of information easy to obtain. Large-scale surveys are normally required to establish the base information against which PES performance statistics can be compared and in measuring the market share of engagements in the labour market, different results are obtained according to whether employers or jobseekers are surveyed.

Another problem shared by market share and overall placement statistics is that both give all placements equal value regardless of their true social and economic value. For example, a casual engagement as a strawberry picker for a few days is given the same value as the long-term placement of a person with serious disabilities. These penetration measures will become even less credible in the future if open systems on the Internet become a major element in PES job-broking activity and where the PES role will be to provide the electronic infrastructure, leaving the selection work to employers and jobseekers themselves. It is significant that the Government in the United Kingdom is currently reviewing PES performance targets and that a House of Commons Committee has suggested moving away from the use of placement-based performance targets. Instead it has proposed that "while data about the number of placements should still be recorded, this should be replaced as the core measure of the effectiveness of the employment services by targets which measure more accurately the value added by the service".[10]

It therefore seems clear that market share will retain a limited value as an indicator of the PES contribution to the transparency of the labour market. Any serious assessment of PES job-broking will require a range of other measures, including customer satisfaction measures (see "Performance management" in Chapter 8). Moreover, in order to assess the PES contribution more generally, it is important to determine the value added by the PES. This approach gives a better prospect of capturing the real worth of the PES to the economy and to society.

Conclusion

The current major trends in PES job-broking services in developed countries involve the extension of self-service facilities for general jobseekers from the display of vacancies in employment service offices to providing access in public places and in the home. This is being achieved by means of kiosks, telephonic job link facilities and lately and most importantly, the Internet. These facilities also offer the potential for developing computerized jobseeker files, career information files and other services. Recent trends also include an increased outreach to employers in an effort to increase vacancy notification, and an increase in intensive and systematic job-search assistance for those at a disadvantage in the labour market (see "Job-search assistance" in Chapter 6).

With the advance of information technology, self-service broking through the Internet (via access to vacancy banks and jobseeker banks) has been introduced by the PES in developed countries such as Canada, Japan, Norway, Sweden and the United States. However, active broking for semi-open and closed vacancies in relation to the hard-to-place is still a major task for PES staff in developed and transition countries (with the exception of Canada) and is often linked with the delivery of job-search assistance services (see Chapter 6).

The electronic revolution is fundamentally changing the nature of job-broking and reducing the intermediary role of the PES. In the most techno-logically advanced countries, jobseekers and employers are increasingly coming into contact with each other through self-service systems on the Internet without the intervention of PES placement officers. As a result, the employer will increasingly register a vacancy directly in the job bank and remove it as soon as no more applications are required. The electronic revolution also means that employers will be able to conduct "electronic interviews" and screen jobseekers with the help of self-service systems. Thus for most transactions, the PES contribution will merely be to provide the self-service infrastructure for employers and jobseekers to use, together with knowledge and training in how to use them. Experience already suggests that once customers have tested self-service systems, they usually prefer them to the traditional service in which they are dependent upon the availability of staff and/or on limited opening hours.

Because an electronic service is relatively cheap to run, it should enable the PES to shift staff from traditional job-broking work to providing intensive assistance to unemployed and hard-to-place individuals who cannot find jobs through the electronic services. Thus there is a trend towards a tiered system differentiated according to the needs of clients. In countries such as the Netherlands, this approach has already been formalized.

As we enter the new century, the PES faces important strategic decisions about achieving the proper balance between an approach that focuses on maximum labour-market transparency and one more focused on disadvantaged groups. In addition, it needs to maintain credibility as a supplier of competent labour and as a body capable of meeting social policy objectives. These decisions will be affected by the relationship between the PES and unemployment benefit and this is discussed in Chapter 7. The strategy adopted will also affect the management and organization of the PES as well as its employees' profile and training. This issue is discussed in Chapter 8.

Notes

[1] C. Almén: *New technology in the Swedish public employment service: Development of customer service self-service on the Internet*, Unpublished Report (Solana, September, 1998), p. 6.

[2] M. Tixier Essec: "Les outils de recrutement en Europe: Evolution de leurs spécifités", in *Humanisme et Entreprise*, No. 231, 1998, pp. 82–83.

[3] U. Walwei: *Placement as a public responsibility and as a private service* (Berlin, Institute for Employment Research, 1996), p. 7.

[4] G. Schulz and B. Klemmer: *Public employment services in English-speaking Africa – Proposals for re-organization* (ILO, Harare, 1998), p. 19.

[5] In some countries positive discrimination in favour of certain disadvantaged groups (e.g. people with disabilities) is explicitly authorized.

[6] ISCO-88 has been designed to serve as a model for national standard classifications of occupations and to facilitate international communication about occupation and comparable statistics. The standard classifies and defines groups of occupations at different levels of aggregation (detail) and is designed to organize all jobs according to the main tasks and duties of the work performed. The main similarity criteria used to define groups are the skill level and the skill specialization required. Four broad skill-level groups are distinguished while skill specialization is defined both broadly and in detail.

[7] FOREM is the acronym used by the OECD for *Office Communautaire et Régional de la Formation Professionnelle et de l'Emploi*. This is the vocational training and employment service for the Walloon region and German-speaking community in Belgium.

[8] ILO: *The United States public employment service country study* (Geneva, ILO, 1998; mimeographed), p. 39.

[9] U.Walwei: *Performance evaluation of public employment services*, Labour Administration Branch Document No. 47 (Geneva, ILO, 1996), pp. 26–30.

[10] United Kingdom House of Commons Education and Employment Committee: *The performance and future role of the employment service*, Report and proceedings of the Education and Employment Committee, Vol. 1 (London, Stationery Office, 1999), p xiii, para. 23.

LABOUR MARKET INFORMATION   5

Canada's PES has placed a high priority on labour market information (LMI) over the last two decades. In part, the rationale was theoretical. Labour markets, like other markets, work most efficiently and fairly when there is a timely flow of accurate information available to all participants. There were also some practical reasons. Workers and employers are better educated than ever before and therefore more able to absorb and use information. Partly because workers and employers are more self-reliant and partly because of resource pressures, the PES has been emphasizing self-service. One of the most valuable elements of self-service is labour market information.[1]

Introduction

The development of labour market information (LMI) is a fundamentally different function for the PES from the other PES functions discussed in this study. The products and services which it generates are more indirect in their impact on people than other PES products. The work processes that produce them are largely administrative and often indirect, unlike other PES work. Moreover, while jobseekers and employers are important customers for LMI, there are many other customer groups. At the same time, there are clear linkages between LMI and the other PES functions. Administrative information from the other functions can provide input for LMI products. Likewise, external LMI products also provide input into the planning and management of the other PES functions. Finally, neither the PES nor other government agencies is the sole producer or analyser of labour market information.

The ILO has defined labour market information as:

....any information concerning the size and composition of the labour market or any part of the labour market; the way it or any part of it functions, its problems, the opportunities which may be available to it, and the employment-related intentions or aspirations of those who are part of it.[2]

The demand for information has created private markets as well. The principal challenge for the PES is to determine the need for LMI from a national perspective, a factor which varies depending on a country's development and the complexity of its economy. Furthermore, it also needs to determine the appropriate role for the PES in providing it.

This chapter looks at the role of the PES and the production of LMI from the following contexts: as a by-product of other PES functions; the PES as a producer of primary labour market statistics; and the PES as the synthesizer, interpreter and distributor of LMI. It also looks at current delivery trends in the services, in particular the increasing demand for information, alternative LMI service providers, innovations in LMI analysis and finally, innovations in the dissemination of LMI and in self-service LMI.

PES roles in labour market information

The Employment Service Convention, 1948 (No. 88) provides a broad mandate for the PES in the area of LMI. It charges the PES to:

> ...collect and analyse, in co-operation where appropriate with other authorities and with management and trade unions, the fullest available information on the situation of the employment market and its probable evolution, both in the country as a whole and in the different industries, occupations and areas, and make such information available systematically and promptly to the public authorities, the employers' and workers' organizations concerned, and the general public.[3]

In practice, the role of the PES in providing LMI differs widely from country to country but three main roles can be identified. Most often, the PES produces LMI as a by-product of its other functions. In some countries, the PES is the main organization responsible for producing primary labour market statistics; in most countries, however, a central bureau of statistics or a ministry of planning fulfills this role. The PES may also assume the role of analyser, synthesizer and distributor of value-added LMI rather than as a producer of basic statistics. These three roles are not mutually exclusive. The PES may carry out one, two or all three of them. Each of these three roles is now examined in more detail.

LMI as a by-product of PES functions

Jobseeker and vacancy information is registered accurately, timely and continuously in the PES and can therefore provide useful information of short-term fluctuations in labour demand and supply. Practically everywhere, the PES collects and produces information on the individual labour market transactions it delivers, namely the registration and posting of reported job vacancies, the registration of the unemployed and jobseekers and the hiring of jobseekers for vacancies (see Chapter 4). However, such PES administrative records cannot provide a comprehensive picture of situations in the labour market for several reasons. Firstly, jobseeker and vacancy registers are primarily constructed to assist job-broking rather than LMI. Thus, the definitions and classifications used in the registers have to reflect the often changing rules and regulations of the PES and these may not correspond to the needs of some of the users of the LMI statistics. Secondly, as was noted in the previous chapter, the PES covers only information on jobseekers and employers who have been in contact with its offices. This means that the information provided by PES registers can be rather limited because in most economies, much recruitment takes place without PES involvement. However, in countries such as Norway and Finland, the PES have systematically registered all vacancies advertised in public media such as newspapers, journals and web sites, even when these have not been directly reported to the PES. As a result, a better service can be provided to jobseekers and the resulting statistics on vacancies will have a much better coverage.

Although PES administrative records have limited coverage, they can still provide useful insight into developments in the labour market. If information is collected and processed promptly and correctly, it can give useful information on trends in the labour market, in particular the part of the labour market which is served by the PES. To a limited extent, information from the PES can be used to project trends for a particular segment of the labour market. In particular, it is useful for small areas covered by a local employment offices. Such areas are normally so small that reliable results cannot be provided from national labour force surveys.

In addition, unemployment benefit records are often used as a source of LMI. In the United States for example, the employer record database of unemployment insurance is the most comprehensive register of employer information for labour market statistics purposes. This file provides the universe of employer records from which samples are drawn for various establishment surveys. Administrative statistics from labour market adjustment programmes can also be used to enhance the understanding of labour market dynamics.

Norway uses its own PES administrative data to gain a better knowledge of the career paths of the unemployed. The Directorate of Labour has established a panel database named LARS, which tracks all people registered by the PES after 1988. This information is useful for assessing how labour market and labour market policies function. Up till recently, the PES has occasionally presented analyses based on the panel database, but as of the second half of 1998, it was planned to include panel observations in its monthly bulletin. In terms of restructuring micro-level PES data from the labour exchange for LMI purposes, France has embarked on an ambitious project called the *Fichier historique* (FH) or "History file" project. This involves the PES using administrative data for analysis of labour market and programme trends. A description of this project can be found in Annex IV.9.

The PES as a producer of primary labour market statistics

In a few countries, the PES itself collects and aggregates primary labour market statistics on the basis of sources other than its own administrative records. This is achieved by means of regular censuses, regular surveys, administrative data and periodic ad hoc surveys. There are three important sources of statistics for labour market analysis.

Firstly, regular household surveys, in particular labour force surveys, provide a variety of data on the economically active population, on informal sector activity, on household incomes and expenditures, and on other topics related to the work situation of the population and their working conditions. The usefulness of these survey results depends on the type, size and reliability of the sample. In contrast, population censuses have limited value for tracking trends in the labour market because they are carried out infrequently (every ten years or so), but they do provide useful background information on structural features and are particularly relevant for small groups and local labour markets.

Secondly, regular establishment (employer) surveys draw upon the business records kept by employers and use these to collect statistics on such features as the number of paid employees, hours of work, wages, labour cost and labour productivity. These may also include information on recruitment, conditions of work and training activities and needs. The usefulness of such data depends upon the completeness of the register from which the establishments are selected and the type, size and reliability of the sample.

Thirdly, periodic (ad hoc) employer surveys are conducted to gather in-depth employer views on current and short-term labour market situations. These may be carried out for specific industries or in specific geographic areas. These analyses are useful, particularly when combined with more comprehensive trend analyses.

In the United States, the Bureau of Labour Statistics contracts with all state employment service agencies to conduct the primary data collection for four national business establishment surveys: the current employment statistics programme; the occupational employment statistics programme; the employ-ment and wages programme; and the mass lay-off statistics programme. This means for example that for a state with a population of 5 million, the state employment service distributes, collects and tabulates approximately 150,000 survey responses annually.

In Norway, there is a central statistical agency that collects the majority of labour market statistics. But the Norwegian PES conducts its own primary labour market research by surveying employers every year to obtain their assessment and expectations concerning changes in demand for labour. The sample of 10,000 enterprises from all over the country includes all enterprises with more than 100 employees (except for Oslo). Employers are asked to compare current estimates of the number of employees in their own enterprises with the following year and they are asked for which occupational groups they expect increased demand. Additionally, they are asked whether they see recruitment problems for specific occupations in the coming year. The county employment offices are responsible for collecting the information and the Directorate of Labour prepares analysis at the national level.

Synthesizing, interpreting and distributing labour market information

The third role of the PES in relation to LMI is the conversion of information from various sources into value-added products that meet the needs of various customers. Regardless of the statistical sources, the PES may develop expertise in providing a coherent picture of how the labour market is operating in a comprehensive, accurate, timely, accessible and usable manner. The ultimate value of this information is to assist customers in making informed decisions on public policy, business or individual career decisions. Customers for LMI and the purposes for which they use information can be categorized as follows:[4]

- *National policy makers and planners.* These need information on employment, unemployment, and under-employment and the underlying trends so they can build sound strategies and policies with a view to influencing the evolution of the labour market and in particular, to adjust current and future manpower supply and demand.
- *Employers' and workers' organizations.* These rely on information about wage levels and differentials, labour turnover, productivity, cost-of-living indices and manpower surpluses and shortages. They need this information to formulate policies for collective bargaining processes and wage

negotiations and to help them formulate standpoints on public manpower and employment issues.

- *Educational and vocational training planners.* These need to know what short- and long-term labour demand and supply will be in order to correlate manpower development policies and programmes with expected requirements.
- *Vocational guidance services.* These rely on occupational information about the changing fortunes of different occupations or clusters of occupations to help them to provide meaningful advice about current and expected job opportunities and employment conditions for jobseekers, students and pupils.
- *Employment services.* These need to know where vacancies and available labour resources exist or are likely to arise and what jobseeker qualifications are in demand. This is important to help them underpin job-broking processes and job-search assistance and avoid waste of time and effort by those in the labour market.
- *Individuals and organizations and the wider public.* These need information on manpower supply and demand in their localities, travel-to-work areas and other areas. They need the information to facilitate informed and rational decision-making and to promote equity in the search for employment and access to jobs.

While the PES almost everywhere publishes these kinds of statistics on the basis of administrative data, one of the key indicators that distinguishes the more advanced from the less advanced PES is the capacity to use LMI from a variety of sources to analyse trends in the labour market and on the basis of the analyses, to orient employment policy and programmes. Table 5.1 presents a breakdown of data sources for LMI products developed in partnership between HRDC and the Canadian province of Alberta and illustrates how LMI from a number of sources is combined to produce sophisticated products for a variety of purposes.[5]

Denmark and Canada are two countries where the PES has given extensive attention to the importance of LMI in the overall management of the human resource development system of the country. Descriptions of the organization of their frameworks for the development of LMI are presented in Annexes IV.15 and IV.16 respectively. The frameworks differ in the choice of customers. In the case of Denmark, the chief customer described for LMI development is the PES itself; it uses the data in the planning and management of labour market policies and programmes. In Canada on the other hand, the PES produces LMI for a variety of customers external to the PES establishment.

Table 5.1   Data sources for LMI products in Alberta, Canada

LMI product category	Source of data	National statistics agency	PES administrative data	Other government data	Other private data	LMI analyst
Occupational profiles and forecast	Canadian Occupational Projections System (COPS) /Job futures		X	X	X	
	Statistics Canada: Census data	X				
	Wage and salary survey			X		
	Media and personal contact					X
Community profiles	Statistics Canada: Census data	X				
	Environment Canada: Climatic data			X		
	Canadian Business Information (CBI): Data on local employers				X	
	Municipal data collected locally (services, attractions, etc.)			X		
	Media and personal contact				X	
Human resource profiles	Statistics Canada: Census data	X				
Industrial/sectoral profiles	Statistics Canada: Standard industrial classification	X				
	Revenue Canada: Employer database			X		
	Canadian business information: Employer database				X	
	National Employment Service System (NESS): Job orders, foreign worker requests		X			
	Data on local associations (collected locally)				X	
	Media and personal contact				X	

Table 5.1   Data sources for LMI products in Alberta, Canada (contd.)

LMI product category	Source of data	Category of data source				
		National statistics agency	PES administrative data	Other government data	Other private data	LMI analyst
Wage and salary data and conditions of employment	Wage and salary surveys	X		X		
	National Employment Service System (NESS)		X			
	Data obtained from newspapers, professional associations and local contacts					X
Vacancy and employment opportunities	National Employment Service System (NESS)		X			
	Data obtained from newspapers and personal contacts with employers					X
Labour market reviews and trends	Statistics Canada: Labour force survey	X				
	Employment insurance summary data		X			
	Data obtained from media and personal contact at the local level					X
Occupational demand	Employment insurance summary data		X			
	Data obtained from local personal contact with firms and associations					X
Potential employer lists	Canadian business information database			X		
	Industry association handbooks			X		
	Local contact with employers by the local analyst					X
Major project updates	Provincial economic development departments: surveys			X		
	Local contact with firms developing major projects					X

Table 5.1   Data sources for LMI products in Alberta, Canada (contd.)

LMI product category	Source of data	Category of data source				
		National statistics agency	PES administrative data	Other government data	Other private data	LMI analyst
Learner information about training providers	Government of Alberta: EdInfo web site			X		
Other local economic development	Media reports and personal interviews					X

Trends in service delivery

Increasing demand for information

In general, one of the consequences of the changes in the labour market described in Chapter 2 has been to underscore the value of systematic LMI for all actors in the labour market. Increasing awareness of the changing labour market demand and supply has created a demand for improved LMI to track these changes, to interpret them and to project them into the future. In addition, data on the supply of labour and its labour market characteristics is important for employment policy development and programme planning. Moreover, it is important for implementation and evaluation.

Alternative labour market information service providers

The transformation of PES administrative data into useful LMI is normally carried out by the PES itself and the production of primary labour market statistics is also carried out by the PES or a central statistics agency. In the context of this, the synthesis of labour market statistics into value-added LMI products may be carried out by a number of public and private organizations. Universities or government agencies such as the ministries of planning or even private firms specializing in economic analysis may carry out similar activities, either in addition to or instead of the labour-market analysis conducted by the PES.

One example of an alternative agency that conducts LMI synthesis, inter-pretation and distribution is employment observatories. These can be set up at an international, national, provincial or even local level. At an international level, the Employment Observatory of the Economic Commission is the best known. At a national level, a few French-speaking African countries such as Côte d'Ivoire and Senegal have established employment observatories. The role of an employment observatory is to provide timely and relevant information on various aspects of labour market functioning including:

- projections of future employment development;
- demographic change and mobility;
- emerging skills shortages;
- problem groups in the labour market;
- needs and availability of further training and retraining;
- wages (e.g. distributional issues, development and collective bargaining systems and so forth);
- monitoring international employment trends;
- gathering information on labour market policies, programmes and measures; and
- various economic news relevant to the labour market such as investment plant closures, sales or mergers of enterprises.

Other examples of organizations that provide value-added LMI products are those public and private sector organizations that provide vocational guidance and occupational and career information. In countries such as the United States, Canada and Germany there are a large number of public and private businesses that transform various kinds of data (e.g. occupational projections, salary and wage data, descriptive information on occupations and information on training resources) into user-friendly materials for vocational guidance and career counselling for young people or adults. Increasingly, these products are being developed as computer applications, available on a for-sale basis or via the Internet.

Innovations in labour market information analysis

Innovations in information technology have made new and more powerful types of LMI possible. In terms of the manipulation and analysis of information, automation has made it possible to access sources of administrative data that were not formerly available. Moreover, more sophisticated software, particularly relational databases, have made it possible to combine and analyse multiple sources of data in ways that were not feasible in the past. In the United States, there has been an overall enhancement of state LMI systems in the past five years due to special federal funding. The infusion of these special funds has fuelled the development of a number of new LMI analysis tools and products, often available in electronic rather than print formats.

The development of the occupational network of employment and training (O*NET) in the United States is an example of a very powerful new LMI tool that was impossible to imagine even ten years ago. O*NET is being designed to replace the *Dictionary of Occupational Titles*. Besides being more flexible and easy to update, this new automated database will include more information on individual occupations, in particular more extensive information on skill requirements, than did the previous print dictionary. It will also be made available in files that allow users to manipulate and customize information to meet individual needs.[6]

Innovations in LMI dissemination/self-service LMI

It is in the dissemination of LMI that the impact of information technology has been most pronounced. Increasingly, sophisticated LMI is being made available electronically, particularly on the Internet. Electronic access allows it to be delivered faster and in a way that allows it to be manipulated as needed by the user. This has fostered more of a self-service approach to LMI.

The PES in Canada and the United States have pioneered the introduction and development of many LMI web sites. In the latter, America's Career InfoNet (ACINET) web site of nationwide LMI complements at a national level the national open-job vacancy and jobseeker databases: America's Job Bank (AJB) and America's Talent Bank (ATB). Most states in the United States are also creating comparable LMI web sites that make a variety of state and local labour market statistics available in flexible formats. In addition, there are a number of more specialized career information web sites available.

In Canada, Human Resources Development Canada (HRDC), the umbrella federal agency that encompasses PES activities, also has an extensive set of web sites that link national, regional and local LMI with career information and business development information.[7]

Conclusion

The PES may play one of three possible roles in the delivery of LMI and its choice of role(s) must balance the demand for information with the capacity of the PES to respond. In all countries, the PES has administrative statistics that are primarily developed in connection with other PES functions. However, not every PES takes advantage of these statistics as a source of information to help describe the functioning of the labour market. This is the starting point for the PES in developing a LMI capacity. It has to be recognized, however, that PES administrative registers of job vacancies and jobseekers are not representative of total labour-market activity because the PES does not serve all jobseekers or employers. Care must also be taken when using administrative information from unemployment benefit and labour-market adjustment programmes for LMI purposes: adjustments need to be made to account for distortions created by the programme regulations that govern these programmes.

The second possible role, that of a nationwide collection agency for primary labour market statistics, is a very serious commitment for the PES and should be entered into with great care. This role depends a great deal on the overall govern-mental statistical information collection framework and how the collection of labour statistics fits into that framework. Where the PES undertakes this role, it involves heavy investment both in funding and staff expertise. It also demands insulation from political influences to avoid jeopardizing the integrity of the statistics.

The third possible role of the PES, as synthesizer and interpreter of LMI, is a distinctly different one. Unlike the aforementioned roles, in this situation the PES enters into a competitive environment with public and private agencies and these have a diverse set of customers with varying needs. The PES must be selective about deciding to assume responsibility in this area and needs to evaluate such factors as the following: the nature of customers and the information they need; whether existing agencies already supply this information; and what resources exist to support the function. In the case where public funds are not available, the PES needs to assess whether customers are willing to pay for value-added resources or user charges.

There are several prerequisites for a high-quality PES labour market inform-ation service. A high political priority should be given to the monitoring of the labour market and there should be a significant development in PES staff capacity, particularly in terms of the provision of a greater technical and analytical capacity and computerized working tools. In addition, the PES would need an organiz-ational framework to support cooperation at local, regional and national levels and also to support cooperation with other producers and users of LMI.

In developing countries with very limited human and financial resources, it is even more important to realistically assess the support for and the capability of the PES to undertake a role in LMI. In the 1980s, an ILO interregional technical cooperation project funded by the Danish International Development Agency (DANIDA) identified four major types of obstacles to building a LMI capacity in developing countries:[8] first, there were inadequate relationships between information customers and producers; second, there was an under-use of existing sources of LMI; third, there was an information gap in the informal sector; fourth, there was inadequate understanding of methodological considerations and preoccupations. Some ten years later, the ILO found similar problems in its technical cooperation activities in English-speaking Africa.[9] In particular it pointed out that a lack of coordination between the producers of

LMI was compounded by a lack of information about the informal sector. Furthermore, delays in the processing and the publication of data were compounded by incomplete and unreliable data. These problems were all underscored by an absence of political support and consequent shortage of funds, equipment and qualified personnel.

Notes

[1] ILO: *The public employment service in Canada* (Geneva, ILO, 1998; mimeographed), p. 27.

[2] This definition was quoted by L. Richter: *Upgrading labour market information in developing countries: Problems, progress and prospects* (Geneva, ILO, 1989), p. 2. See also G. Schulz and B. Klemmer: *Public employment services in English-speaking Africa: Proposals for reorganization* (Harare, ILO, 1998), p. 43.

[3] Convention No. 88, Article 6 (c).

[4] This is taken from L. Richter: *Upgrading labour market information in developing countries: Problems, progress and prospects* (Geneva, ILO, 1989), pp. 1–2.

[5] ILO: *The public employment service in Canada*, op. cit., Annex 8a. Also subsequent correspondence from Avrum Lazar of Section 3, HRDC.

[6] A detailed explanation of the O*NET tool is available at the web site listed in Annex VI.1A (United States).

[7] For further details, see web site addresses in Annex VI.2.

[8] Richter, op. cit., Ch. 3.

[9] Schulz and Klemmer, op. cit., p. 45.

ADMINISTRATION OF LABOUR MARKET ADJUSTMENT PROGRAMMES 6

There is a general agreement on the need to shift the focus of labour market policies from the passive provision of income support to more active measures which assist reemployment.[1]

Introduction

The earlier chapters of this study describe how the increase in unemployment from the 1970s onwards has led to a broadening of the role of the PES. Where previously the PES had been preoccupied with job-broking and to a lesser extent with unemployment benefits, it has now become involved in the delivery of special employment measures which tend to cost substantially more than that allowed for in previous budgets. The terms used to describe such measures vary. The term, "special employment measures" conveys the notion of an emergency stopgap measure introduced to alleviate an unemployment crisis. But as unemployment has persisted, governments have become interested in more long-term policies as a means of tackling it. Since the early 1990s, the OECD has advocated "active labour market policies",[2] a term implying more continuous policies and which can be distinguished from "passive" intervention in the form of unemployment benefits. Nevertheless, the latter continue to command more resources in most countries than active policies (see Annex III).

In this study, the term "labour market adjustment programmes" is used for two reasons. Firstly, this conveys the important idea that government intervention is necessary in the labour market if it is to adjust to changes such as redundancy and unemployment which cause upheaval. Secondly, this term implies the idea of substantial intervention or programmes that go beyond standard job-broking or unemployment benefit systems, neither of which can correct a major disequilibrium in the labour market like the kind many countries have experienced since the 1970s.

This chapter focuses on the issues relating to labour market adjustment programmes. First, we discuss why government should introduce programmes to adjust the labour market and assesses what role the PES might play in these programmes. We then go on to discuss the various types of adjustment programme. These programmes include: job-search assistance; training/ education programmes and lifelong learning; direct job creation and work experience; and various integrated programmes. The chapter ends with an analysis of the effectiveness of labour market adjustment programmes.

Governments and labour market adjustment programmes

Certain economic liberals believe that the labour market is ultimately a self-regulating mechanism if left to its own devices, but such a model is remote from the reality of modern economies. In practice, market failure occurs because workforces are ill-prepared for change. Moreover, in developed, transition and developing countries, employment plays a central role in public and private life. Accordingly, the provision of employment opportunities for people is an important task for all governments.

When developing employment policies, governments face a dilemma. On the one hand the maintenance of existing employment opportunities is difficult because as we saw in Chapter 2, structural changes occur all the time because of economic and technological developments. This leads to the displacement of large numbers of workers from their employment and there is a real danger that these workers may sink into long-term unemployment without government intervention. On the other hand, it is not easy for governments to create viable jobs to replace those that are lost through structural change. Thus, while government employment policies have often continued to pursue direct job creation, they have also sought to create a climate which is conducive to the development of new jobs in the labour market. In addition, they have also introduced measures to increase the employability of unemployed people.

This was very much the approach adopted in an OECD study on jobs, which made recommendations concerning macroeconomic policy and which encouraged technical development and the reforming of employment security provision amongst other things.[3] The report recognized a place for adjustment programmes and urged that programmes should be targeted at specific client groups or be designed to remedy specific labour market problems. The report also argued that the extension and upgrading of worker skills and competencies needs to be a lifelong process if OECD economies are to foster the creation of high-skill high-wage jobs. It went on to say that education and training policies should be directed at furthering this goal in addition to achieving other fundamental social and cultural objectives.

The report further argued for the reform of unemployment benefit systems, suggesting that with the growth of long-term and recurring unemployment, these systems have drifted towards quasi-permanent income support in many countries, thus lowering work incentives. Accordingly, an increasingly important thrust behind labour market adjustment programmes has been "welfare-to-work", the idea of weaning people away from benefit dependency so that they can become competitive and independent in the labour market. In some countries, an element of compulsion underlies such adjustment programmes in the sense that continued state-funded income support is dependent upon participation in the programmes.

The PES and labour market adjustment programmes

Involvement in adjustment programmes has probably been the biggest single change for the PES in recent decades. In many countries, however, it would be wrong to assume that the PES is the sole or even the primary deliverer of labour market adjustment programmes; instead, this is an area of competition between public and private service providers. In effect this means that the development of programmes may be outside PES control and the PES may be ignored when it comes to implementation. Alternatively, it may mean that the PES plays a key role in relation to some programmes but plays no part in others. Despite this, the PES often has strong claims to be both involved in the design of adjustment programmes and to be entrusted with their delivery. Several good reasons lie behind the claims: the PES has a good general knowledge of the labour market; the PES is familiar with individual employer and jobseeker needs; the PES has a local service delivery infrastructure; and the PES has links with both the training and education network and the social assistance/welfare network. For these reasons, the PES has in some countries been given a central role in delivering adjustment programmes and has become both the gateway and the gatekeeper for these programmes.

Kinds of adjustment programmes

Labour market adjustment programmes may be designed to fulfil a variety of objectives including: correcting labour shortages; reintroducing people to a working environment; overcoming social obstacles to re-employment such as drug or alcohol addiction; overcoming educational barriers to re-employment such as illiteracy and poor numeracy; and overcoming employer resistance to taking disadvantaged or long-term unemployed people. The common aim in all these cases is to increase the employability of jobseekers and to help them move into employment. This is especially true where certain disadvantaged groups such as women, the long-term unemployed, unemployed young people, retrenched workers, elderly workers and workers with disabilities are concerned. The following section focuses on three types of adjustment programmes: job-search assistance; education/training programmes and lifelong learning; and direct job creation and work experience. There is also a discussion of how the various strands of these programmes can be brought together into integrated programmes. The relative importance of these programmes in OECD countries in terms of public expenditure as a percentage of GDP can be seen in Annex III.

Job-search assistance

From the beginning, the PES has been perceived not just as a job-broking organization, but also as one that offered people access to more intensive services such as vocational guidance and training.[4] But this was not a major aspect of PES work in most countries until the rise in unemployment in the 1970s and 1980s. It was discovered then that with jobseekers greatly out-numbering vacancies, there were severe limits to what the PES could achieve through its job-broking services. In conditions of labour surplus, employers made less use of jobcentres because they could easily find candidates in other ways, though this may not have entirely been the case for posts requiring specific qualifications. As we have seen, one PES response to this was active marketing. A second was for the PES to focus less on active job-matching and to rely more on providing job vacancy information and job-search assistance.

The idea inherent in this is that many unemployed people can manage their own job-search if the proper information is made available to them. However, some unemployed people need assistance in how to use the available information and need to learn job-search techniques. The emphasis of the PES has gradually evolved from one of placement of unemployed people towards one of teaching them how to find jobs and this was achieved by providing additional services to the job-matching function. As Mr. Göte Bernhardsson, former Director-General of Swedish Employment Service, noted:

> (The PES) role will certainly change. We will be not so much needed anymore
> for simple matching activities. But in our societies knowledge and competence
> will be more and more important. The role of the employment service will be
> more of counselling and guidance, we shall have to offer more qualified services
> than today. And this will enable us to do more for those people who really need
> our assistance. Not everyone will be able to make use of information technology,
> but (will) require guidance.[5]

From an economist's point of view, job-search assistance seeks to influence the supply of labour. It includes services that are provided to advise and support jobseekers in finding work, often in combination with PES job-broking services. It is also the gateway to training, retraining and job creation services because these services depend upon a clear assessment of jobseeker skills, abilities and interests.

The organizational locations of job-search assistance can vary. Frequently, it is provided with the labour exchange function, as is the case in France. This model is particularly useful where resources allow it to be provided for a broad spectrum of the population. It is also increasingly linked to the administration of unemployment benefits (see Chapter 7) where there is a strong incentive to tie job-search obligations to the receipt of unemployment benefits as is the case in the United Kingdom, the United States and Norway. In other countries, intensive job-search assistance is more often tied to specific programmes for targeted groups and may be bundled with training or education programmes or job creation services. Different forms of job-search assistance are associated with different levels of service and the customization of activities to meet the needs of groups of jobseekers with special needs. Three are worthy of note: (1) universal and self-service provision; (2) group activities; (3) individual or intensive assistance.

1. Universal and self-service provision

Because of the costs associated with providing one-to-one counselling for large numbers of unemployed people, there has been a considerable development of much cheaper forms of delivery. The least costly methods of assisting people with job-search customarily consists of providing a resource room or resource centre where a variety of information such as general occupational information, related education and training opportunities information, and job-specific information is made available on a self-service basis. More recently, a great deal of this information has been made available on computer, particularly on the Internet, for easier access by a variety of individuals. In Canada for example, self-service provision for job-search assistance has been highly automated. This automation includes the following:

- an electronic career exploration system (job-search) on the Internet and in PES offices;
- an additional electronic resource with a wealth of labour market and human resource service information (WorkInfoNet);
- an interactive computerized system (COMPASS) to provide assistance to young people in entering and adjusting to the labour market; and

- a computerized, heuristic[6] occupational information and career exploitation system (CHOICE) to assist people in acquiring knowledge and understanding of specific types of occupations so as to assist their employment and career development.

For jobseekers who need more assistance, PES staff conduct an interview that determines service needs.

Declining PES budgets over the past decade in the United States has led to fewer and fewer general employment counselling staff being available in local offices. In some states, there are no longer any general counselling staff at all unless they are funded by programmes targeted at specific groups such as dislocated workers and veterans. Their place has been taken by electronic career information tools that can be accessed in PES offices, secondary schools, vocational colleges, universities and on the Internet. These systems have proliferated and grown much more sophisticated with advances in information technology.

2. Group activities

Since many of the barriers to employment are common to all jobseekers, the PES can simultaneously assist many jobseekers by grouping them. This is cheaper than providing one-to-one counselling and it also has the advantage of bringing people in the same situation together so they can learn from each other and build up their own networks. "Job clubs" are probably the best known and most effective group provision. They were devised by two behavioural psychologists[7] in the United States in the mid-1970s and were first implemented on a large scale in the United Kingdom in the 1980s. Since then, they have been launched in several other European countries such as Belgium,[8] France, Hungary, Ireland, Poland,[9] and the Netherlands. Job clubs encourage jobseekers to take responsibility for their own situation and to work with a group of other jobseekers by sharing information and ideas. The idea behind them is to encourage jobseekers to increase their chances of finding jobs by looking for them more actively. In particular, jobseekers are encouraged to contact employers directly and to take advantage of the fact that many jobs are never publicly announced or notified to the PES.

A job club needs fairly spacious and attractive premises equipped with essential job-search tools such as free telephones and fax machines and also computers for creating well-presented resumés or curriculum vitaes. The provision of these tools is important since many jobseekers do not have access to such facilities at home. Free stationery and postage are also provided. The participants are guided by job club leaders who combine a positive outgoing personality with good knowledge of job-search techniques.

Job clubs have been one the most successful adjustment programmes introduced in recent years, but there are limits to the scale on which they can operate in particular labour markets. Often, too many unsolicited phone calls to employers can prove counterproductive. The most rigorous evaluation of job clubs was carried out in the United Kingdom. It found that job clubs were very efficient when used on a small scale: for three pilot job clubs set up in 1984, the success rate in getting jobs was 75 per cent. However, when introduced on a larger scale, their effectiveness decreased: figures from 1996/97 show that about 40 per cent of participants obtained jobs in this case. An evaluation study relating to 1994 suggested that job clubs had a positive effect on employment outcomes but that these effects were concentrated on women.[10]

Another common type of group activity is the "Job fair". Job fairs bring employers and jobseekers together within a limited time and space, allowing them to approach each other directly with the PES only playing an organizing and facilitating role. Job fairs make possible direct links between both sides of the market. Jobseekers can informally sound out employers about work content and working conditions while employers can assess the degree of interest among jobseekers and the availability of staff with the right qualifications. Hong Kong, China for instance, organizes "Job bazaars" jointly with the Employee Retraining Board and other major employer associations while Poland organizes inter-institutional job fairs.

Group courses or workshops on job-search techniques, employment conditions and occupational and career information help jobseekers to define their job objectives and discover employment possibilities. Training can range from several hours to several weeks. These group courses are addressed either to general jobseekers or special target groups. There are many types of group courses and workshops offered by the PES in many countries. Sweden provides group training courses on how to apply for a job and how to raise self-motivation. Norway organizes group-based information and counselling to both provide jobseekers with information on their duties and rights as unemployed and to provide guidance towards job-search techniques. The United Kingdom organizes job-plan workshops for long-term unemployed people, with a five-day programme of individual assessment, job-search guidance and confidence building. Hong Kong, China conducts group briefings for major job categories and for small groups on basic skills in job-search techniques such as self-analysis, market positioning, networking, interviewing skills, access to public and private employment services, and access to training and retraining courses. It also organizes recruitment seminars and exhibitions on career choice.

Tunisia conducts meetings for initiation into job-search techniques, and in Argentina the "image project", targeted at groups with low skills levels, provides short, 15-hour courses that focus on job-search and spontaneous application techniques. In Canada, work orientation workshops provide disadvantaged students and drop-outs with a developmental training experience.

3.   Individual or intensive assistance

Intensive one-to-one assistance[11] can take one of several forms. It can be offered as vocational guidance, it can be offered as intensive counselling or advice to unemployed people or it can be offered as specialized counselling to particular groups of disadvantaged jobseekers.

Vocational guidance

Vocational guidance is a process in which a trained counsellor draws information from individuals about their abilities, aspirations and temperament and provides information about appropriate employment opportunities and education and training routes into jobs. The aim is to help individuals to make worthwhile career choices by giving them better information and understanding about the labour market, about educational and training qualifications and about their own interests and abilities. The process may include psychological tests to assess interests and aptitudes. The administration of such tests has traditionally required a trained psychologist or at least a tester who has received specialized training. Because of the need to reach more jobseekers and achieve a favourable response, simpler client-administered print and automated systems are increasingly replacing the earlier approach. Traditionally, vocational guidance has been provided mainly for students in full-time education, but in a number of countries, a similar approach has been used to address the problems of people who have been made redundant or who want to change the direction of their careers.

Effective vocational guidance is extremely demanding. It requires diagnostic skills, a good knowledge of the education and training system and good local and national labour market information, in other words, knowing which occupations are growing and which are in decline. This is important, as the growth of unemployment and the pace of change in the labour market that was described in Chapter 2 have made it much more difficult than it used to be to predict long-term opportunities in particular occupations.

Vocational guidance has been used in various ways in several countries. In Belgium for example, the *Centre d'accueil, d'orientation et d'initiation socio-professionnelle* of FOREM provides counselling, vocational guidance and basic training for the unemployed but does not select trainees with a view to placing them rapidly in jobs. In Norway, the PES has published a vocational guidance book[12] which contains a survey of upper-secondary and higher education in Norway. It has also published information on education abroad and on financial support for education. It aims to provide jobseekers with opportunities to choose an occupation according to their interests and abilities thus encouraging them to undertake more education. In Tunisia, vocational guidance is limited to applicants for training and uses psycho-technical tests as the main tool to evaluate candidates' aptitudes and motivation. In the future, guidance and psycho-technical tests will be extended to young, first-time jobseekers and enterprises. In the United States, vocational guidance and aptitude testing are provided for veterans. Other examples of vocational guidance include the provision of specialized vocational counselling and guidance to young first-time jobseekers in countries such as Canada, France, Japan, Tunisia and Hong Kong, China. In Hong Kong, China, specialized vocational counselling is also provided for jobseekers with disabilities and in Canada, for women.

While vocational guidance provision has declined in countries such as France due to a reduction of resources, it has been increased in transition countries such as Poland. Its vocational counselling system was established with six vocation information centres (including a mobile vocational information centre), 200 vocational information and group guidance rooms and 480 fully trained vocational trainers.

Individual intensive employment counselling

The trend in individual employment counselling services is towards the development of more structured systems to assist unemployed people. Sometimes this is referred to as a "case management approach", as advocated by the EU. It involves the development of a plan which is agreed between the adviser and the jobseeker with obligations for both the jobseeker and the PES. Such a plan goes under various names including "a contract", "an agreement", "a re-integration plan" or "an employability development plan". Progress is checked at regular intervals and additional job coaching and counselling is provided where appropriate. The scheme is linked with policies designed to ensure that unemployment benefit claimants return to work as soon as possible. (These policies are discussed further in Chapter 7; see "Job-search assistance or re-employment services".)

The United Kingdom has developed one of the most structured systems for this kind of job-search assistance service. The service is built around a "Jobseekers agreement", which is drawn up the moment a jobseeker registers as unemployed. This establishes a contract between the jobseeker and the PES, with specific job-search and other service obligations undertaken as a condition of receiving unemployment benefit. Progress is reviewed at regular intervals with more services made available the longer an individual remains unemployed. Likewise in the New Deal programmes, each jobseeker is assigned a personal adviser with whom they have a series of intensive interviews in an effort to develop plans for job-search, training and so forth

In Belgium, a guidance plan called the *Plan d'Accompagnement des Chômeurs* or PAC[13] was introduced in 1993 by the federal authorities to maintain contacts between the unemployed and the labour market. The guidance plan combines a preliminary diagnosis of the situation of the unemployed individual with an assessment of his or her chances of being re-integrated into the labour market. After a month, this is followed by the establishment of a concrete action plan based on age, professional competence and other factors. The action plan is drawn up in writing in the form of a contract and lists the action proposed such as participation in job-search counselling, vocational training measures or a subsidized employment pro-gramme. The contract also provides for continuous evaluation.[14] In Finland, an individual job-search plan was introduced in 1998 as part of the improvement in service process by the PES. It aims at shortening the duration of unemploy-ment periods, increasing the job-search activity of the unemployed and directing jobseekers' activities more effectively into re-employment in the open labour market. (For more details, see Annex IV.17.)

In France the ANPE offers guidance towards employment (*Accompagne-ment à l'Emploi*) for the unemployed and for jobseekers who have problems directly linked to employment and the labour market. It requires profound and lasting intervention in order to enable the client to diagnose his or her own strengths and weaknesses and to provide advice and support. It is not, however, linked to unemployment benefit claims. (The approaches adopted by the ANPE are detailed in Annex IV.18.) In Norway, PES staff call in unemployed people every three months for individual consultations or for group-based information and counselling. They also prepare action plans or employability development plans in full cooperation with jobseekers which describe the different steps the jobseeker should take for improving his or her chances in the labour market. The PES in the Netherlands, Portugal and Spain also provide re-integration plans or individual assistance plans for structuring a return to work for unemployed people. In Hong Kong, China, a job-matching programme offers intensive proactive employment service to help the unemployed to find jobs.

Specialized employment counselling

Intensive counselling for the unemployed sometimes includes tackling personal problems such as drug or alcohol addiction, homelessness, child care or debt problems – all of which can be obstacles to re-employment. Such specialized employment counselling goes beyond PES competencies and requires specialist help. Links to social assistance services may also be vital. The PES in many countries such as Japan, Norway and Hong Kong, China provides selective job-search assistance services for special categories of jobseekers. The range of these selective services is quite diverse, depending on the priorities in national employment policies. Hong Kong, China, provides priority services such as counselling, briefing and career guidance for elderly jobseekers, retired civil servants, applicants of comprehensive social security and single parents. For jobseekers with disabilities, it provides in-depth interviews, vocational guidance/assistance, trade tests, accompaniment to job interviews and follow-up after placement. For new arrivals from China, it created two employment and guidance centres in September 1997 to provide them with the following: briefing on employment conditions and career guidance; labour market information; employment counselling; job referrals for placement; and intensive job-matching. For secondary school students and clients of youth centres it provides: career education (information and guidance); career counselling; large-scale career exhibitions with exhibitors from different trades and training institutes; workplace visits; and quizzes on contemporary careers information and activities.

Japan provides a comprehensive amount of services. For example, 25 Talent Banks have been established in the major cities for white-collar and elderly workers and 12 "Hello Lady" work offices have been established in major cities to assist re-entry of women who are willing and able to work. In addition, a "U-Turn" centre has been established in Tokyo to provide employment, lifestyle information and vocational counselling for those wishing to return to their home towns. It supports the programme by holding joint-interview meetings (called U-turn fairs), arranging interviews using video conferencing technology, and also provides aid to employees of an establishment which moves from a major urban area to a non-urban area.

Training and education programmes

As we saw in Chapter 2, there is increasing recognition by modern governments and international institutions such as the OECD, the EU and the ILO of the need for the continual updating of people's knowledge and skills which is often summed up in the term, "lifelong learning". With a rapidly changing and increasingly flexible labour market, training and education are becoming increasingly important. The PES has the potential to become a gateway for lifelong learning because of its close interaction with jobseekers and employers. Education and training programmes therefore play a significant part in labour market adjustment programmes in all developed countries. They are intended to help provide basic education to those who lack basic skills, to help unskilled workers qualify for jobs and to help skilled workers change their occupation in response to economic change. Such programmes can be provided in a number of ways such as through off-the-job and classroom-based courses, through on-the-job training in a work context or through a combination of both, such as in the apprenticeship model. They may be customized to fit the immediate labour market needs or to target particularly disadvantaged groups.

While education and training programmes are important in many developed countries, they are not necessarily seen as one of the core functions of the PES. Indeed, the PES role may be confined to the recruitment and selection of candidates for such programmes and to helping with placing candidates in employment after their programme is completed. The role of the PES in providing training is becoming increasingly contractual, seeking as it does training services from other public and private sector agencies. The training contractor may also provide additional counselling services and may be required to accept a negotiated responsibility for placement of a portion of the trainees in jobs. In some countries, however, the closeness of the PES to the labour market is considered to be one reason for giving the PES a greater role in the planning and supervision of such programmes. Annex V describes the way in which such programmes have developed in recent years and the degree to which the PES has been involved in them.

The variety of job training and retraining policies and programmes and their effectiveness has been well researched.[15] There are a number of important policy and programme management issues regarding training programmes with several recurring ones concerning training targeted at the unemployed or those at risk of unemployment. First of all, there is the issue of selection of participants. Even in programmes targeted at serving hard-to-place individuals, there is often a strong bias towards serving the least hard-to-place in this category. This is particularly true because the most hard-to-place unemployed often have poor education and learning experiences. This bias is also known as "creaming".

A second issue is the difficulty in finding training institutions that are flexible enough to meet both the individual needs of the hard-to-place unemployed and the changing demands of the labour market. As large public sector training institutions in particular have in-built institutional rigidities, many countries have begun to outsource training. A third issue involves training programmes that have been used on a large scale during periods of high unemployment. These have been criticized for providing "parking places" for the unemployed. This is particularly true where the training provided is not relevant to labour market needs. Finally, there is the issue of incumbent worker training. While workers with limited skills may be employed, should labour market programmes also devote resources to upgrade the skills of the current workforce in order for them to remain competitive and to prevent future unemployment? Should this responsibility be borne by the government or the private employer?

Direct job creation programmes

The primary objective of job creation programmes is to improve the demand for labour; a secondary objective may be to improve employability of unemployed people by giving them work experience. Three categories of job creation programmes can be distinguished: public sector programmes; programmes that promote self-employment; and employment incentives or wage subsidies.

Public sector programmes create jobs in the public or quasi-public sectors in non-market activities. These also include more modest community projects aimed at creating employment in intermediate labour markets via re-integration enterprises or community businesses. In countries undergoing economic restructuring, the PES is increasingly being asked to play a more active role in local community development projects. This role consists of helping to screen workers and of providing specialized training for workers in firms which agree to make new investments that assist with community development.

PES involvement in programmes that promote self-employment differs from country to country. One way in which the PES helps is by providing limited capital and technical assistance to unemployed individuals seeking to start small-scale enterprises through local PES offices. However, evidence suggests that the PES has limited expertise and time to administer such programmes. In countries like Indonesia and Mexico, the design and implementation of small enterprise development are left to NGOs. They can provide technical assistance (such as evaluation of the initial aptitudes and interests of the unemployed), or provide access to facilities or credits to the unemployed. Another approach is to provide income support to new self-employed workers in place of unemployment benefits. This was the principle underlying the enterprise allowance scheme in the United Kingdom which was successfully run by the PES during the 1980s.

Employment incentives or wage subsidies to employers are used to create jobs, to hire exposed groups of unemployed or to maintain employment in the regular labour market. The PES may actually manage these programmes themselves or they may assist other public or private agencies by recruiting participants. Evidence is mixed regarding the cost-effectiveness of temporary wage subsidy programmes. It is clear that they are effective in redistributing employment opportunities but there is disagreement about how much they speed up the adjustment process through the creation of additional jobs per se.[16]

The prominence of job creation programmes in national labour market policies varies widely from country to country (see Annex III). In some countries, job creation is a major component of labour market policy. In the Netherlands for example, job creation programmes comprise a large part of the labour market policy strategy. The number of subsidized jobs planned for 1998 corresponded to 3 per cent of the active workforce and 12 per cent of public sector jobs (most subsidized jobs are in the public sector). Programmes include a sheltered employment for people with disabilities, a youth guarantee scheme, a labour pool for the long-term unemployed, and work experience in the public sector.

Moreover, the role of the PES in the administration of these services differs from country to country. In the United Kingdom, the PES has played a major role in planning and managing job creation programmes including employee subsidy programmes. In 1994, the "Workstart" pilot began and this was expanded in 1997. Subsidized jobs are now one element in the New Deal strategy for 18–24 year-olds and for the older, long-term unemployed. Under these programmes, employers are given subsidies in return for a commitment to hire long-term unemployed people or young people for a period of six months. (For more information on the New Deal, see Annex IV.19.)

In the United Kingdom, the PES also manages the "Work Trial" programme which enables employers to try out long-term unemployed people for three weeks without incurring the usual employer costs. In 1998–99, 15,000 people participated in a Work Trial of whom 9,000 were subsequently placed in work. In addition, employment in home services such as cleaning are being promoted through wage subsidies and tax reductions. The goals are to promote employment for low-skilled people and to discourage illegal work. An evaluation of the process found that Work Trials had a very positive impact on job chances for the long-term unemployed and that the programme seemed particularly able to encourage entry into full-time and permanent jobs.[17] However, the researchers were not sure that the results would be so positive in a larger scheme.

In Germany, the PES is actively involved in the administration of job creation programmes, aided by local steering committees which oversee the management of the programmes. At the local level, the PES has the authority to move up to 20 per cent of available funding between job training and job creation programmes, depending on local circumstances. In addition, a new programme permits unemployment benefit entitlements to be redirected to wage subsidies for the long-term unemployed in certain types of social and environmental projects. This programme was originally adopted in the eastern part of Germany.

Job creation programmes in Norway are managed by the PES and Norway is a good example of how public job creation programmes are organized. The Norwegian programme provides work experience and training for the long-term unemployed. Municipalities, counties, the state and voluntary organizations are the employers and for each participant, they receive a fixed amount every month which supports approximately 87 per cent of the total costs. Participants receive ordinary wages for the 85 per cent of the time when they are working and receive no compensation for the 15 per cent of the time when they are in training. These programmes are overseen by a steering committee at the local level. In addition, wage subsidies are paid in Norway to private sector employers for employing the hard-to-place. Employers receive a subsidy for up to one year which varies according to the target group and there is no formal obligation to retain the participant after the subsidy expires. Norway also has a unique job rotation scheme where the unemployed can work as substitutes for employees on educational leave. The participant receives an ordinary wage for the period of the leave and the employer is reimbursed for a flat amount.

In Canada, research has shown that wage subsidies and self-employment are the most effective labour market adjustment programmes. As a result, the PES has placed special emphasis on targeting wage subsidies, earnings supplements and self-employment assistance while also promoting job creation partnerships or work experience. In the United States, the public service employment programmes of the mid-1970s have been terminated, although subsidized employment continues on a more modest scale in more recent programmes such as the current welfare reform initiatives. A major evaluation of public service programmes in the United States during the mid-1980s drew several conclusions about them.[18] Firstly, it suggested that the programmes should be prescribed for only a limited period to avoid dependence by participation on the one hand and excessive budgetary substitution by local governments on the other. Secondly, it argued that higher than normal subsidies should be considered for the programmes given the greater than usual employment barriers to participants in comparison to others in training programmes. However, limits should be placed on subsidies to control costs and to ensure that there is sufficient incentive for participants to seek other employment. Thirdly, it suggested that the eligibility criteria should be defined by income level and employment experience and not by target group membership nor educational qualification. This was because the main objective of this activity was to provide work experience for those capable of holding a job.

It is notable that in developing and transition countries such as Argentina, Indonesia and Tunisia, the emphasis is placed on public sector programmes (in particular employment intensive works of public and social utility) and self-employment programmes through the development of small and medium enterprises (SMEs). In Argentina, six programmes (namely the "inter-institutional programme of work of social interest", the "social interest employment programme", the "joint employment programme", the "intensive afforestation programme" and the "temporary employment programme") target all workers having difficulties entering the labour market and are intended to carry out public works and community services. In Tunisia, the focus is on assisting young entrepreneurs in setting up small enterprises with technical and financial assistance. In Argentina, a "micro-enterprises project" targets those with only a secondary education or those displaced from the public or private sector since 1989. It provides both training and technical assistance.

Innovations and good practices in integrated market adjustment programmes

While individual labour market adjustment programmes may be pursued individually, there are advantages to bringing them together to create integrated approaches, especially for special groups such as workers with disabilities, dislocated or retrenched workers, the long-term unemployed, welfare recipients and unemployed young people.

Vocational rehabilitation programmes

With regard to groups with disabilities, vocational rehabilitation programmes are often provided by bodies other than the PES. In Austria and Germany for example, these are provided by offices for social affairs and people with disabilities. Exceptions in this respect are Portugal, Norway and Sweden. In Portugal one vocational rehabilitation centre is directly managed by the PES and the other, which provides training for people with disabilities, is jointly managed. In Sweden, vocational training is seldom given in separate institutions for people with disabilities; its "employability institutes" focus on ability testing, counselling and individual workplace adjustments. It also has the largest shelter-work programme among OECD countries. In Norway, the PES has been responsible for managing vocational rehabilitation programmes financed by both the Ministry of Labour and the national insurance scheme (NIS) since 1994. The NIS decides the eligibility for participation in vocational rehabilitation programmes while the PES is responsible for the selection of appropriate programmes. The PES is also responsible for re-integrating people with disabilities (for both medical and social reasons) because of its links with labour markets. The PES registers jobseekers with disabilities and assesses the prospects for rehabilitation. If the disability is deemed to be too severe for the employment services, the PES refers the individuals back to the NIS for a disability pension. They can also refer them to other health or social service institutions for more appropriate help. If the PES assessment shows that rehabilitation is appropriate, an action plan is drawn up between the PES and the jobseeker in question. When all actions described and agreed in the action plan have been carried out, the rehabilitation process is completed. The rehabilitated individual is assessed again and then transferred to either active or passive labour market solutions.

Several countries have a legal quota system requiring most employers to have certain proportions of people with disabilities on their payrolls. The figure is 4 per cent in Austria and 6 per cent in Germany. In the United Kingdom, the quota has recently been replaced by legislation making it illegal to discriminate unfairly against people with disabilities.

Mass lay-off programmes

In countries experiencing the type of economic restructuring that involves mass lay-offs, the PES provides proactive mass lay-off services for retrenched workers.[19] It is supported by advance notice of plant shutdowns or large lay-offs and backed by PES guidance and support services. In a number of countries such as Canada, France, Poland, the United Kingdom, the United States and Hong Kong, China, the PES set up special mass lay-off service teams which can deliver services on site as early as possible before the shutdown or lay-off date. These services include the following:

- providing pre-lay-off services;
- providing worker orientation sessions after notice of lay-off;
- providing early assessments of the needs of affected workers;
- providing extended employment and self-employment counselling and retraining;
- providing redeployment assistance, special mobility assistance and extended unemployment benefits to dislocated workers; and
- providing advice for firms and communities about how to solve practical labour problems.

It is particularly important to assess the scope for upgrading the skills of redundant workers in order to fit them to available vacancies.

A further example of this kind of programme includes the Industrial Adjustment Service in Canada which was designed to assist employers, workers, representatives of industry and communities and provinces/territories to establish and operate adjustment committees (composed of some or all of these parties). The programme is designed to develop and oversee the implementation of measures designed to remedy an actual or potential work-force adjustment problem. In Hong Kong, China, the Outreaching Placement Service (OPS) was introduced in June 1995 and offers placement assistance to workers displaced in large-scale retrenchments. It provides services such as the following: seminars to promote open employment for people with disabilities; annual large-scale exhibitions to disseminate the latest information on career choice; recruitment seminars; and job bazaars (jointly organized with the Employees' Retraining Board and major employer associations) to help jobseekers better understand the labour market and apply for jobs on the spot with employers.

A further option for displaced or redundant workers is relocation assistance or job mobility programmes which consist of paying the costs of fares for job-search, providing lodging allowances and household removal expenses, and making a contribution towards the cost of house sales/purchases. However, an evaluation carried out by the OECD[20] suggested that the use of job mobility programmes among displaced workers was less than anticipated and that mobility assistance is a difficult, often paradoxical area for policy makers. Relocation is a last resort for policy makers in most displaced workers communities just as it is for workers themselves.

Welfare-to-work programmes

Other examples of integrated programmes can be found in the welfare-to-work programmes introduced in the Nordic countries in the early 1990s, in Australia in the 1990s, in the United States in 1996 and in the United Kingdom in 1997. (The background to these programmes has been discussed earlier in this chapter.) Such programmes aim at helping socially excluded people (whether they be unemployment benefit claimants or recipients of other welfare benefits) to move from unemployment into sustainable work. These programmes are a product of the reform of social protection and the activation of labour market policies, as recommended in the OECD *Jobs study* project. However, the extent of the social protection reform and labour market policy activation varies from one country to another. In his review of these programmes in the Scandinavian countries, Pekka Kosonen found important differences between countries in terms of control and discipline.[21]

It is difficult to draw firm conclusions from experiences in Australia since the ambitious "Working Nation" programme operated only briefly there. Bearing some resemblance to the New Deal of the United Kingdom, it was introduced by the Labour Government in 1994 but was then abandoned by the incoming Liberal Government in 1996. Long-term unemployment fell 20 per cent in the first 18 months of the programme, but employers failed to respond to the offer of job subsidies and some participants returned to unemployment. It has been argued that the programme was inadequately integrated with economic development strategies.[22] Subsequent initiatives in Australia have involved the further complication of putting PES work out to contract

Annexes IV.19 and IV.20 give descriptions of the welfare-to-work programmes instigated in the United Kingdom and the United States. The groups targeted by these programmes were initially different from each other: the Temporary Assistance for Needy Families (TANF) programme targeted welfare recipients in general while the New Deal in the United Kingdom initially targeted young people in the 18–24 age bracket, though its coverage has since been extended. Both programmes use a blend of the various labour market adjustment methods already described in order to entice socially excluded groups off welfare and back to work. Both programmes are administered by the PES through a public/private partnership.

In the United States, one-stop systems (see Chapter 8) were introduced for implementing the TANF programme and are responsible for the placement of welfare recipients. As the implementation of these programmes is still recent, their long-term impact remains to be seen. Nevertheless, two critical issues faced by the PES were detected within a year of the programme implementation.[23] Both relate to the uneasy relationship between the PES job-broking and job-search assistance programmes on the one hand and the programmes created under the TANF to assist the disadvantaged on the other. Firstly, the work requirements, time limits and the potential for state-determined sanctions which were added to national welfare law (1996) created the potential for a larger than usual pool of hard-to-place former welfare recipients who required job-broking and job-search assistance services from state PES agencies. It is likely that those former welfare recipients with the closest existing ties to the labour market were the first to get jobs, and that the hardest-to-place under the TANF programme will ultimately be the victims of the welfare time limits.

Secondly, the full consolidation of employment services and welfare programme administration within the same PES agencies (as illustrated by the Utah and Wisconsin experiences) necessarily implies that PES employees must act both as social service providers and job-brokers for welfare recipients. There is, however, a potential conflict between these two types of services. The

PES through its job-broking and job-search assistance services expects workers to adapt to the needs of employers, while welfare programmes are accustomed to serving the needs of clients. As the two functions coalesce, job-broking officers are concerned that the image of the PES may be compromised if employers are presented with a large number of under-prepared former welfare recipients; social services officers on the other hand are concerned that their clients' complex needs may be overlooked in the process of moving them quickly into the labour market. It is believed that there is room for compromise on both sides of the issue and future evaluation will show how successfully such integration can be accomplished. In addition it will show how successful welfare reform placement efforts are in the long run.

It is too early to reach a firm judgement on the effectiveness of the New Deal programmes in the United Kingdom and a full evaluation will not be available until late 2000. The programmes have been introduced on a large scale for a wide range of disadvantaged groups including lone parents and the partners of unemployed people who had been previously neglected. The programme design combines many of the separate ingredients discussed in this chapter and draws on the experience which has been built up in recent years. Large numbers of those on the programme have moved into educational courses. Large numbers have also moved into subsidized or unsubsidized employment.

However, the New Deal programmes give rise to several issues. Firstly, what will the effect be on the previously seamless service of the PES of having to deal with different groups under different New Deal programmes given the added complication that some programmes in some localities are contracted out to private agencies? Will the proliferation of programmes create new barriers and rigidities for the PES? And, as was the case with the TANF programme, what will the impact of all these high profile New Deals be on the normal work of the PES and its other clients? The second issue is: what effect will the threat of benefit sanctions have on young people who are already alienated from society? Will it simply serve to shift them even further away from the legitimate labour market?[24] Thirdly, the programmes assume that if employability can be improved, people can move into jobs. But the programme options only last six months, including the education courses. Is this a realistic assumption for unemployment blackspots? Where jobs are very scarce, does the New Deal need to be linked to substantial additional investment in economic regeneration?

Effectiveness of labour market adjustment policies

This section summarizes the major conclusions of the OECD *Jobs study* work since 1994 with regard to two issues: firstly, the contribution that labour market adjustment programmes can make as part of a strategy to combat high and persistent unemployed;[25] secondly, the measures that should be taken by the PES to increase the efficiency of labour market policies.[26] It was felt that a summary of the OECD conclusions would contribute to an understanding of what is expected from the PES, particularly in relation to performance management and evaluation (see Chapter 8) undertaken for accountability reasons.

As can be seen in Annex III, public spending on active labour market programmes (e.g. job-broking, labour market information, labour market training for both unemployed and employed adults, youth measures, subsidized employment creation and measures for people with disabilities) absorbs a significant percentage of national resources in many OECD countries. It ranges from a low of under 0.01 per cent of GDP in the Czech Republic to a high of over 5 per cent of GDP in the Netherlands.

What works?

The OECD review[27] of what works and what does not for each category of labour market adjustment programme is based on the two types of evaluation of the outcomes of individual programmes: a) the ex-post evaluation of the impact of programme participation on individuals' employment and earnings; b) the evaluation of the net effects of programmes on aggregate employment and unemployment by estimating deadweight, substitution and displacement effects. The review highlights five principles which should guide the selection of labour market adjustment programmes in order to maximize their effectiveness.

- Rely as much as possible on in-depth counselling, on job finding incentives such as re-employment bonuses and on job-search assistance programmes. However, it is vital to ensure that such measures are combined with increased monitoring and enforcement of the work test.
- Keep public training programmes small in scale and well-targeted to the specific needs of both jobseekers and employers.
- Early interventions, reaching back to pre-school, can pay dividends for disadvantaged young people. These measures should include steps to reduce early school-leaving among at-risk students combined with policies to ensure that such people leave the schooling system equipped with the basic skills and competencies recognized and valued by employers. It is also important to improve poor attitudes to work on the part of these young people and adult mentors can help in this regard.
- As the duration of unemployment spells lengthens, various forms of employment subsidies may serve to maintain workers' attachment to the

labour force. However, employment subsidies should be of short duration, properly targeted and closely monitored.
• Use subsidized business start-ups for the minority among the unemployed who have entrepreneurial skills and the motivation to survive in a competitive environment.[28]

Other evaluation studies have also shown that job-search assistance alone is more cost-effective than training and job creation programmes in reducing unemployment. An evaluation study carried by the World Bank[29] concluded that retraining programmes for those laid off en masse and for the long-term unemployed in OECD countries are generally no more effective than job-search assistance in increasing either re-employment probabilities or post-intervention earnings. Moreover, they are two and four times respectively more expensive than job-search assistance. In addition, well developed job-search assistance, particularly employment counselling, has also been found to make other labour market adjustment programmes more effective through better targeting.

To the five OECD principles, a sixth can be added, that is the training of employed workers should be reviewed in the light of lifelong learning for all citizens.[30] This is an important component of a policy strategy aimed at overcoming structural barriers to job creation and economic growth. With a national strategy for making learning opportunities available to citizens in place, the PES could have an important role as guide and gateway for these opportunities and for how they relate to developments in the labour market.

The OECD also recommends that more countries begin to systematically evaluate their labour market adjustment programmes. Evaluation should be built into the design of programmes from the beginning rather than being viewed as an ex-post exercise. It should also be undertaken in a rigorous way.

Conclusion

This chapter has shown that high and persistent unemployment in a number of countries has given rise to a wide range of labour market adjustment pro- grammes which are constantly changing, with only a few countries having a stable set of labour market adjustment programmes. In response to new perceptions and political concerns, countries are continuously changing the programme mix and superimposing new programmes without phasing out old ones. This leads to a strange proliferation of programmes, many of which overlap or cancel each other out, making them costly to administer and confusing to firms, to the PES and to the unemployed they are supposed to assist.[31]

The essential tool for rationalizing this state of affairs is evaluation. As the OECD noted, the United States and Canada have a longstanding tradition of evaluating labour market adjustment programmes (mainly the major ones). Other countries such as Norway, Sweden, the United Kingdom and Australia have also carried out rigorous evaluations of their own programmes. In most other countries, however, the most common method of evaluation consists of simply monitoring the "gross" results of individual labour market adjustment programmes.[32]

Recently, a number of researchers have developed evaluation methods and approaches[33] and undertaken evaluation of labour market policies.[34] These suggest that most methods of evaluation are best suited to assessing individual programmes and this tends to reinforce an approach of generating specific programmes (often in response to particular political concerns) which are not linked to one another. Moreover, a major flaw in evaluation is the lack of reliable and valid empirical data. In future, there is a need to develop a systematic approach to evaluation that stresses not alone the effectiveness of individual programmes, but also how these programmes relate to one another. Moreover, there is a need to establish effective monitoring systems[35] to enable researchers to combine analyses of net employment effects with data on financing, organizational and regulatory structures.

The PES can contribute to programme evaluation by strengthening its performance management (see Chapter 8), by increasing the transparency of its service delivery system and by commissioning periodic independent evaluations of PES-managed programmes – in particular, of what works and why it works. These evaluations can be undertaken either by a PES evaluation unit (if such a unit exists) or by outside labour market research institutes. Besides the need for streamlining and evaluation, there are two other vital factors that differentiate labour market adjustment programmes from the other core functions of the PES. The first is the administrative role of the PES in these programmes and the second is the broad variability of activities. Each of these factors contributes to the diversity of issues confronting PES managers in administering these programmes.

As noted earlier, the PES has no presumptive right to run these programmes so the PES can take nothing for granted: it must compete with other organizations in the public and private sector. But of all the competing organizations, the PES is often the one with the most to offer because of its labour market knowledge, its delivery infrastructure and its external links. Indeed, the presence of the PES in so many localities may well be the clinching argument in favour of its suitability; it can enable a new programme to be set up quickly to meet tight political deadlines. Another decisive factor may be its ability to develop partnerships with other public and private sector agencies.

This can be useful whether the PES is in the lead or is simply one of many service providers. (For a discussion of external relationships, see Chapter 9.)

There are four basic roles, or a combination of roles, that may be played by the PES in the administration of labour market adjustment programmes: the PES may have policy input into programmes run by other organizations; it may simply refer participants to programmes run by others; it may be funded to provide a certain service or package of services; or it may have overall management responsibility for a programme that it may wholly run or may subcontract to other service providers. The fact that different institutional relationships may exist at the national, regional (or state) and local levels complicates this further. For example, at a national level the PES may have policy input into a programme administered by another agency but may be funded to manage the programme overall at the regional level and may choose to contract out some of the services to other agencies at the local level.

The second complicating factor for the PES is that labour market adjustment programmes include a smorgasbord of activities that can be selected and combined in almost infinite ways to meet specific objectives. Among the variables that affect the design of programmes are the following:

- The overall scale of the programme.
- The timing of the intervention.
- Is the programme to be a preventative or re-integrative one? Is it intended to activate jobseekers (move them from passive measures to active measures) more quickly?
- The choice of clients. Will these services be provided on a universal basis to all customers and if not, what should the target group be? There are numerous examples of rationing services on an income (means tested) basis and on a target group specification basis.
- Will the target group be selected on the basis of demographics and characteristics such as age and relative ability or will they be selected on the basis of a more general assessment of the functional barriers to re-integration into the labour market?
- Will the programme use demand or supply side strategies or a combination of both?
- Will the programme concentrate on a single service or as is more commonly the case, will a variety of activities be bundled together as in the integrated strategies described earlier in this chapter?
- What level of intensity will programme resources allow? Should fewer people be served by more intensive services or should more people be served with less intensity?

Critical to the planning and management of these programmes is sophisticated labour market information. An accurate diagnosis of the labour market and factors affecting it is necessary to sensibly answer the questions set out above.

To summarize, if the PES is to play an effective role in these programmes, it has to achieve the following. First, it must be prepared to work in partnership with other bodies, in particular to purchase training services (see Chapter 9). Second, it must ensure an integrated service delivery system and a better targeting of selected groups. Third, it must ensure effective use of labour market information. Fourth, it must build up an expertise in selecting appropriate applicants, procurement, and management of these programmes so that they can successfully bid for this work. Finally, it must develop robust monitoring and evaluation strategies.

Notes

[1] OECD: *Jobs study: Facts, analysis, strategies* (Paris, OECD, 1994), p. 47.

[2] The OECD since the late 1980s has done much to conceptualize and popularize a distinction between passive and active labour-market measures. According to the OECD, the latter seek to rapidly redeploy labour and develop new skills and employment opportunities for workers. They aim at preventing unemployment or remedying it by returning displaced workers to productive jobs. Active measures include job-broking, job-search assistance and labour-market information services to assist workers to find jobs and employers to find qualified workers. Other measures which fall under this heading are those generally intended to improve worker productivity, promote investment, and facilitate mobility. Training and retraining programmes, assistance for small-enterprise development and other job creation schemes can also be included. Passive measures help to reduce the short-term costs of economic adjustment to individuals and communities by providing income support and maintenance programs. They aim to alleviate the hardship of job loss and to reduce poverty. Passive measures include unemployment benefits, family and maternity allowances, social welfare payments, pensions, and protection of health benefits during unemployment. Related programmes such as wage subsidies and relocation allowances to encourage geographic mobility can also be included. In this study, we define labour-market adjustment programmes as part of active labour market policies, but exclude job-broking and labour-market information from this category. See "Glossary of Terms" in Annex I.

[3] OECD, op. cit., pp. 47–49.

[4] For instance, Article 6 (a) (i) of the Employment Service Convention, 1948 (No. 88) states that the PES should assist (workers) where appropriate to obtain vocational guidance or vocational training or retraining.

[5] See "Information technology as an asset in competition", An interview with Mr. Göte Bernhardsson, Director-General of AMS Sweden in *Public Employment Service*, Vol. 2, 1997, p. 20.

[6] A heuristic system of education is one in which students are trained to find out things for themselves.

[7] Namely, N. Azrin and V. Besalel.

[8] They are called "active job-search clubs" in the Walloon region (a total of 6); "active job-search workshops" in the Brussels-Capital region; and "job club" in Flanders (a total of 38).

[9] In 1995, the PES operated 333 job clubs in Poland serving 28,000 jobseekers. See ILO: *The public employment service in Poland* (Geneva, ILO, 1998; mimeographed), p. 61.

[10] M. White et al.: *The impact of public job placing programmes* (London, Policy Studies Institute, 1997), p. 83.

[11] For details on the employment counselling process, see C. Kasserly: *Employment counselling, career guidance and occupational information provided through a public employment service*, Labour Administration Branch Doc. No. 40.2 (Geneva, ILO, 1994).

[12] Norway Labour Market Services: *More education? Vocational guidance* (Oslo, Directorate of Labour, 1999) or @ http://www.you.nls.no.

[13] Initially it concerned unemployed people under 46 years of age but since 1995 has been restricted to people without an upper-secondary education diploma.

[14] See OECD: *The public employment service: Belgium* (Paris, OECD, 1997), pp. 51–53.

[15] See G. Schmid et al.: *International handbook of labour market policy and evaluation* (Cheltenham, Edward Elgar, 1996).

[16] There is considerable debate among economic experts as to the extent to which subsidies paid to employers generate additional jobs. Additionality can be reduced by "deadweight" (unemployed who would have moved into jobs anyway), "substitution" (employers hire subsidized workers instead of unsubsidized workers) and "displacement" (subsidized firms take business from unsubsidized firms). Some experts recommend subsidies in order to redistribute opportunities in favour of unemployed people and improve their employability. See OECD Working Party on Employment: *Measures to assist workers displaced by structural change* (Paris, OECD, 1986), pp. 36–37. See also National Economic Research Associates (NERA): *Right to work assessment: An independent inquiry requested by the Prime Minister* (London, NERA, 1996), paras. 3.3, 5.3.4, 5.4.3 and 5.5. This study estimated that 305 of the jobs subsidized under the United Kingdom "Workstart" scheme might be "additional".

[17] White et al., op. cit., p. 37.

[18] D. Fretwell and S. Goldberg: *Developing effective employment services*, World Bank Discussion Paper (Washington, DC, 1994).

[19] For further information on prevention and re-employment measures to assist retrenched workers, see ILO: *Worker retrenchment: Prevention and re-employment measures* (Geneva, ILO, forthcoming).

[20] OECD Working Party on Employment: *Measures to assist workers displaced by structural changes...*op. cit., pp. 34–35.

[21] See P. Kosonen: "Activation, incitations au travail et *workfare* dans quatre pays scandinaves", in *Travail et Emploi*, No. 79, 1999, p. 13.

[22] D. Finn: *Working nation: Welfare reform and the Australian job compact for the long term unemployed* (London, Unemployment Unit, 1997), p. 1; p. 5.

[23] S. Lazerus et al.: *The public employment service in a one-stop world*, Policy Issues Monograph (Baltimore, Maryland, Johns Hopkins University Press, 1998), pp. 16–17.

[24] See T. Bentley and R. Gurumurth: *Destination unknown: Engaging with the problems of marginalized youth* (London, Demos, 1999). This is a study of the relatively large group of young people in the United Kingdom who are "off-register" or outside the system and are often engaged in the informal economy. It recommends solutions drawing on international best practice.

[25] See J. P. Martin: *What works among active labour market policies: Evidence from OECD countries' experiences*, Labour Market and Social Policy Occasional Paper No. 35 (Paris, OECD, 1998).

[26] See OECD: *Economic outlook survey by country* (Paris, OECD, 1998 and 1999).

[27] See Martin, op. cit.

[28] Ibid., p. 22.

[29] A. Dar and I. S. Gill: "Evaluating retraining programs in OECD countries: Lessons learned", in *The World Bank Research Observer*, Vol. 13, No. 1, 1998, pp. 79–101.

[30] A review of the concepts, principles and policy targets of lifelong learning in the perspective of labour market policy and educational policy can be found in A. C. Tuijnman and K. Schöman: "Life-long learning and skill formation", in G. Schmid et al.: *International handbook of labour market policy and evaluation* (Cheltenham, Edward Elgar, 1996), pp. 465–467.

[31] For instance, in the United States the troublesome features of such proliferation are: duplication of resources with many programmes offering the same services and sharing common goals; different programmes serving the same groups; different definitions of eligible groups; programmes operating on different planning cycles thereby hampering the ability of programme administrators to coordinate assistance. Moreover, apart from some of the major federal programmes, little is known about the cost-effectiveness of many programmes. See OECD: *The public employment service in the United States* (Paris, OECD, 1999), p. 128.

[32] See C. Brinkmann: *Controlling and evaluation of employment promotion and the employment services in Germany*, Labour Market Research Topic No. 36 (Nuremberg, Institute for Employment Research, 1999), pp. 1–28.

[33] E. Nesporova et al.: *Evaluation of labour market policies in transition countries* (Geneva, ILO, 2000).

[34] A state-of-the-art account of research on evaluation methods and approaches as well as on evaluation of labour market policy, vocational education and training is provided in Schmid et al., op. cit. See also W. Norton Grubb and P. Ryan: *The roles of evaluation for vocational education and training* (Geneva, ILO, 1999).

[35] P. Auer and T. Kruppe: "Monitoring of labour market policy in EU member States", in Schmid et al., op. cit., pp. 899–923.

UNEMPLOYMENT BENEFITS AND THE PUBLIC EMPLOYMENT SERVICE   7

The exchanges and unemployment insurance were complementary. They were man and wife, mutually supported and sustained by each other.[1]

Introduction

During the course of the last 90 years, a close relationship has existed between the PES and unemployment benefit. Unemployment benefit systems are the passive component of labour market policies and income support for the unemployed is their chief aim. They stand in contrast to active policies such as job-broking and labour market adjustment programmes which are aimed at re-integrating or re-employing the unemployed. The balance between active and passive policies is a source of continuing public policy debate and is one in which the PES plays a pivotal role.

This chapter focuses on employment benefits. We first describe the main forms of benefit and the general policy issues that these give rise to. There follows a discussion of the role played by the PES in unemployment benefit which focuses on topics such as job-search assistance or re-employment services, continuing eligibility and job-search verification, and overall unemployment benefit programme administration. We conclude with an outline of current trends and issues.

The main forms of unemployment benefit

The term "unemployment benefit" is used in this chapter to describe all forms of income support for unemployed people. These benefits divide broadly into two categories: "unemployment insurance" where benefits are principally financed by contributions and "unemployment assistance", where the benefits are normally financed by taxation and dependent upon needs or means testing.

Unemployment insurance is a system in which workers are entitled to compensation for lost income based upon past contributions. It covers the risk of loss of a certain level of income and is often based on the concept of a replacement rate. The system is financed wholly or mainly by pay-related contributions and benefits are normally paid out for a limited period of time. As was noted in Chapter 1, the payment of unemployment insurance began with trade unions, mutual benefit societies and other worker associations in countries such as Germany, France and the United Kingdom where members contributed to funds from which benefits were provided. The entry of the government into unemployment benefit schemes evolved over the first half of the twentieth century, usually inspired by strong political conflicts or economic upheavals. In continental Europe, unemployment insurance was often the last piece of social security legislation to be enacted. This was because of its complexity and because it intervenes more directly into the world of work by establishing minimum conditions of work in the labour market.[2]

The 1911 National Insurance Act in the United Kingdom was the first national compulsory unemployment insurance programme. It was followed in 1919 by the setting up of a programme in Italy which covered most manual workers. After the First World War, several countries adopted unemployment benefit programmes and some countries subsidized voluntary schemes. The economic depressions of the 1930s and the post-Second World War period stimulated the strengthening of existing programmes and the introduction of new ones. Examples of the latter include the 1935 Social Security Act in the United States, the 1940 Unemployment Insurance Act in Canada and the 1947 Unemployment Insurance Law in Japan. From this period through to the early 1970s, countries adapted their systems by extending coverage or increasing benefits. Some countries adapted their objectives for the programme by trying to integrate it into a broader labour market policy. The international economic crises of the 1970s and the widespread rise in unemployment increased the cost of benefits which led to governments tightening the stipulations for benefit and actually reducing the benefits in the 1980s. Over the past decade, unemployment insurance systems have not changed substantially in the G7 countries, although there have been modifications in response to economic and political events such as the reunification of Germany.[3]

Unemployment assistance on the other hand is paid to unemployed people based upon need, regardless of their work history. It compensates for a lack of income by subsidizing objectively assessed expenses and needs and is based on the concepts of minimum income. The system is taxpayer-financed and is more often than not, limited to a specific period of time.[4] Unemployment assistance benefits are based on a welfare principle which has its roots in religious charity and "relief for the poor" which was supported by local government. These activities have increasingly been taken over by national governments, particularly in financing and standard setting. Some countries operate a guaranteed minimum income (social benefit). This may be in addition to or as an alternative to employment assistance and is available to all those in need, irrespective of whether they are available for paid employment or not. Some countries also provide a combination of unemployment insurance and unemployment assistance/social benefit, with the latter often being paid when contribution-based entitlements are exhausted. Moreover, in some countries there is a social benefit system.

Table 7.1 illustrates the incidence of unemployment insurance, unemployment assistance or social benefit and combined unemployment insurance/unemployment assistance programmes among the 12 countries reviewed for this study. The table also highlights those countries where the entire system of benefits is administered by the PES. In those countries where the PES does not administer unemployment benefit, the PES is still involved in job-search assistance or re-employment activities and also continuing eligibility and job-search verification. This will be discussed shortly.

Unemployment benefits: General policy issues

The purpose of unemployment benefits is to reduce the costs of economic adjustment to individuals, enterprises and communities by providing income support. As we have seen, the benefits may be financed by contributions (from workers or employers or both), by taxation or by a combination of the two. Unemployment insurance may be voluntary or compulsory but the latter is more common. The programme may be managed by the PES, by another state institution or by the social partners. Basically, unemployment benefit is a replacement wage paid during the time required by a worker to find a new job. To receive benefit, workers must prove that they are unemployed and that they are looking for a new job.[5]

Beyond these overall objectives, emphases may vary somewhat from country to country and within each country and it may also vary over time. France, the United Kingdom and Germany pay particular attention to people experiencing long-term unemployment, while Italy and Japan provide temporary wage subsidies for workers in depressed industries. Canada and Japan strongly stress re-entry into employment.

This study does not address the complex policy and administrative aspects of unemployment benefits. Programme variables are numerous, but can be summarized as follows:

Table 7.1   Unemployment insurance, unemployment assistance and social benefits in the 12 countries, and territories covered by ILO country studies, 1998

Country	Unemployment insurance (UI) only	Unemployment assistance or social benefits (UA/SB) only	Combined UI and UA/SB system	PES administration of system
Argentina	X			No
Canada	X			Yes
France			X	No
Hong Kong, China		X[1]		No
Japan	X			No
Netherlands			X	No
Norway	X			Yes
Poland	X			Yes (partial)
Spain			X	No
Tunisia		No programme		
United Kingdom			X	No
United States	X			Yes

[1] This is means-tested social assistance, not exclusively for the unemployed.

Source: ILO: *Twelve unpublished public employment service country studies* (Geneva, ILO, 1998; mimeographed). The countries and territories surveyed were: Argentina, Canada, France, Japan, the Netherlands, Norway, Poland, Spain, Tunisia, the United States, the United Kingdom and Hong Kong, China. References are made to the individual country studies in this study.

* the degree of state control of the system;
* the distribution of the financing burden among employees, employers and government;
* the work history required for eligibility;
* the relationship between benefit amounts and past earnings;
* the adjustment of benefit duration according to economic conditions;
* the coverage for new labour force entrants and re-entrants;
* the availability of means-tested benefits for the long-term jobless; and
* the amount of job training activities in the system.[6]

Since the mid-1970s, a number of countries such as Germany, France and Spain have reacted to the increase in long-term unemployment and the widening deficits in unemployment benefit funding by raising the minimum period of employment and/or linking the duration of benefit entitlement more closely to the length of previous employment. In the majority of OECD countries, the maximum duration of benefit entitlement now varies according to the length of previous employment. In some cases, the age of the person involved is also a factor. The benefit duration can be as much as five years for older workers with many years of paid contributions in countries such as France and the Netherlands, or can be virtually unlimited as in Belgium. In a number of countries such as Greece, Ireland and the United Kingdom, benefit entitlement does not commence until after a waiting period of several days. For countries in which unemployment benefit is wage related, the level of benefit at the start of the period of unemployment varies. In Italy, Ireland and Greece, this varies between 20 and 50 per cent of the last gross wage; in Denmark it is as high as 90 per cent. The level of benefit is subject to somewhat atypical regulations in Germany and the United Kingdom: in Germany it depends not on gross but net wages and in the United Kingdom, unemployment benefit is not wage related but is paid as a flat-rate allowance. In countries such as Belgium, Spain and France, the level of benefit falls with increasing duration of unemployment. This is a response to the rise in long-term unemployment.[7]

Unemployment benefits present some of the most politically controversial issues that the PES has to face. On the one hand, benefits help to prevent poverty and indeed have a labour market rationale by providing unemployed workers with support during a period of enforced job-search. In addition, they also help workers maintain their morale and self-respect. On the other hand, there are widespread fears that significant periods of benefit dependency may blunt the will to work and undermine incentives. The PES tends to be the main instrument charged with preventing benefits from having adverse consequences on the motivation to work.

The PES role in unemployment benefit

For the purposes of this study, we need to focus on the three possible roles for the PES in relation to unemployment benefits: the provision of job-search assistance or re-employment services; continuing eligibility and job-search verification; and the overall administration of the unemployment benefit programme. The first two roles are most common for the PES as the emphasis upon re-integration into the workforce is consistent with the objectives of other PES functions. However, though the overall administration of unemployment benefits is carried out by the PES in countries such as the United States, Canada, and Norway, it is often handled by a separate administrative authority in other countries.

Job-search assistance or re-employment services

The purpose of these services is to facilitate the re-employment of unemployment benefit recipients and a variety of activities can be conducted to achieve this aim. (For a description of the various activities associated with these services see "Individual or intensive assistance" in Chapter 6.) In addition, job-broking provides an important service for getting unemployed claimants back to work (see Chapter 4). What distinguishes the activities in various countries in relation to unemployment benefits are differences in expectations for re-employment. These can relate to the duration and level of income support provided, the intensity of active job-search efforts demanded and the targeting of re-employment efforts on certain jobseekers.

The variation of active job-search assistance methods used in member countries was reviewed by the OECD in 1999.[8] Out of the 24 countries that responded, a variety of methods was noted. With regard to the initial registration of unemployment benefit claimants, virtually all countries required registration with the PES for job placement as a precondition for benefit payment. In some countries, there were efforts made to immediately place claimants, but in most countries this activity was not carried out at initial registration. Detailed registration for job placement purposes and an explanation of the rights and duties of the unemployed occurs in most countries within one week of the initial registration, but in some countries such as Austria, Belgium (Wallonia), Denmark, Finland, New Zealand, Poland, Sweden and Switzerland, there may be a delay of two or more weeks. Australia and the Netherlands use this interview to implement a profiling instrument while Austria, Belgium, Finland, New Zealand, Switzerland and the United Kingdom use it to establish action plans.

Group information sessions on topics such as job-search methods, jobseeker rights and benefits, labour market programmes and self-employment promotion are normally scheduled at an early stage in the unemployment period in Australia, Belgium (Flanders), Canada, Denmark, Finland, Hungary and Poland. These sessions are conducted on a more selective basis in Austria, Greece, Luxembourg, Portugal, Switzerland, the United Kingdom and the United States.

The frequency of compulsory intensive interviews during the unemployment period varies. A few countries such as Australia, Finland, the Netherlands, Spain and the United Kingdom schedule interviews at fixed points during the unemployment period. Others such as Austria, Denmark, Germany, New Zealand, Norway and Sweden have a fixed rule for the maximum interval between interviews. Making claimants maintain contact as a prerequisite for continued benefits also takes the form of an intensive interview in the Republic of Korea, Switzerland, Spain and Hungary. Although voluntary interviews may be just as common as mandatory interviews in Luxembourg, Portugal and Sweden, this is not the case in most other countries.

Individual action plans for employment are established for all unemployed within a month or so of initial registration in Austria, New Zealand, Switzerland and the United Kingdom. It is carried out on a very selective basis (based upon profiling or another selection method) in Australia and Poland, and it is offered on a voluntary basis in Canada and Hungary. An action plan is established after four to six months of unemployment in the Czech Republic, Finland, the Netherlands, Norway and Portugal. In the Republic of Korea, Germany, Poland and Spain, an action plan is rarely used even for the long-term unemployed. The focus of these action plans varies greatly. Some countries provide assessment and advice, others stress job-search efforts, while others stress that placement in a active labour market programme follows when employment is not secured.

Mandatory placement in an active labour market programme occurs in Denmark after 12 months, in Luxembourg after 6 months, in Sweden after 6 months, in Switzerland after 7 months and in the United Kingdom after 24 months.[9] In Australia, the Netherlands and Norway, about half the unemployed are likely to be placed in a programme after 12 months. In countries which do not have precise stipulations for entry into active labour market programmes, PES counsellors may determine compulsory entry according to individual circumstances.

Once an unemployed person is placed in an active labour market programme, the monitoring of job-search activity changes in some countries: in the Netherlands, participants are no longer required to apply for jobs during training or subsidized work; in Denmark and Luxembourg, participants may still be referred to a vacant job; in Denmark, the benefit sanctions for refusal of work become harsher. In Switzerland and in some Australian programmes, participants must still report independent job-search activity although the frequency of monitoring is reduced.[10]

Recent programme developments in the United Kingdom provide a more detailed illustration of how requirements for active job-search have been strengthened. With the passage of the Jobseekers' Act in 1995, the United Kingdom moved to consolidate their unemployment insurance and unemployment assistance programmes and link active and passive components of labour market policy. While the vast majority of programme participants qualify through unemployment assistance (means tested) provisions rather than the insurance (contributory) route, people from both categories are served in Jobcentres by employment services and benefits agency staff working in tandem and using what is known as an "active benefits regime" – a condition for receiving an allowance. Registration takes the form of a "new jobseekers interview", where a "jobseeker's agreement" is negotiated between the jobseeker and the employment service adviser.

This agreement is monitored according to a schedule of biweekly check-ins, supplemented by an in-depth interview after 13 weeks and an in-depth "restart interview" after six months, with additional activities prescribed after 12 months or 24 months where necessary. If an adviser believes that a jobseeker is not fulfilling the conditions for job-search assistance, he or she can refer the case to an adjudication officer who then decides if the jobseeker should be disqualified. This regular and increasingly intensive contact with the employment service is designed to encourage jobseekers to find jobs or improve their employability as early as possible. It also enables the employment service to identify those who require further help and to refer them to the range of more intensive employability measures on offer. Superimposed on these arrangements now are a range of New Deal programmes. (See "Welfare-to-work programmes" in Chapter 6.)

In some countries, job-search assistance services are offered on a more selective basis to those deemed to be in the greatest need of them. Even though in some countries the provision of re-employment to unemployment benefit claimants is universal, the targeting of particular subgroups of the unemployed population for intensive intervention may also occur. In the Czech Republic, Spain and Poland, a large proportion of the population is identified as being particularly vulnerable. In the Netherlands, many claimants may be classified by a profiling instrument as not being immediately employable, and in need of extra assistance. (See "Innovations and good practices by the PES" in Chapter 4.) In the United States, approximately 30 per cent of new registrants are assessed by a profiling instrument. In the United Kingdom, the scope of the various New Deal programmes and the procedure of caseloading have the effect of prioritizing entry to particular groups or individuals. In Belgium, education, age and occupational experience are used as criteria in establishing target groups. Australia has a number of programmes targeted at specific groups and New Zealand prioritizes those with Maori ethnic origins. People with disabilities are an important priority group in Sweden.[11]

Several countries have explored the possibility of using statistical methods to target individuals who may experience long periods of unemployment and thus could benefit from re-employment and other services early in their employment period. A few countries, principally Australia, Canada and the United States, have introduced variations on this concept into existing programmes. The concept referred to as "profiling" in the United States is designed to reduce the cost of assessment and referral and to provide a means of integrating services more effectively.

Through the profiling initiative in the United States, formally named the Worker Profiling and Reemployment Services (WPRS), states are taking preemptive action to help unemployment insurance beneficiaries shorten their time out of work. The programme identifies – primarily through statistical methods – those unemployment insurance recipients who are most likely to exhaust their benefit entitlement and refers them to compulsory re-employment services. Beneficiaries are then referred to re-employment services in order of their ranking until the capacity of local agencies to serve them is exhausted. Unemployment insurance beneficiaries then receive re-employment services that are tailored to individual needs. For state employment security agencies, this new programme marks a significant change in the way they allocate resources and deliver services. Programmes similar to the WPRS have been considered in other countries but to date only two countries, Australia and Canada, have implemented programmes that use a statistical method for early identification of those most likely to experience long spells of unemployment. Some countries, such as the United Kingdom, have found that the predictive accuracy of their statistical profiling models has been lower than desired.

Profiling is most relevant in countries that are selective in offering jobseekers access to training and job-search assistance during the early stages of an unemployment period. As a result, countries such as France, Germany and Sweden which offer services to all unemployed as soon as they register, find little use for profiling as a management tool to prioritize who receives services. However, these countries may find profiling useful in assessing the needs of clients and in recommending the most effective and cost-efficient combination for individuals.[12]

Continuing eligibility and job-search verification

The second role of the PES in the context of unemployment benefits is continuing eligibility and job-search verification. This involves developing standards and enforcing sanctions to ensure that unemployment benefit claimants look for work and that they accept suitable job offers. The purpose of this activity is to offset the disincentive to work created by the availability of income support and to guarantee that claimants are exposed to work opportunities. To accomplish this purpose, unemployment benefit claimants are usually required to register as jobseekers with the PES. Various standards are applied (after determining ability and availability for work) for unemployment benefit claimants to report their job-search activities and to compel them to accept job offers. In some cases, unemployment benefit claimants are required to accept a suitable job referral as a condition of continued receipt of benefits. The application of work test sanctions are directly tied to the provision of job-search assistance or re-employment services.

The variation in continuing eligibility and job-search verification methods employed by member countries was reviewed by the OECD in 1999.[13] In the 24 countries that responded there was a considerable variation in procedures. Basic claim continuation reporting occurs most often on a biweekly or monthly basis, although overall it can range from weekly in New Zealand and the United States to once every three months in Spain. In the Netherlands and Hungary, the reporting frequency is left to local discretion. The Czech Republic and Germany have no separate procedure for claim continuation. Continued claims reporting is carried out by telephone in New Zealand and in many areas of Canada and the United States, while it is carried out by mail in Denmark, Finland, Norway, Portugal, Sweden and some areas of Canada and the United States. Personal visits are required in Australia, Austria, Belgium, Greece, Hungary, the Republic of Korea, Luxembourg, Poland, Spain, Switzerland and the United Kingdom.

The type of job-search reporting also varies. In Australia, the Republic of Korea, the Netherlands, New Zealand, Switzerland, the United Kingdom and the United States, job-search initiatives are part of the continued claims reporting procedure. However, in Austria, Denmark, Germany, Norway, Poland and Sweden, it is reviewed infrequently and then often as an individual item in a general interview. In Belgium, the Czech Republic, Finland, Greece, Hungary, Luxembourg, Portugal and Spain, there is no requirement for reporting independent job-search activities. Countries also differ in the evidence of job-search activities required. This can range between verbal accounts, employer contact lists, reports from employers or letters of application.[14]

A more detailed description of procedures is provided by the example of Norway. Unemployment insurance claimants mail in a report card every two weeks to report their employment status. They are required to actively search for jobs and be immediately available for work. A claimant who refuses a reasonable job or labour market programme offer is denied further benefits. The PES has uniform rules for when an unemployment insurance claimant can reasonably be expected to move or accept a lower salary as a condition of employment. The enforcement of these rules has been strengthened by the improvement in the Norwegian economy over the past few years.

Overall unemployment benefit programme administration

As Table 7.1 shows, in three of the 12 countries reviewed for this publication the PES administers the entire unemployment benefit system. In all three, the programme involved is an unemployment insurance programme not an unemployment assistance programme or a mixed programme. In Canada and the United States, the administration of unemployment insurance (or "employment insurance" as it has been renamed in Canada) has always been an integral function of the PES.

The fundamental unemployment insurance administrative functions are tax collection, benefit determination, benefit payment, and continuing eligibility and job-search verification. With regard to the three functions not addressed in the previous section, reform initiatives in recent years in countries such as Canada and the United States have mostly been taken to improve efficiency or to streamline financing methods. One of the most dramatic initiatives in the United States has been the development of a telephone claims service system. (See Annex IV.21.)

Canada is using self-service computers in local offices as a means of filing claims in its drive to create innovations in its administration of unemployment insurance. Claims can be filed using a paper application or increasingly, electronically via a computer terminal in a local office. Filing by remote computers is also being tested. Biweekly job-search verification/refiling report cards are also required. They can be dropped off at a local office but increasingly, they are being filed telephonically by interactive, touch-tone, voice-response systems.

In addition to revolutionizing the benefit application process for benefit applicants, advanced countries are exploring methods such as the Internet in an effort to streamline tax collection and reporting requirements for employers.

Conclusion: Trends and issues

Unemployment benefits raise important policy issues, many of which are beyond the scope of this publication. Here we focus on those issues which affect the future of the PES. As Chapter 1 showed, the relationship between unemployment benefits and the PES has been central to the history of the PES. Churchill's observation that the PES and unemployment insurance were like man and wife has some truth to it but as in many real marriages, there are often tensions between partners. Job-broking requires an entrepreneurial approach and a strong emphasis on building up close relations with employer and jobseeker customers. Benefit systems by their nature require the rigorous enforcement of rules including at times, the imposition of sanctions. In one sense, the PES is well placed to play a policing role because of its position as an intermediary in the labour market. But playing this role also risks alienating both employers and jobseekers and thus making the PES less effective in its other functions. As Chapter 1 showed, concerns about this risk led governments in Canada, the United States and the United Kingdom to separate benefit from employment work for a time.

The pendulum has now swung back. The danger of undermining the image of the job-broking service is considered to be less important than the danger of relaxing efforts which encourage unemployed people to return to work. The fundamental issue is to find the proper balance between the conflicting goals of providing income support and promoting re-employment. Strategies include the tightening of benefit eligibility rules, limiting the duration of benefits, tightening of job-search requirements and the better enforcement of fraud controls. In addition, stronger linkages with labour market adjustment programmes through profiling and other activities as advocated by the OECD are aimed at the same purpose.

This does not necessarily mean that the PES should administer unemployment benefits. There may be sound administrative reasons for entrusting the administration of benefits to another body. But the current opinion tends to favour a close partnership, at least between benefit administration, the PES and the one-stop concept of co-locating the functions at a local level.

In order to promote a closer partnership, there is a need for continued analysis of which unemployment benefit claimants are most in need of re-employment services and which services are most effective for which groups. In particular, it must be remembered that unemployment benefits developed largely in response to cyclical unemployment. Some countries are facing the difficult challenge of adapting their unemployment insurance systems to cope with structural unemployment. This entails more profound and permanent career dislocations for many workers.

For those countries pioneering automated claims filing processes, it will be important to monitor the impact of these innovations in terms broader than improved administrative efficiency and cost control. Even as the United States and Canada are implementing telephone claims processing, discussion and research are underway about how to provide claims services electronically. It may soon be possible for unemployed workers to file a new claim for unemployment benefits via the Internet. When security issues are resolved, it will be relatively simple to provide unemployed workers with the option of completing an unemployment claim form from their personal computer or from a computer available in a one-stop centre, library or other public facility.

Before these new automated systems become widespread, some important issues need to be dealt with. In the United States where these administrative innovations are most advanced, some employers have been expressing concerns that telephone-initial claims may increase the vulnerability of the unemployment insurance system to fraud and abuse and have demanded that the impact of a telephone claims system on programme cost, error rates, and duration of claims be evaluated. A broader issue is whether less person-to-person contact between unemployment insurance claims-recipients and claims administrators will reduce incentives to re-employment, or whether there are more effective methods to promote the same objective.

As in some countries, long-standing unemployment benefit programmes are being administratively streamlined and programmatically integrated with other PES programmes. These programmes are being introduced for the first time in other countries, including a number of central European countries and more recently, Asian countries such as the Republic of Korea. These countries, which have experienced rapidly rising unemployment and poverty for the first time in decades, consider the introduction of such programmes to be part of a social safety net to combat the effects of the introduction of a market economy and the exposure to a more volatile global economy. However, these countries are also aware of the need to build in incentives for unemployed people to quickly return to work and this has led to the simultaneous introduction of other active labour market adjustment programmes to complement unemployment benefits.

In conclusion, PES administrators need to maintain close contact with developing policies on unemployment benefits. In the modern world, they are unlikely to be able to disengage themselves from benefit issues whether they actually administer the entire unemployment benefit system or not. Instead, they need to be sure on the one hand that the PES is fulfilling the wishes of politicians and policy makers in playing its full part in helping and encouraging people to move from social welfare into work. On the other hand, they need to be vigilant about the potential adverse effects that an involvement in benefit control could have on customer attitudes to their other services and take what remedial action they can. Tensions between these different functions will remain, but PES administrators need to be aware of them and seek to minimize them.

Notes

[1] Winston Churchill in the House of Commons on 19 May 1909. Quoted in R. S. Churchill: *Young statesman: Winston S. Churchill 1901–14* (London, Minerva, 1991), p. 311.

[2] G. Schmid et al.: *Unemployment insurance and active labor market policy* (Detroit, Wayne State University Press, 1992), p. 70.

[3] See C. O'Leary and S. Wandner: *Unemployment insurance in the United States: Analysis of policy issues* (Kalamazoo, Michigan, W. E. Upjohn Institute for Employment Research, 1997), pp. 600–602.

[4] OECD: *The public employment service in Belgium* (Paris, OECD, 1997), p. 68.

[5] S. Ricca: *Introduction to public employment services: A workers' education manual* (Geneva, ILO, 1994), p. 19.

[6] O'Leary and Wandner, op. cit., p. 603.

[7] European Employment Observatory Mutual Information System on Employment Policies (MISEP): *Policies, No 43F* (Berlin, European Commission, Autumn 1993). In addition, a somewhat dated but lucid and detailed discussion of these issues can be found in OECD: *Employment Outlook 1991* (Paris, OECD, 1991), Ch. 7.

[8] OECD: *Interventions in the unemployment spell managed by the public employment service*, ELSA Committee Discussion Paper (Paris, OECD, 1999).

[9] In the United Kingdom, this is earlier for those eligible for New Deal programmes, e.g. young people under 25 who enter a mandatory programme after 6 months.

[10] OECD: *Interventions in the unemployment spell managed by the public employment service* (Paris, OECD, 1999), p.13.

[11] Ibid., p. 14.

[12] European Employment Observatory Mutual Information System on Employment Policies (MISEP): *Policies, No 60F* (Berlin, European Commission, Winter 1993).

[13] OECD: *Interventions in the unemployment spell...* op. cit.

[14] Ibid., p. 7.

ORGANIZING AND MANAGING THE SERVICE   8

...life has become so hard for established institutions and those that work for them: the ground can disappear so rapidly from beneath their feet. Competition and radical innovation can suddenly emerge to threaten the identity and purpose of established institutions...institutions have to learn rapidly and reinvent themselves repeatedly.[1]

Introduction

Turbulence is a fact of life for many public institutions today and the PES is no exception. Managing the PES has become a most challenging undertaking. Competing needs, limited resources and powerful influences impose seemingly unending demands on the time and resourcefulness of senior PES managers and these managers are uncomfortably aware that they cannot satisfy all the demands that are being placed upon them. Senior PES managers play a dual role. On the one hand, in partnership with governmental representatives, social partners and their own managers and staff, they may be involved in the design of labour market interventions of various kinds. On the other hand, once the nature of these interventions has been determined, they may become responsible for delivering the results.

The PES role in both design and delivery can no longer be taken for granted. The character of government planning of labour market policies is changing and becoming more strategic, with a greater emphasis being placed on flexibility, competition, decentralization and sensitivity to the needs of customers and the labour market. In the eyes of central government, the PES may just be one of a variety of potential delivery agencies in an environment where complex partnerships and contracting arrangements may be necessary for effective delivery.

Producing results in such an environment calls for a different approach to management and for profound changes in organizational culture. Most of the well-established PESs have been through the phase of organizational life where

111

a standardized and structured set of services, procedures, and processes were the norm throughout local offices. This meant working within a standardized command structure at regional and headquarters level regardless of the economic and social environment. In recent years, there has been a recognition that a standardized organization fails to produce the desired results. It has been, or is being replaced by a more flexible and decentralized service-delivery approach tailored to the conditions and needs of local areas. A significant part of this restructuring includes the implementation of a quality culture within the organization, with a sharp focus being placed on customer needs. Within this changing framework, PES resources have to be skilfully deployed. These resources include the motivation and expertise of staff, new information and communications technology and the appearance and quality of PES offices; the latter can communicate a great deal about an organization to its customers.

In this chapter we look at the context within which the PES is managed and at the ways of responding to the organizational and management challenges which confront it. Our information is based on a review of practices in a number of countries, but good practices are not confined to these countries: the scope of the review had to be limited for practical reasons. The topics that are dealt with are manifold. Under governmental framework and accountability we look at stakeholders, strategic and operational planning, performance management and the evaluation of programmes. Organizational issues such as decentralization, integration of services and competitive service delivery are discussed as are management strategies such as quality management, information and communications technology, facilities planning, internal communications and staff training and development

Governmental framework and accountability

Stakeholders

Before looking at internal management, we need to look at the accountability of the PES and how it receives its remit. The PES manager's world is made up of a variety of stakeholders: the politicians and civil servants who oversee the PES; the direct customers of PES services; the staff of the PES and those organizations which provide labour market services; the taxpayers who finance the services; and finally, there are stakeholders who represent the various customer groups indirectly through the political or advisory processes. To achieve anything, the PES manager must be adept at dealing with all of these.

The importance of stakeholder support for the PES cannot be overestimated. It is likely to determine to a large extent the eventual success of any new initiatives. Public support in particular is essential if political support and funding are to be made available to achieve the vision of the organization. A positive perception of programmes strengthens the position of the PES and significantly increases the probability of being successful.

The PES is normally accountable to a political leader who is its most powerful stakeholder. In parliamentary systems this is usually the Minister of Labour, but the civil service advisers surrounding the minister may also wield considerable influence. There are other political leaders with whom the public manager must contend, particularly the representatives comprising the legislative body. Elected representatives may have little or no interest in the day-to-day details of programme implementation or operations, but their interest can increase dramatically if significant employment problems arise, particularly in the area that they represent. Moreover, the relationship between PES managers and political leaders may be complicated because each uses different measures of success.

Customers are very important stakeholders. For the PES, customers are a very diverse group and often compete with each other to demand service. Customers include jobseekers, employers and other organizations. Various subgroups of jobseekers also compete for services. Moreover, customers may not only express views directly to the PES, but may also express them to elected representatives and to the representatives of the social partners.

There are three other significant groups of stakeholders. First, there is the staff of the PES itself. Without their support, the best efforts and intentions of PES managers can be undermined and the desired results not materialize. Moreover, they may be organized in staff unions with whom PES senior managers have to negotiate. Second, there are organizations with whom the PES cooperates to deliver services (see Chapter 9) or with whom it may contract for services (this is discussed later in this chapter). Finally, there are the supervisory or advisory boards including the social partners and others. (A discussion of their roles can be found in Chapters 3 and 9.)

Strategic and operational planning

The political leaders of any government bring certain values and policies to office that set the direction of the PES. Generally, these values and policies are articulated in broad visionary language, lacking in specific outcomes or expectations. The PES administrator is expected to turn these into more specific plans in partnership with the minister's more immediate advisers and other stakeholders, and then communicate them throughout the organization and to the public.

Traditionally, the PES in most countries has developed annual or biennial operating plans for directing PES services. This process is often carried out in conjunction with the budget process. In the United States, the federal government has routinely required biennial plans for major programmes, including those of the PES. In most European countries, annual operating plans are a common feature. The need to adapt more quickly and effectively to external change, however, demands a longer term planning approach. It is becoming increasingly common for the PES to be involved in strategic planning not just to align its internal planning with government economic and employment policies, but also to align this planning with the realities of the labour market and pressures from other stakeholders.

Strategic planning is a structured way of applying strategic thinking to the organization in order to develop a plan for the future and it is usually influenced by the concept of "management by objective". The latter tries to answers three basic questions: Where are we now? Where are we going? How do we get there? Strategic planning can take many forms and the following example involves four phases:

- The "assessment phase" involves reviewing the current organization, identifying customers and assessing how their expectations are being met. It also involves identifying the trends affecting the organization including those likely to affect customer satisfaction in the future, for example changes in technology, customer demographics, demand for services and budget constraints. This enables the existing guiding principles for the PES to be reviewed.
- The "vision phase" uses information from the assessment phase to develop a vision of where the organization should go. This vision needs to be shared by leaders because each must support actions that will make it a reality.
- The "targeting phase" sets goals (with a time horizon of up to 5 years), objectives (3–5 year horizon) and "action steps" (up to one year).
- The "implementation phase" is the phase in which PES managers become "champions" and manage improvement and change based on the strategic plan.

The organization needs to repeat the planning process periodically, perhaps every three years. In the intervening years, there are intensive quarterly or semi-annual reviews that focus on validating what is planned and updating as necessary.

Sweden initiated a discussion process along these lines in 1998 and enlisted the participation of staff at all Swedish PES offices. The process was given the name "Dialogue 98" and the product of the year-long process was a workbook which addressed issues such as the uniformity of services in relation to staffing enterprises, developing knowledge of occupations and the enterprise sector, and the relevance of ecological thinking.[2] In France, a *Contrat de Progrès* or progress agreement between the ANPE and the ministries of Labour and Finance sets the direction of the agency for a four-year period.[3] This agreement has the objective of transforming the ANPE into a modern, client-oriented service provider and of enhancing its effectiveness. The agreement contains a number of qualitative targets such as widening the range of services, fighting against social exclusion, modernizing computer equipment and decentralizing budget management. Other targets include increasing the market share of notified vacancies out of the total vacancies in the economy, tripling the number of notified vacancies for executive positions and reducing the incidence of excessive long-term employment.

In Austria, strategic and operational planning have been very carefully integrated. Broad, labour market policy targets with a three-year time horizon, are agreed between federal and state organizations for the PES. These are then broken down into annual outcomes with concrete targets. Performance indicators based on these targets are then monitored quarterly as the plan is implemented.

As a result of the passage of the Workforce Investment Act of 1998 in the United States, all states are required to develop workforce development plans to guide implementation of the new legislation. A number of states have used a strategic planning process to develop a broader framework for future service delivery. At one stage removed from national strategic planning, the European Union has implemented a strategic planning approach by the adoption of common European Employment Guidelines: each EU member State is required to develop a national action plan and report regularly on its progress (see Chapter 3).

Performance management

Performance management is also relevant to accountability and to the relationships between the PES and its political stakeholders. The plans agreed through strategic and operational planning normally include defined outcomes which need to be embedded in a performance management system. In addition to reflecting the accountability of the whole organization, performance management is also a valuable internal tool for the PES to improve programme performance by systematic assessment of the progress being made toward goals. Performance indicators generally fall into one of four categories:

Measure	Outcome
Labour market outcomes	Placement
Distribution of outcomes by target group	Percentage of service to a particular target group, e.g. the long-term unemployed
Work process	Vacancy fill time; number of programme completers
Customer satisfaction	Satisfaction level with service rendered

The first two categories of measures are primarily concerned with PES effectiveness in implementing labour market policy and achieving employment goals, these being the chief concern of policy-makers responsible for funding these measures. The other two categories focus on PES efficiency in delivering services to customers.

The purpose of these measures is to provide statistical evidence of success or failure in reaching current goals and to facilitate systematic feedback to the respective steering levels.[4] In addition, performance management that is properly conducted can offer valuable learning experience for PES managers as it deepens their understanding of their business. A performance review therefore should not be conducted as an inquisition nor as part of a blame culture; it should be conducted instead in a constructive, problem-solving spirit in which PES managers can celebrate successes and explore together ways of overcoming difficulties.

The selection of relevant performance indicators is a difficult art and needs to be tied to the goals set out in the planning processes described earlier. It is vitally important to set measures which are both appropriate in relation to the underlying aims of the organization and to the culture that is most conducive to achieving those aims. Performance targets have a powerful influence on staff behaviour for good or ill and badly chosen targets do more harm than good. For instance, at one time the PES in the United States used a measure that was based on the number of individual placements made by each employee. While on the surface this seemed to be a legitimate measure, in practice it encouraged employees to behave selfishly to the detriment of the service. They found ways of hoarding easy-to-fill job orders and well qualified jobseekers. It was later found that teamwork based on sharing information yielded far better overall results.

The system of measurement used should enable comparisons to be made. These comparisons can be made in relation to the targets set in the course of planning, to historical data or to the performance of other agencies. A sample of PES programme performance measures taken from several countries include:

Job-broking	Number of job placements Number of job placements as a proportion of the number of vacancies reported directly to the PES Number of temporary work placements Labour market penetration rates
Labour market adjustment	Proportion of people with occupational disabilities programmes covered by initiatives for them Proportion of people previously classified as "occupationally disabled" now in work-related activities Attainment of a recognized qualification or credential relating to the achievement of educational skills Proportion of people no longer receiving unemployment benefits through labour market initiatives
Unemployment benefits	Proportion of unemployment benefit cases processed within 21 days
All programmes	Entry into unsubsidized employment Number retained in unsubsidized employment for six months Earnings received while in unsubsidized employment Customer satisfaction
Cost-effectiveness	Cost per placement Placements per staff unit

In the United States, the PES has begun to tackle the issue of developing new performance indicators for an electronic labour exchange. The performance indicators that have been proposed as a result of preliminary discussions include:

1. For self-service strategies	Holdings (job vacancy listings and jobseekers resumé listings) Users Transactions

2. For facilitated self-help strategies	Number of jobseekers using self-help service Customer satisfaction
3. For staff-assisted service strategies	Measures of jobseeker customer services • Entered employment rate Measures of employer customer services • Job listing return-business rate • Business assistance service return-business • Referral response time • Average time lapse to successful referral • Job order fill rate
4. For system measures	Cost per entered employment Duration of benefits compensated[5]

The performance of the PES can be measured or monitored in a number of ways and examples from a couple of countries show the extent of these. In Norway, there is a quarterly assessment of the disparity between goals and results. This operates at and between every level in the PES: between the Ministry of Labour and Administration and the Directorate of Labour; between the Directorate of Labour and the county employment offices; between the county employment offices and the district employment offices. After assessment, guidance is given to subordinate levels on how to reduce the gap between goals and results.

In Hong Kong, China, the PES reports monthly on the number of jobseekers and vacancies registered, referrals made and placements achieved. A new measure allows for the empowerment of local managers to make operational decisions best suited to local circumstances. The results are released to all local offices and then reviewed at a monthly management meeting. A more in-depth process occurs every six months with an emphasis on improvements made since the previous semi-annual review. Monthly and six-monthly results are reported to senior management. Interestingly, government agencies are required to make their performance pledges known to the public, thus enabling the public to monitor service quality. More recently, the PES has initiated focus group meetings with major clients who came up with innovative ideas for improving services.

Evaluation of programmes

Whereas performance management provides a regular check of progress against plans, evaluation goes much deeper. It offers a critical and detached look both at the underlying objectives of a programme and at how these objectives are being met. In short, it is concerned with the impact or outcome of a programme of activity. In Chapter 6, the importance of evaluation as a means of ensuring that money was well spent on labour market adjustment programmes was noted, and this has a part to play in relation to all PES functions. However, because it is an expensive and time-consuming activity, there needs to be a careful selection of programmes to be subjected to rigorous evaluation. Evaluation is particularly useful in pilot schemes designed to assess the effectiveness of a politically sensitive new programme and the techniques used in it, prior to the introduction of the programme on a large scale. Ideally, evaluations need to be built in at the initial programme design stage. The discipline of drawing up an evaluation plan can help to identify ambiguities or inconsistencies enabling these to be corrected before launch. In the PES in the United Kingdom, evaluation has been built around a ROAMEF statement covering the following items:

Rationale: the reason for government intervention.

Objectives: the objectives of the programme and how they relate to other government objectives.

Appraisal: why does the programme take this particular form?

Monitoring: what information will be collected to assist evaluation?

Evaluation: how will success be measured against the objectives?

Feedback: how will the evaluation results be fed back into future policy decisions?

Organizational issues

To PES staff, it can often appear that their organization is in a state of perpetual reorganization and in recent years there has been some truth to this perception. Frequent organizational adjustments have been needed to accommodate not only new employment policies and programmes, but also to accommodate other changes in the methods of administering public employment services. The three most notable changes have been decentralization, integration of services and competitive service delivery.

Decentralization

One of the most notable trends in the modern PES is the decentralization of authority and responsibility. The emerging trend is for the centre to maintain control of such features as primary funding, general policy development, systems development and monitoring and evaluation of operations. At the same time, much of the detailed design work is being tailored to local conditions. Overall employment policies are set at national level, but regional and local offices have increasing flexibility to supplement those policies so they can address the specific needs in each area. In this way, the services become more accessible and better adapted to customers in various segments of the labour market.

This major change in the organization and mix of PES services has been caused in part by political pressures (e.g. in Canada and Spain), and in part by a growing recognition of the pace of change in the labour market and the diversity of needs among the PES clientele. Very different labour market conditions can exist in different local labour markets. Some markets or regions may have a shrinking economy and many long-term unemployed while others face labour shortages – all within the same country. Each local PES office or group of PES offices needs to pursue a strategy appropriate to local labour market circumstances.

The number of countries pursuing this decentralized strategy is increasing. For instance, in a recent OECD publication,[6] 13 countries (Belgium-Flanders, Canada, the Czech Republic, Denmark, France, Italy, Mexico, New Zealand, Poland, Sweden, Switzerland, the United Kingdom and the United States) were identified as being involved in the decentralization of PES services to regions and provinces and in the use of local management for the design and implementation of employment policies. This approach requires a different kind of oversight, with less detailed operational control, more reliance on performance measures and better communication between central management and local or field managers. It is a risky environment in which to manage. The culture both at the centre and in the regional or local offices is affected: central management must give sound policy guidance and thereafter trust in local judgement by avoiding the temptation to interfere; regional or local managers have to be ready and equipped to decide things for themselves. Moreover, local discretion often includes a degree of flexibility in the use of funding that previously would have been forbidden.

Decentralization has long been a feature of the PES in the United States. While the national government retains broad policy discretion and major funding responsibilities, each state is given broad latitude to create an employment system that meets its individual needs. Further latitude is granted to most local offices within each state to organize the services that best respond to the labour market in each of their respective communities. Norway has a similar structure with county employment offices having authority to decide on the organization of the local offices on the basis of Directorate of Labour guidelines. These guidelines may include such items as strengthening recruitment assistance, mainstreaming the services for people with vocational disabilities or reducing the number of managers in a local office. In Germany too, local employment offices are being given more discretion to spend funds in ways that best meet local needs.

In the United Kingdom, there has also been a move toward greater local discretion. This first took the form of programme centres which enabled local management to vary the mix of programmes in an area according to local needs. The United Kingdom is now introducing the concept of "Employment Zones" in which benefit money and programme money would go into a local pool to be deployed in ways that optimize movement into sustainable employment.

Integration of services

The second major organizational issue confronting the PES is how to integrate services so as to promote the most synergetic functioning of labour market programmes. Given the fragmented legislative development of many programmes, particularly labour market adjustment programmes, this is not an easy undertaking. But all four PES functions are increasingly being shaped by common guiding principles which demand stronger interconnectivity between programmes. For example, there is increasing emphasis on individual responsibility in the use of self-service facilities and in more rigorous job-search requirements for unemployment benefits. Likewise, there is an increasing emphasis on viewing jobseekers' working lives as a series of work and learning commitments as part of a lifelong learning continuum. Accordingly, customers need access to good quality labour market inform-ation, job-search counselling and help from other labour market programmes. In addition, they may need income support at different stages. There is also an increased emphasis on improved customer service either through greater sensitivity to customer needs and aspirations or through maximum use of compatible information technology systems. Last but not least, there is greater emphasis on increasing the cost-effectiveness of social welfare expenditure by securing a better balance between active and passive labour market policies.

These changes in emphasis do not necessarily constitute institutional integration, but they do mean greater functional integration or working more closely together. It may also mean that the PES is not always engaged in direct delivery in relation to these services, but may instead be an allocator of public resources, a coordinator or a facilitator. Three major approaches to service integration can be found in the PES today: institutional integration; customer-focused integration/one-stop centres; tiered service delivery.

Institutional integration

As we noted in Chapters 1 and 3, the OECD *Jobs study* of 1994 recommended integrating three related functions under the PES:[7] job-broking (including job-counselling); payment of unemployment benefits; and active labour market programmes (including training). Chapter 3 cited examples in Canada and the United States where this integrated approach had been expressed in legislation (see "Functions" in Chapter 3). This presumably does not mean that all three functions must be delivered in the same institution; the same objective of integration could also be achieved by close partnership. In reality, the three functions are organized in a variety of ways in different countries. Germany combines job-broking, unemployment benefit and labour market adjustment programmes in a single insti-tution. The United States on the other hand combines job-broking, labour market information and unemployment benefit administration in a single institution, one which also carries out some of the adjustment programmes. Sweden combines job-broking, training and labour market measures but leaves unemployment insurance to the trade unions. In France, there are three separate institutions (ANPE, AFPA and UNEDIC) for handling the three functions of placement, administering unemployment insurance and participating in labour market adjustment programmes.[8] In the United Kingdom, the employment service is responsible for job-broking and most labour market adjustment measures, but unemployment benefit and training are at present separately administered. How-ever, the Government proposes to make the employment service responsible for training the unemployed (see "Funding and administering training programmes" in Annex V, p. 238). As part of the next stage of welfare reform, it has announced that the employment service is to be merged with that part of the benefits agency concerned with welfare benefits for people of working age.[9] Since there are frequently problems in achieving coherent local services whether these are delivered by the same institution or not, two new approaches have been developed: "one-stop centres" (customer-focused integration) and "tiered service delivery".

Customer-focused integration/one-stop centres

The one-stop centre is an important example in collaboration: here, a number of services are delivered from the same premises in order to assist the customer. This reflects a growing acceptance of the difficulties which customers can face when dealing with a variety of different public bureaucracies whose services overlap and interact with each other. If local delivery occurs from a single site, it is much more likely that interface problems can be quickly resolved and unemployed people receive integrated help to aid them return to work.

The United States government has been a pioneer of the one-stop approach and has used federal funding to extend it across the country. One-stop career centres have been introduced with the aim of ensuring integration of programmes and services, universal access, customer choice and outcome accountability. The functions embraced by the centres include job-search assistance; employment counselling; job referral and information; assistance in filing unemployment insurance claims; and information on education and training opportunities. A range of different partners are thus using common local sites, with one or more of them being selected by a local board to operate the site.

In the United Kingdom, the local Jobcentre is recognized as the one-stop for employment services, referral to training and unemployment benefits: in these offices, benefit agency staff work alongside PES staff. The Government is now experimenting with a much more ambitious experiment called ONE.[10] This experiment brings together the PES, the benefits agency, local authorities and in some pilot schemes, private and voluntary sector partners. The programme has been designed to offer a seamless and coherent service across welfare providers, giving benefit claimants a wide range of information on work, benefits and other government services – all in the one place. The aim of this programme is to put work at the heart of the benefit system, in other words to encourage people to consider not just benefits but also how they can become more independent. There have been similar developments in France and the Netherlands. In France, *Espace Cadres* (see Annex IV.22) have been set up to bring together in one place all services for managerial and technical staff. *Espaces Jeunes* have been set up with a similar objective for dealing with young people. In the Netherlands, there are plans to introduce centres for work and benefits throughout the country by 2001.

The one-stop shop is a powerful concept which is likely to change and improve the interface between public services and their customers. This is a mixed blessing for the PES. On the one hand it constrains the PES choice of local premises, making it less likely that the PES will be able to operate in prominent city centre sites. On the other hand, the one-stop concept offers scope for improving services to disadvantaged people by much better local integration.

Tiered service delivery

A third way of organizing service integration is to organize PES services according to the level of intensity of service that is needed to either remove barriers to employment for jobseekers or to assist employers to fill vacancies. In this "tiered services" approach, customers receive services better tailored to their personal needs and interests. It offers, for instance, a way of confronting the dilemma of differentiating between the services needed by self-reliant users who can take advantage of self-service tools on the one hand and those in need of greater support on the other (see "Self-help services and enhanced personalized services" in Chapter 4). It can also ensure that scarce resources are allocated as efficiently as possible, with those in need of the greatest support receiving the most assistance. Moreover, it helps to make the optimum use of new technology.

Sweden has adopted this tiered approach to service delivery. Its employment services are divided into four categories. The self-service category is the most dynamic of these with the number of individuals accessing the PES via the Internet each month now corresponding to 6 per cent of the total labour force; half of these are not formally registered with the PES. This number is increasing and the Internet will soon become the preferred method of making contact with the PES. The use of self-service systems is facilitated by an information service which takes the form of customer workstations at PES offices that are backed up by staff specializing as information "pilots" rather than information providers. The system is complemented by the establishment of call-centres at both national and regional levels. The PES in Sweden also provides an individualized service and intensive assistance. The former category provides job-search assistance, vocational guidance, referrals to active programmes and other services where the activity at the PES is of limited duration. The latter provides services where the jobseeker needs more continuous support over a longer period of time, such as in vocational rehabilitation and other forms of case management.[11]

The PES in the United States has also advocated the adoption of a tiered service delivery approach, although the implementation of this varies by state. In Wisconsin, for example, there are three levels of service for jobseekers and employers alike: self-service, light service, and intensive service. Fig. 8.1 illustrates how services are organized. France has also structured its job-search assistance activities according to a tiered approach of free access services and intermittent support service. (This is described in Annex IV.11.)

In a tiered system, a number of customers (jobseekers or employers) may opt for self-service or information-only services that require a minimum of staff intervention. But for those jobseekers that need more staff-intensive individual-ized service or intensive assistance, an accurate assessment process is important. This is generally conducted as part of the job-search assistance activity. It often becomes the access point for training, retraining and job creation schemes, mainly because these services depend upon a clear assessment of jobseeker skills, abilities and interests.

In order to determine a more consistent method for selecting jobseekers for resource-intensive activities, the PES in a number of countries is evolving policy guidelines. For example, Chapter 4 describes the new administrative

Figure 8.1 US State of Wisconsin: Partnership for full employment

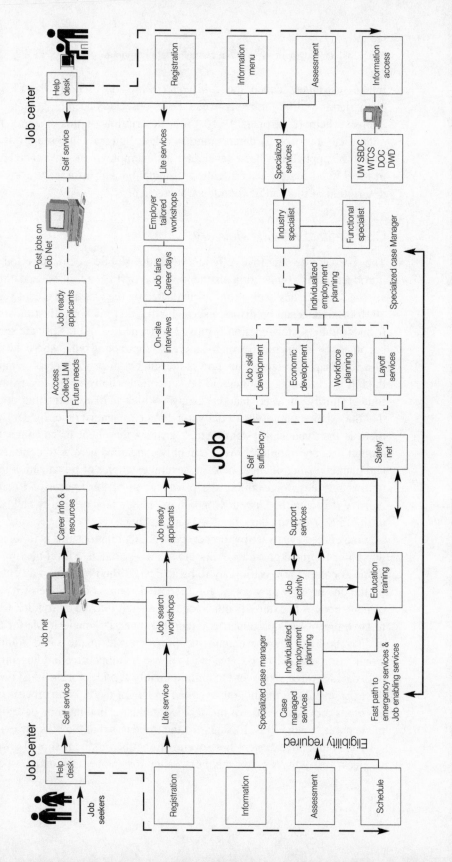

intake instrument called the *Kansmeter* which is used by the PES in the Netherlands to differentiate between those jobseekers needing greater or lesser intensive help (see Annex IV.10 for a description of this system). A more quantified approach to determining to whom intensive job-search assistance should be applied has been developed for unemployment insurance recipients in the United States. This is called "unemployment insurance profiling". (A description of this can be found in Chapter 7.)

Competitive service delivery

The pressure to improve efficiency in the public sector has led to the introduction of competition in the delivery of PES services, and this is an approach which has been strongly advocated by the OECD in recent years.[12] In all, four models can be distinguished. Firstly, there is "privatization", where a former public sector function is moved permanently into the private sector and becomes self-financing. Secondly, there is "contracting out", where the delivery of a former public sector function is the subject of private sector competition, though the function continues to be supported wholly or mainly from public funds. Thirdly, there is "market testing", which is like contracting out except that the existing public sector deliverer competes against other bidders. Finally, there is the "voucher system" which enables the client or customer to shop around between suppliers. We are mainly concerned here with contracting out and market testing, though there are several examples of privatization in labour market services, for example the privatization of the Executive Recruitment Agency (PER) in the United Kingdom in 1988, which originally had been part of the PES. We also take a brief look at vouchers.

One of the keys to setting up new contracting relationships is to separate the purchaser from the provider. Without such a separation, a level playing field in terms of competition is unlikely to be achieved. The PES may play either role: on the one hand, it may act as purchaser and contract out some of its existing or new services to external bodies; on the other, it may be a provider, tendering to government for a particular contract. However, it is undesirable for the PES to play both the purchaser and the provider role in the same competition. Contracting out and market testing both use a competitive bidding process to help decide who can deliver the highest quality services for the most people for the least cost. Determining the eventual winner of the bidding process can be a laborious process because of the detailed standards that must be developed and made public by the PES. It is against the standards that the bids are evaluated.

The competitive system has several strengths. Firstly, it should ensure that services are delivered for the best value for money. Secondly, specifying services can be a healthy discipline. Thirdly, competition may open up access to skills which are not resident among the existing staff. Finally, competition may enable additional workloads to be absorbed at a time when there are constraints upon expanding PES staffing.

The system also has its drawbacks. Firstly, it can be difficult to give specifications for services in a rapidly changing situation and contracting out is unlikely to work well unless the outcomes desired can be clearly specified. Secondly, the competitive process itself can be relatively costly and new obstacles to communication may be created which previously did not exist. Thirdly, there may also be a loss of in-house expertise and continuity. Finally, introducing competition in a service that has long been provided by the PES is likely to create considerable morale difficulties for PES managers and staff. To counter this, senior management needs to keep staff fully informed to avoid false rumours and ensure confidence in the fairness of the process; this in itself can be a distraction from other priorities.

Contracting out or purchasing services has been used extensively in relation to training. For example, the PES in Sweden is obliged to purchase training services both from the public labour-market training centres and from private providers. As a result, the public labour training centres have seen a drop of almost 50 per cent in their market share over the last ten years and a drop of nearly 20 per cent in the cost of training during the same period.

Contracting out can also produce complicated arrangements. For example, there has been criticism of the contracting arrangement surrounding the Training and Enterprise Councils (TEC) in the United Kingdom.[13] Sometimes, details regarding the cost of developing and monitoring contract performance are not always built into the cost equation. Moreover, far too often the PES fails to develop an evaluation process to determine how trainees have benefited from the arrangement. In short, while savings may result from the contracting out process, it is important to understand both the indirect costs and the effectiveness of the purchased services.

The extreme case of introducing competition into the delivery of PES services is Australia. In 1998, the PES was replaced by a job network of 310 private, community and governmental organizations which were paid to place clients in jobs. The functions covered by the new network include job-broking and intensive employment assistance for unemployed people. As agencies receive a fee for each unemployed person they place in a job (with extra fees for long-term unemployed placements), the system is strongly driven by outcomes. It is understood that as a result of the second tender round, the role of the public sector organization involved (Employment National) is being cut back and that the largest contribution will now be made by non-profit organizations run by the churches and other voluntary bodies.

As a Committee of MPs in the United Kingdom has commented, the Australian example is "a unique step which is being watched closely by employment ministers around the world".[14] It is still too early to judge the effectiveness of the system. Such a radical approach seeks to exploit expertise in labour market delivery outside the PES in order to ensure a focus on outputs and to ensure value for money. But the Australian Government took considerable risks in introducing such a far-reaching a reform so quickly. Moreover, such a comprehensive change could lead to the loss of a wealth of carefully acquired expertise in the PES. It is this rather intangible factor, the "corporate memory", which often enables the PES to introduce and deliver new programmes for governments at short notice.

A more cautious approach to competition is reflected in the Canadian experience. Here the PES has been committed to making greater use of community and other organizations to deliver programmes and services through partnership arrangements. Such arrangements normally consist of detailed and legally enforceable contractual relationships between the PES and the organizations. But while there have been transfers of responsibility, there has been no transfer of accountability. The PES remains accountable for the effectiveness of the programmes and services and is required to make a detailed monitoring report to Parliament each year on progress against targets.

In sum, introducing competition is not an easy process. For it to bring worthwhile results, several conditions need to be fulfilled: firstly, the staff overseeing the process need appropriate skills; secondly, a level playing field must be established between public and private sector providers; thirdly, where jobseekers receive some services from the PES and other services from an outside provider, links between the service providers are vital. Finally, new competitive arrangements can prove costly and should be reviewed from time to time to determine whether the benefits outweigh the costs.

While contracting out services involves many risks and there is scope for considerable improvement in the way it is carried out, it will continue to be a feature of the PES world. It can bring rewards in terms of efficiency, in terms of clarifying the outcomes which are being sought and of delivering those outcomes in a way that is beneficial to society. At the same time, there is a strong case for maintaining a core in-house capacity to preserve expertise and continuity.

The final form of competitive service delivery that we look at in this section is the voucher system. This is a competitive means of making services available to recipients which are more relevant to their specific needs. In principle, these enable the recipient to shop around for the service provider willing to offer the most attractive service at the most reasonable cost. Frequently, a government voucher covers most of the cost of the service while the remainder of the cost is assumed by the purchaser or service recipient. In France for example, an executive unemployed for less than six months can receive a voucher to purchase an assessment of his or her job competencies and the executive becomes responsible for approximately 10 per cent of the cost.

A recent OECD study noted that there is little conclusive evidence about the impact of vouchers though several unanswered questions remain.[15] In particular there is the question of how much information is available to the voucher holder and whether the voucher holder, particularly if long-term unemployed, is sufficiently motivated to take advantage of the opportunities available. There is also the question of the extent to which the voucher system allows access to a truly competitive market. Despite these reservations, vouchers are a competitive strategy which may be applicable to certain situations and to certain clients, but they are unlikely to find universal application.

Management strategies and tools

We now turn from questions of accountability and organization to the management strategies which the PES can follow in order to achieve success. The important issues to be considered here are the following: quality management; information and communications technology; facilities planning and management; internal communications; and staff training and development.

Quality management

Principles

Quality management is a strategic, integrated set of organizational values and management practices for achieving customer satisfaction. The aim is to please the customer and create a service enterprise. Quality management involves all managers and employees and uses structured methods to analyse work processes. Adopting a quality management culture is fundamentally different from traditional management and is more than just a minor refinement of past managerial practices; instead it offers a genuinely new perspective on how best to combine or re-engineer the resources, the people, the budgets, the programmes and the processes that comprise the PES. The hallmark of quality management is a commitment to continuous improvement. In addition to adopting a unique set of principles, this involves the development of new roles for senior management and co-workers alike and the adoption of a whole array of practices and techniques. It recognizes that process redesign techniques are not sufficient in themselves to achieve results: organizational values and behaviour must change as well.

Any organization considering introducing a new culture based on quality management principles needs to fully understand current conditions and also the desired conditions when the transition is completed. The following set of contrasts compares the characteristics, values and behaviour of organizations before and after adopting a commitment to quality management:

Old culture	New culture
Many different and often conflicting goals among its divisions and departments	Common vision shared by everyone
Punishes mistakes, covers up or rationalizes problems	Openly discusses problems, sees defects as opportunities for improvement
Rewards according to established policies	Rewards risk-taking and creative thinking
Short-term problems drive and dominate activity	Focuses on long-term continuous work improvement
Relies on inspection to catch mistakes before customers receive the product	Improves work processes to prevent the mistakes from occurring
Gives management full authority for top-down decisions for change	Trusts and empowers employees to contribute to decision making
Accepts the inevitability of "turf battles"	Facilitates and rewards cross-functional cooperation
Makes decisions arbitrarily	Bases all decisions on objective data
Has a negative or indifferent self-image	Feels like a winner, with achievements creating good morale

Quality management involves measuring and analysing customer needs, analysing and restructuring the interaction between organization and customer, and developing and monitoring standards for service. The methods that can be used to achieve quality management include:

- Customer-based planning
- Work-process analysis methods such as ISO 9000, the European Foundation Quality Model (EFQM) or "process re-engineering"
- Benchmarking or the development of customer-based performance targets

All three activities are interdependent. Success depends on the positive impact of work-process reforms on the achievement of targets, which are based in turn on an accurate assessment of customer needs. For all these activities, the quality of management leadership and of staff involvement is critical.

Customer-based planning

Central to quality management are the concepts of customer-based planning and service delivery though which the customer becomes the focus of the organization. But the PES has a diversity of customers with different needs. Primarily there are employers and jobseekers but jobseekers can be broken down into further categories: the newly unemployed, the long-term unemployed, new entrants into the labour market, redundant workers, workers with disabilities, and those already employed who are seeking to upgrade their standard of living. Some take this concept a step further and identify government itself as a customer, for instance in the application of work tests for unemployment benefit purposes. In this section, however, we are primarily concerned with employers and jobseekers as the customers of the PES.

The United Kingdom offers an interesting example of culture change linked with the need for a more customer-oriented approach. When the Labour Government took office in 1997 and David Blunkett became Secretary of State for Education and Employment, he quickly decided to use the PES for the delivery of the Government's high-profile New Deal programmes. But he was concerned that after many years of pursuing benefit control policies under the previous Government, the culture of the PES might not be positive enough in its attitude towards unemployed clients. Blunkett launched a major culture-change process through which the PES would renew itself. This involved discussions with staff at every level and also with external stakeholder and customers. The PES adopted a new set of values: quality, service, achievement, partnership and "valuing our people". Early in 1999, Blunkett commented:

> Many people have commented to me how much the Employment Service has changed for the better over the last 18 months. My constituents, fellow members of Parliament, and partner organizations with whom we are working, have noticed a real difference.[16]

In France, the ANPE also implemented a programme dedicated to providing quality services for an increasing number of beneficiaries. Each jobcentre adopted a set of five key principles: first, customer satisfaction was to be the main concern; second, quality standards were to be supervised by management; third, there was to be a permanent action plan for quality services and the delivery of good results; fourth, the approach and tools had to be familiar to everyone; finally, clarity had to be assured in external communications.

Each of the successful French jobcentres that were reviewed revealed one characteristic in common: they had all made a significant commitment to the employers or enterprises they served. It was clear that each of the centres recognized the value of the employer in the process. They had agreed with employers about the level of services they wished to obtain and on the basis of this, had issued a quality guarantee from the centre. This high-level attention and commitment to a major customer has produced significant results and is a testimony to the quality culture implemented by the ANPE. The ANPE is not unique in this commitment to quality, although its commitment is exemplary.

In Germany, a similar reform was initiated after the adoption of a new organizational concept called "Employment Office 2000" in 1995. The main principles behind this reform of the entire German PES were to orient services to customer needs, to provide services effectively and economically and to promote the job satisfaction and occupational success of its employees. The activities chosen to carry out reforms were the establishment of customer-oriented staff teams, the delegation of organizational and budgetary tasks, the spatial decentralization of service delivery and the realignment of state and local employment office structures.

Essential to successful customer-based planning is research on customer needs and customer satisfaction. This research can be carried out in a number of ways. In an informal manner, the PES in Hong Kong, China developed a particularly effective approach to building relations with employers by appointing a dedicated team to make contacts, obtain job vacancies and follow up on recruitment needs. The feedback from employers has been positive and they show a readiness to make use of the free recruitment service provided by the PES. The PES plans to increase its outreach efforts to those employers who have not yet used the free service (for more details of this programme, see Annex IV.23). The Slovenian PES has adopted a simple but effective customer satisfaction procedure. A complaint book is maintained in every regional and local PES office and customers are encouraged to provide complaints, compliments and make suggestions for improvement. The PES staff periodically review these comments in order to improve service delivery.

Customer surveys and focus-group surveys are techniques that have been used by the PES in various countries in a structured approach to customer satisfaction. The Swedish PES has been conducting customer satisfaction surveys annually since 1991. Forty thousand interviews are conducted, divided equally between jobseeker and employer customers. Approximately 40 factual and attitude questions are asked of each group of customers to determine how they feel about the services provided by the PES and to see what they think of the treatment they receive. Telephone interviews are conducted using computer-assisted telephone interviewing technology. Although the survey is conducted centrally, results are broken down by region and local office. In addition to these approaches, customer survey methods are also extensively used in the ISO certification and work process reform efforts that are described shortly in this chapter.

Work process redesign and service standards

Various work process analysis and redesign methods are used by organizations to introduce quality management. These methods include ISO 9000, EFQM and process re-engineering. The PES in many countries, including Austria, the Netherlands, Japan, Germany, the United Kingdom, the United States and Canada have applied one or more of these methods and while their approaches have varied, the intent has consistently been the same. The Austrian PES used the ISO 9001 certification process to implement quality management principles. Fundamental reform was initiated in the early 1990s to transform the Austrian PES into a more customer-oriented and market-driven service. One region, Upper Austria, decided to achieve ISO certification for the services it delivers to enterprises. There were several reasons why the organization decided to do this: first, it wanted to develop a more precise definition of PES services, second, it wanted to gain a closer proximity to the market; third, it wanted to develop clearer targets and greater transparency in the organization; fourth, it wanted to improve communication; fifth, it wanted to develop more internal responsibility and external communication; and finally, it wanted to promote the PES with customers. The ISO standard comprises a set of quality specifications which focus on identifying, documenting and monitoring the flow of work to achieve conformity with certain rules. By the application of this structured process, the PES in Upper Austria learned to integrate customer orientation in very fundamental ways. As a result of their efforts, the process has now been more widely adopted in Austria.[17]

The PES in Denmark is using the European Foundation Quality Model (EFQM), or Business Excellence Model, to structure work analysis and promote quality management. The model is a framework for analysis and understanding. It consists of nine elements which demonstrate the relationship between enablers and results in a development-oriented perspective. Enabling elements include leadership, policies and strategy, human resources management, resources and work processes; result elements include performance measure achievement, user satisfaction, staff satisfaction and impact on society. The

EFQM model will be used to develop the performance contracts that will be introduced in 2000 to govern the relationship between the Ministry of Labour and the PES at both national and regional levels.[18]

Process re-engineering, on the other hand, is a technique that involves a radical re-evaluation of specific workflow processes. It goes beyond evolutionary change of continuous improvement to question the entire operation of a process from a customer's point of view. For example, the planning of telephone claims-processing for unemployment benefits by the PES in the state of Wisconsin was conducted using process re-engineering.

What links the assessment of customer needs and process reforms is the development and monitoring of standards for service improvement. The establishment and monitoring of these standards is intended to ensure that the reforms introduced do indeed improve customer satisfaction. In the United Kingdom, for instance, the PES adopted a "Jobseekers' Charter". This charter included such standards as seeing customers on time when they have an appointment or within ten minutes without one. Should the customer make contact by telephone, the charter specifies that the call should be responded to within 20 seconds.

Benchmarking

Benchmarking is an additional programme improvement technique. It can be defined as the search for practices that lead to superior performance. It offers a method for comparing aspects of a product or service against an appropriate point of reference by which that activity can be measured.[19] The comparison can be internal, that is between parts or subunits of an organization; external, in other words between an organizational unit and other organizations with similar characteristics; or it can be functional, that is between specific tasks or processes.[20] Benchmarking involves not only identifying best practices but meticulously analysing the processes that produce superior results and comparing these to the current processes of an organization, the goal being to develop improvement strategies. In the public sector, benchmarking often demands the cooperation of research, policy-making and programme operations units.

An innovative benchmarking project is currently underway in the EU, with the public employment services of Belgium (Wallonia), Sweden, France and Austria all collaborating with a research institute in Belgium in an effort to improve their performances in how they deal with enterprises. The objective of the project is to identify the best performance of similar organizations and to build upon their successes while adapting this to individual country needs and priorities. The process involves several steps. Participants first study the mechanisms set up by the PES to improve its performance towards enterprises and draw up an inventory of PES products and services it provides to these enterprises. They then identify innovations and good practices as well as potential transfers of good practices and analyse how the PES measures and follows the performance of these mechanisms. Finally, they are to provide an inventory of performance indicators and develop the first steps toward a coordinated approach in the EU.[21] The results of the project are expected to be presented in late 2000.

The use of information and communications technology

Previous chapters have shown how innovation in information and communications technology are transforming the operation of the PES. Two principal changes were identified: changes in the way in which the PES manages its information and communication internally, and changes in the way in which PES customers access information directly. The use of information technology for internal management purposes is not new to the PES in most countries. Virtually all of the developed countries have used computer technology for many years to manage and control the various activities of the PES. However, more sophisticated and powerful applications are continually being developed. The following is a list of some of the applications that are currently being used to improve internal management:

- Electronic mail. This is now being extensively used for internal and external communications. Intranet systems are also giving staff access to increasingly sophisticated internal information.
- Executive Information System (EIS). This is being used by the Irish PES to draw information from legacy databases that provide comprehensive reporting, analysis, statistical forecasting and modelling to assist in making informed business decisions.
- Case management systems. More sophisticated systems are being devised which merge client records from multiple administrative records systems for the use of staff serving jobseekers and employers.
- Data collection. Computer-assisted telephone interviewing technology is being used instead of mail surveys in the United States to collect labour market and employer survey information. In Sweden, it is being used to collect customer survey data. Internet survey data collection is also being tested.
- Enhanced computer data manipulation and analysis. These techniques, particularly the greater use of relational databases and data warehouses, have greatly improved labour market information products.

- Electronic cash transfer. This facility is available in some countries and facilitates the direct payment of benefits into claimants' bank accounts.

Advances are also being made in the calculation, payment and control of unemployment benefits to speed up payment and reduce error and fraud.

The second, and perhaps more radical, way in which information technology is transforming the PES is by allowing PES customers to access information more directly through the use of open systems and in particular, via the Internet. The Internet is already beginning to have a radical impact on the way services are offered. The PES in an increasing number of countries provides customers with an electronic labour exchange through internet access (see "Innovations and good practices" in Chapter 4). Examples of self-service customer technology applications include the following:

- Job vacancy banks. These allow employers to list jobs and allow jobseekers to find jobs. They are accessible via the Internet, teletext, kiosks (limited-feature computer information terminals located in public places), or PES office computer terminals. (See the Canadian kiosk innovation described in Annex IV.1.)
- Jobseeker banks. These allow jobseekers to list CVs or resumés and allow employers to consult them directly.
- Self-service labour market information. This can be accessed on the Internet and provides more timely and flexible information that can be more easily customized for a variety of uses.
- Career or vocational guidance information. This can be presented in media-enhanced, youth-friendly formats.
- Databases of training opportunities. These can be made directly available to jobseekers and also to service delivery providers.
- Interactive voice-response systems. These allow benefit claimants to file for benefits by telephone or receive payment information about the status of a claim.
- Distance learning technologies. Internet and satellite can now be used to deliver on-the-job training programmes.
- Customer surveys or feedback mechanisms. These are often built into internet-delivered services, allowing automatic and immediate feedback on customer satisfaction.

A detailed description of the customer self-services that can be accessed by the Internet in Sweden can be found in Annex IV.6. America's Labor Exchange (ALX) is described in Annex IV.8 and a description of how the Internet has been used to disseminate a variety of information to jobseekers and employers in

Slovenia is described in Annex IV.5. The evolution of the PES information system in Japan and the employment service information system in Mexico are described in Annexes IV.3 and IV.4 respectively. In addition, details of the electronic labour exchange are given in Chapter 4, advances in labour market information are described in Chapter 5 and direct access to unemployment benefit information is described in Chapter 7.

The introduction of technology offers many benefits, but it brings with it the inherent stresses of major change. To minimize the stress on an organization, extensive analysis, careful planning and the use of skilled professionals are required to achieve a successful undertaking. Where technology is approached incorrectly, an organization may suffer for years. The time and resources required to plan, develop and implement a new technology are frequently underestimated and this often causes disappointment and a loss of confidence. Once a design phase has been completed, it is advisable to first pilot the new system before embarking on an organization-wide implementation. This provides the opportunity to identify and solve problems on scales that are manageable and correctable. Organization-wide implementation should be approached incrementally, first verifying results for accuracy and assessing outcomes before moving on to the next step or location. The introduction of new technology is a formidable challenge for management, but the benefits can be enormous when it is done properly.

Frequently, there are concerns among staff about new technology, partly because of the disruption it can bring and partly because of fears of redundancy. There have been examples such as in the United Kingdom where the introduction of new technology has been justified on the basis of staff reductions, though normally natural wastage has prevented redundancy from arising. This highlights the importance of careful planning, good communications and proactive personnel policies to retrain and redeploy staff where necessary.

Facilities planning and management

PES services have traditionally been delivered through a network of local offices. As we pointed out in Chapter 4, the development of delivery through the Internet and through automated telephone links provides powerful alternative ways of communicating with the public. Nonetheless, we believe that for many customers the local office will remain important as a resource centre and as a local access point to services.

Usually, the PES is tied to a network of local offices through long-term investment commitments. Nonetheless, there is a need to periodically review the network and to make sure that it still meets the needs of the service and its customers. Several factors need to be taken into account when determining the optimum network and location of offices. First, there is accessibility for the potential customer base. Usually this is more critical for jobseekers as employer contact tends to be mainly done by phone. Moreover, changing population patterns also need to be taken into account. Second, one-stop policies may require co-location with other services such as unemployment benefit. Third, the need for prominent sites for marketing purposes needs to balanced against the potential extra costs involved. Fourth, the optimal size of the office can be important. In the early 1990s, the PES in the United Kingdom closed several large offices on the grounds that smaller offices were easier to run and performed better. Finally, the implications of tiered service delivery discussed earlier in this chapter needs to be taken into account as do the implications of the outsourcing of certain PES services.

Decision making about local premises is made easier where national guidelines exist which take the latest policy thinking into account. For example, in France the ANPE has established a facility guideline. In this, a team of seven to eight placement staff are attached to a free access zone or resource centre. This facility provides information about career and training opportunities and also displays job vacancies. The facility is designed to provide economies of scale in the use of space, furnishings and computer equipment. Guidelines like this need to be reviewed regularly, however, as services evolve.

Appearance and layout are critical to the success of a local office. They have an important effect for good or ill on both PES employees and customers. The experiences of local office redesign in France, Finland, Norway and the United States, have indicated that upgrading from a compact, cluttered, dimly lit office space to a well-organized open plan office that is spacious and has good lighting made a significant difference to the attitude, morale and effectiveness of employees. The change was almost immediate, with customers and elected leaders noticing an increased professionalism. Not only was there a change in employee attitude and behaviour, but there was also a marked change in the response of customers. Employers also noticed the difference. They were far more interested in working with the local PES than before and spontaneously notified more vacancies.

Internal communications

Establishing honest, open communications in both horizontal and vertical channels is probably the single most important factor in successfully creating an effective continuous improvement process. When employees continue to discuss issues and problems among themselves, problems can be worked through, barriers overcome and encouragement and support can be discovered.

An organization in the process of significant change must use every communication means available. Employees – particularly those who have served the organization for a long time – often struggle with the new roles, rules and accountabilities that can be linked to underlying changes in social, political and economic realities. Communications are more vital than ever if momentum towards meeting an organization's vision is to be maintained. Leaders must establish an open door policy that encourages input and feedback from every employee in the organization. In the United Kingdom, some senior PES managers go beyond this: they work at a desk alongside other staff rather than occupying a private space. They also make themselves available to answer phone queries from any employee on certain designated days.

The traditional ways of maintaining communication in an organization have been meetings or through print communications such as policy and procedure handbooks, internal memos, internal newsletters or staff magazines. However, e-mail is complementing and rapidly replacing internal written communication and intranet systems are making a broader range of internal information available in a more timely fashion and in a more flexible format. In developing an effective communications strategy, it is important to create a two-way flow of information. The use of surveys to determine issues important to staff has been effectively used by administrators in the United Kingdom and the United States. These surveys, often carried out on an annual basis, are used to determine staff attitudes about matters such as staff benefits, working conditions and the direction of the PES. They are also used to identify issues and trends that may not be evident through the normal reporting channels.

The "focus group" is another effective method of obtaining staff feedback. Typically, a series of questions on particular topics is prepared and presented to several small groups comprising a cross-section of staff members. The sessions are organized by a facilitator who preferably should not be a local manager or supervisor. Feedback is passed back on a non-attributable basis to senior managers so that it can be taken into account in PES planning. The PES in Sweden has established another communication tool for soliciting input called the "Idea Bank" (see Annex IV.24). Similarly, the Slovenian "Complaint Book" mentioned earlier also provides information upon which meaningful discussions among staff can be based.

Staff training and development

Effective planning and management of all personnel and human resource development activities are essential for an effective PES, but staff training and development are particularly critical. Achieving results depends primarily on having capable, motivated and highly trained employees who feel that their work is appreciated. Staff development involves providing staff with the tools to carry out work in an environment that is conducive to high quality work. The need for staff training and development has become all the greater because of the pace of change. Chapters 3 and 6 describe how the PES role has extended from its origins in job-broking and unemployment benefit into a wide range of services designed to help people to adjust to a rapidly changing labour market. In this chapter we have also stressed the importance of integrated and tiered forms of delivery. All these changes affect PES staff profiles, in particular the professional and technical staff categories such as client advisers, job counsellors, PES local managers and administrative officers. They also affect core competencies such as the following: the capacity to understand the functioning of the labour market and labour market policies; the ability to communicate; the ability to display sound judgement; the ability to organize work and time effectively; the ability to work as part of a team; and the ability to adapt to change and to use information technologies.[22] In a situation where the PES is redesigning its services, its delivery methods or its organization, it is vital to consider the inherent implications for the role of the staff and any new learning needs that arise as a result. This process of updating skills and knowledge is critical to success and is virtually continuous. Moreover, the training and development programmes provided need to be placed in the context of the wider cultural change that senior management is seeking to achieve.

The importance of staff development is evident in the scale of investment being made in several countries. In France, a substantial effort has been made by the ANPE to provide 100,000 staff training days per year.[23] In 1998–99, the PES in the United Kingdom planned to spend £12 million or approximately 2.6 per cent of the payroll on training and development. Although the PES in many countries has made a commitment to staff development, their emphases vary. In developed countries, there is a strategic approach to training for all employees, beginning with basic training for new employees. (Annex IV.25 highlights the emphasis placed on staff development in Canada.)

In Norway, the PES has designed a basic training course for new employees at the local offices. This training course is divided into four modules: the first provides an understanding of the PES goals and the means of achieving them; the second an understanding of how labour market policy is implemented; the third trains the employee in the jobseeker registration process; the fourth is a specialized course in a specific professional area. In Germany, basic training consists of local-office training by means of on-the-job training, working on projects and computer-based training. In addition, new staff must attend the PES training school, take part in study groups and do self-preparation. Continuing training in the local offices can take the form of self-instruction, official instruction, on-the-job assistance, computer-based application training and computer-based training. The training is supplemented by seminars, courses, study groups or correspondence or distance learning programmes.

In the United States, the introduction of the self-service electronic labour exchange and the evolution toward one-stop career centres has resulted in a dramatic re-orientation in the activities and competencies of customer-service staff in local PES offices. In preparation for these changes, staff from several states contributed to a national "workforce development staff skills and training project". An analysis of new customer interactions was carried out to identify a framework of 12 customer interactions for front-line staff. Then the necessary staff competencies were identified for each of the 12 areas. This framework provides a flexible way of identifying competencies for staff working in a variety of areas. (See Annex VI for web site addresses where detailed information on this project can be found.)

The United Kingdom has made an equally strong commitment to the training and development of its PES staff. The PES was one of the first large public bodies in the United Kingdom to achieve recognition as an investor in people, reflecting an examination by external reviewers into the level of commitment, planning, action and evaluation of the organization in developing its people. The PES strategy is to ensure that all staff have the skills and competencies to do their jobs. Much traditional classroom training has now been replaced by computer-based training. While computer-based training is a resource-intensive undertaking, it has been shown to be cost-effective in the experience of the United Kingdom.

Finland also has a comprehensive approach to staff training and develop-ment, which is conducted by a Labour Institute under the Minister of Labour. The institute came up with an interesting set of issues they found relevant to their training.

- better links were needed between strategic planning and the planning of training content;
- core competencies for staff need to be updated to meet future challenges;
- training should be better incorporated with PES pilot schemes in order to disseminate best practices in service delivery more effectively;
- opportunities for training should be distributed more broadly and equitably;
- continuous improvement principles should be applied to the staff training function in order to develop an increasingly coherent training package that facilitates staff self-development efforts;
- the use of alternative learning methods should be expanded; and
- methods for assessing training effectiveness should be developed.[24]

The training of managers is especially important since managers have the responsibility for coaching their own teams. In Norway the six major demands for PES managers have been defined as the following: knowledge of the labour market and labour market policies; the ability to communicate information to working partners and the public; the ability to achieve the aims which are set for the organization; the ability to communicate well and build up networks; the ability to stimulate developments in one's own organization; and the ability to inspire good general attitudes and team spirit in one's own organization.

In France, the ANPE has identified a similar set of competencies for local PES managers, who receive the following training activities: a one-month local office observation period (for external recruits); a week of political orientation; a skills assessment and temporary assignment to work with an experienced manager; an individual training contract including assignment of a mentor and choice of training sessions; formal training sessions; and a skills evaluation. The United Kingdom has among other things introduced access to 360 degree feedback for their managers to identify strengths and areas for additional personal development.

Exchanges of staff between the PES of different countries also provide good opportunities for PES staff members in one country to get to know good practices in another country. It also allows them to try these out and to study them with a view to possible adoption in their own country. Such experimental exchanges first took place in 1998 between the French and German PES.[25] Negotiations between other European countries are under way.

Conclusion

There are several reasons why there is much more interest in improved management methods in the PES today than in the past. First of all, the services managed by the PES have diversified and the choice of the services to be delivered is increasingly determined by customer-driven planning rather than through legal mandate. Secondly, the PES is increasingly operating in a competitive market which demands improved quality and reliability, particularly in services provided to employers. Thirdly, the PES has been influenced by important external trends, such as total quality management. Last but not least, the availability of new information and communication technologies has provided powerful tools for transforming work processes and customer access to information.

The degree of trust between PES senior managers and their most powerful stakeholders, particularly political leaders, has also become critical. Understanding customer needs as they are interpreted by political leaders and advisory bodies is vital to continuing public support and to maintaining the resources entrusted to the PES. In the modern world, no public organization can succeed without a planning process that is both formalized and participatory. This requires understanding the motivations of the political leadership, collecting information from customers and involving staff at all levels. Once plans have been agreed and are being implemented, then progress must be monitored and the plan adjusted where necessary.

The PES is experiencing enormous change in organizational structure. The three major trends driving these changes are decentralization, service integration and competitive service delivery. With regard to decentralization, the central office is taking on the role of broad policy guidance, funding, monitoring and evaluation but more authority and flexibility is being granted to regional and local offices. Similarly, with service integration initiatives such as one-stop centres and the increased outsourcing of services through competitive service delivery, organizations are becoming less hierarchical and rule-driven and more customer-driven instead.

The movement toward customer-based services is part of the widespread adoption of quality management principles in the PES. This in turn is leading to the transformation of many internal management processes. In many countries, the PES is introducing better performance management, continuous staff training and development, improved internal communication, more sophisticated use of information and communications technology and improved facilities management. Continuous staff training and development is the most important challenge for all successful service organizations. New competencies are being demanded of staff at all levels from agency leaders to staff at the client-service level. The most progressive PES organizations are seeking to become learning organizations.

In recent years, managing the PES has become a more complex and formidable task than ever before in peacetime. This chapter has shown on the basis of the experience of many countries, that powerful management tools and techniques are available which can be used to achieve success.

Notes

[1] C. Leadbeater: *Living on thin air: The new economy* (London, Viking, 1999), pp. 23–24.

[2] Swedish Labour Market Board: *The public employment service in the 21st century: A discussion process within the Swedish labour market administration* (Swedish Labour Market Board, ISEKen 1999:7 @ www2ams.se/ams/rapport_eng/index.html).

[3] OECD: *Labour market policies: New challenges – Enhancing the effectiveness of active labour market policies: A streamlined public employment service*, Unclassified Paper presented at the Meeting of the Employment, Labour and Social Affairs Committee at Ministerial Level, 14–15 Oct, 1997, pp. 14–15.

[4] C. Brinkmann: *Controlling and evaluation of employment promotion and the employment services in Germany*, Labour Market Research Topic No. 36 (Nuremberg, Institute for Employment Research, 1999), p. 19.

[5] United States Department of Labor Employment and Training Administration: *Labor exchange performance measures: Notice and requests for comments* (Washington, DC, United States Department of Labor Employment and Training Administration, 1998), p 3.

[6] OECD: *Local management for more effective employment policies* (Paris, OECD, 1998).

[7] OECD: *Jobs study: Facts, analysis, strategies* (Paris, OECD, 1994).

[8] AFPA stands for the *Association Nationale pour la Formation Professionnelle des Adultes* (The National Association for the Vocational Training of Adults). UNEDIC stands for *Union Nationale pour l'Emploi dans l'Industrie et le Commerce* (National Union for Employment in Trade and Industry). UNEDIC is organized as a federation of the ASSEDIC agencies (*Associations pour l'Emploi dans l'Industrie et le Commerce*). These are private, non-profit associations run by the social partners which administer the employment insurance system and pay out on behalf of government, unemployment insurance and early retirement benefits.

[9] The new agency, which will be firmly focused on helping people to become independent, will be established as soon as possible in 2001. The responsibility for its design and development will be held jointly by the Secretaries of State for Education and Employment and for Social Security. See Department of Social Security Press Notice, 16 March, 2000.

[10] Originally known as the "single work-focused gateway".

[11] C. Almén: *Tiers of service: The service delivery system in the Swedish public employment service*, Paper delivered at WAPES Service Delivery Workshop (Washington, DC, 1998).

[12] See OECD: *Labour market policies: New challenges…* op. cit. See also R. G. Fay: *Making the public employment service more effective through the introduction of labour market signals*, Labour Market and Social Policy Occasional Paper No. 25 (Paris, OECD, 1997).

[13] See H. Mosley and C. Degen: *The reorganization of labour market policy: Further training for the unemployed in the UK* (Berlin, Social Science Research Centre, 1994).

[14] House of Commons Education and Employment Committee: *Active labour market policies and their delivery: Lessons from Australia* (London, Stationery Office, 1999), p ix.

[15] Fay, op. cit., p. 15.

[16] United Kingdom Employment Service: *The way ahead: Towards 2000* (London, United Kingdom Employment Service, 1999).

[17] See E. Buchinger: *Achieving ISO 9001 certification in a public employment service*, Labour Administration Branch Document No. 49–3 (Geneva, ILO, 1997), pp. 14–18.

[18] M. Jensen: *The EFQM-model in the Danish public employment service*, Unpublished Paper presented at European Union Quality Networking Conference, Lahti, Finland, 22–23 Nov., 1999.

[19] Ibid.

[20] T. Leonello: "Benchmarking labour market performances and policies", in European Commission European Employment Observatory Mutual Information System on Employment Policies (MISEP): *Policies, No. 61* (Berlin, European Commission, 1998), Sect. 10.1.1.2, p. 2.

[21] M. Siraut: *Comparing customer satisfaction: Case study on employers*, Unpublished Paper presented at WAPES Benchmarking Seminar, Oslo, Dec. 1999.

[22] It is notable that in France and Norway the proportion of professional staff are respectively 80 and 77 per cent while that of administration support staff are respectively 11 and 9 per cent of the total national PES staff. See table 3.1, Ch. 3.

[23] The ANPE staff training programme for 1999 focuses on the following strategic axes: support to the ANPE network in improving the control and quality of service delivery; development of professional and managerial practices; strengthening of staff competencies in support of technical steering; upgrading competencies of ANPE officers/counsellors through professional projects aimed at acquiring a better knowledge of the employment situation or at the preparation of the access to new employment opportunities. See ILO: *Les services publics de l'emploi: Le cas de la France* (Geneva, ILO, 1999; mimeographed); Additional information 1999.

[24] A. Keskinen and I. Millonen: *Staff development challenges in the Finnish labour administration*, Unpublished Paper presented at the WAPES PES Staff Training Seminar, Greece, Oct. 1999.

[25] For details on the approach, see European Commission European Employment Observatory Mutual Information System on Employment Policies (MISEP): *Policies, No 64* (Berlin, European Commission, Winter 1998).

THE PES AND OTHER ORGANIZATIONS 9

The PES will build upon a partnership strategy involving other actors in the labour market.[1]

Introduction

It is a sign of the changing environment within which the PES operates that this subject now merits a full chapter in a study on the PES. Since the earliest days, there has been a recognition of the importance of a close relationship between the PES and employer and worker organizations and this has often been reflected in the membership of the PES supervisory board. But apart from this, the PES was seen as a self-sufficient organization, often having a monopoly position in the labour market. There was always a temptation for the PES to become not only self-sufficient but also introverted, particularly if it had an unpopular policing role in administering work tests for unemployment benefit purposes.

Today, by contrast, it is rare for the PES to have a monopoly. Instead, it has to operate as one of many players in a complex labour market and its success may well depend on how it conducts its relationships with other organizations. The most conspicuous change has been in relations with PREAs, but the PES has to deal with many other organizations besides PREAs. Three factors contribute mostly to the change in climate. Firstly, the increasing influence of economic liberalism and globalization has led to a questioning of the public sector role and to pressures for more competition in the interests of efficiency. Secondly, the complexity of the modern labour market requires a diverse expertise that no authority on its own, either central or local, can offer. Thirdly, there is a recognition that problems like unemployment and social exclusion do not exist in isolation, but are linked with wider social and economic problems that require integrated or combined solutions and need the involvement of a wide range of interested bodies.

In this chapter, we look at the relationships between the PES and other bodies. The bodies in question are the social partners, other governmental agencies, local partners and PREAs. We also look at networking between public employment services.

Relationships with the social partners

Chapter 3 described the various different legal bases for the PES. One common arrangement has been to make the PES an autonomous organization under a commission or supervisory board which includes the social partners. Chapter 1 showed that this model had a long history with for example the foundation of the Federal Institute in Germany occurring as early as 1927. Such arrangements have been changing in recent years however. Both Sweden (1991) and the United Kingdom (1987) have abandoned tripartism while Austria (1994) and the Netherlands (1991) have established quasi-independent employment services with tripartite self-management for the first time.[2] Today, the PES in almost half of all OECD countries has tripartite, autonomous administrations.[3] The attraction in this for the PES is that by involving employer organizations and trade unions in overseeing the PES, it commits them to its support. It should also help to resolve conflict in sensitive areas such as the PES role in the event of strikes. The remit of such administrations varies from country to country with some, such as in Germany and Spain, responsible for a much wider range of labour market issues than just the PES job-broking role. This has the advantages of raising the strategic importance of the commission and making it less likely that it will interfere with day-to-day management.

The success of this kind of collaborative approach depends ultimately on the degree of consensus between the social partners and the government. Without consensus, the arrangement comes under strain and the PES can become a political football in an ideological conflict. This occurred in the United Kingdom in the 1980s where tensions between the Thatcher Administration and the trade union commissioners of the Manpower Services Commission eventually led the Government to take direct control of the PES in 1987. Other countries have dealt with the risk of conflict in various ways. In Norway for example, although the PES is mandated to report to a tripartite board under the Employment Act, the board cannot give instructions to the Director-General. Instead, the board is used as a forum for discussing new ideas and receiving feedback.[4] In the Netherlands, the PES became an autonomous organization under a board that included the social partners in 1991 but in 1996, the government representatives on the board were replaced by independent experts. This was because the government representatives found themselves in an impossible position and impasses on the board were paralysing decision-making.[5]

It is difficult to generalize about what arrangements work best, since this depends a great deal on the wider culture and relationships in each country. What is clear though is that it is in the interest of the PES to cultivate close relationships with the social partners. For example, a formal agreement with the central employers' organization may lead that organization to encourage members to use the PES.[6]

Relationships with governmental institutions and other national bodies

As we have already seen in Chapter 6, one key PES role is to deliver labour market adjustment programmes, but the nature of such programmes is changing. Where previously governments introduced relatively narrow programmes offering a particular service to a particular target group, it is now more common for programmes to be wide-ranging and to address a number of interrelated problems. Such problems may include not just unemployment, but also problems associated with social exclusion and poverty such as benefit dependency, housing, environment, drugs, crime, health and education. These problems cannot be tackled by the PES alone. It is therefore necessary to involve not only the PES, employers and trade unions, but also a range of other government agencies. In addition, municipalities, public and private development agencies and national voluntary/community associations in the social, educational, cultural and environmental areas are involved. Success thus depends on drawing upon a large number of policy-makers and public and private service providers who are responsible for these areas and bringing them into a partnership framework. This partnership is necessary to contribute to the development and planning of government policy and increasingly, to ensure an integrated approach to service delivery.

Relationships with governmental agencies are critical in such an interdisciplinary area. How these are structured depends on the particular functions the PES administers and also on its organizational structure in relation to other governmental institutions (see "Functions" in Chapter 3). At one extreme, the PES can be viewed as a single-purpose agency that manages the job-broking function; at the other extreme, it can be viewed as the focal point for implementing government employment policy. Indeed, the ILO country study on France refers to the ANPE as a central actor in the labour market.[7] Whether the PES can play such a role depends on its reputation and credibility with other governmental agencies.

In the policy-making arena, one PES function that is not often exploited fully is its understanding of labour market information and its power to contribute to the design and formulation of employment policies. The Canadian PES has developed this capability at all levels of government and it has significantly enhanced its value and credibility as a result. (See Chapter 5.)

In the service delivery area, relationships between government agencies can take on a variety of forms. On the one hand, these may be contractual (see "Competitive service delivery" in Chapter 8); on the other, with the rise of service integration strategies (see "Integration of services" in Chapter 8), they may be based on partnership. For instance, the drive to create one-stop centres in the United States or centres for work and income in the Netherlands depends on developing close partnerships at national level. Similarly, the new, tiered arrangements for service delivery (see "Tiered service delivery" in Chapter 8, p. 123) may require national collaboration between various governmental agencies. In such cases, the need for a national decision-making framework for partnership often arises. In countries where supervision of the PES is entrusted to a commission or board of the social partners, this board may be well placed to play the central role in the framework. Alternatively, a new type of formal central partnership body may need to be created

Regardless of the level, cooperative partnerships demand that the terms of the partnership be clearly spelled out. In France, the ANPE has established a partnership charter as a framework for the development of all partnership agreements. This charter specifies several aspects. On the one hand it specifies services to be delegated, the levels of delegation, the conditions for providing training and for the granting of individual recognition to the partner; on the other, it specifies the procedures for subsequent monitoring and quality control, the rules to be adhered to and the financial resources to be provided.[8] Where the delivery of programmes is contracted out to a large number of delivery agents, it is useful to establish other common rules governing such matters as confidentiality, exclusion of charges on participants, equality of treatment and the joint use of assets such as vacancies, job directories, skill evaluation services and so forth. There also need to be nationwide links with central bodies responsible for educational planning and the development of qualifications, drawing upon (among other things) labour market information. Education has an important part to play in remedying problems like social exclusion.

Relationships with local partners

Local partnership brings together employers, trade unions, statutory agencies and voluntary/community groups for the purpose of concrete action. It creates forums where local problems can be solved by people familiar with the diversity of local conditions. Local partnerships are normally as inclusive as possible and seek to enhance labour market policy effectiveness and social cohesion through the combination of a more participative approach and a new form of grassroots democracy. But there are also a number of problems associated with this. These include the potential conflict of legitimacy between partners representing specific interests and representatives of democratically elected bodies; the diffusion of decision-making power between different partners which can lead to conflict; and the problem of auditing, monitoring and evaluating local partnerships using public funds.

At the conference organized by the OECD in Venice in April 1998,[9] it was found that in the area of job creation, training measures and welfare-to-work initiatives, the involvement of decentralized bodies such as the PES, local governmental agencies, local authorities, voluntary/community groups and associations in implementation is becoming increasingly important, irrespective of whether these are financed by central or lower levels of government or not.

The linkage between the PES and local partners takes various forms and varies from one country to another and examples can be found in the papers presented by the participants at the OECD conference in 1998. In Mexico,[10] executive committees in the state employment services (SES) were established in 1992. These committees include representatives of business groups, training institutions, labour unions and state government agencies. They provide guidance for the operation of the SES in every state of the country and together include representatives of 161 business associations, 177 business firms, 152 government agencies, 19 labour unions, 209 training schools and 23 other types of organization. The executive committees in turn form part of the state councils for productivity and competitiveness which are responsible for the coordination of labour market policy between the federal and state governments. They are also responsible for consultation with the productive sectors.

In the United Kingdom,[11] local partnerships are responsible for the assessment of local needs and planning and for the delivery of part or all of the New Deal programme in their locality. For example, the PES and the careers services work locally with bodies that have a track record in helping vulnerable clients such as those with severe learning difficulties. In Bolton, the New Deal partnership established an ethnic minorities forum to help members present the programme to the local community and to support its delivery. In addition to the New Deal, the PES is also a partner in every prototype "Employment Zone". (See "Decentralization" in Chapter 8.) Experience from five of these zones has shown that a wealth of new ideas has emerged from consultations with local groups and these could be used in designing provisions that relate to local needs.

In Hungary,[12] county labour councils comprising representatives of local employers' organizations, employees and municipalities develop short- and long-term labour market adjustment programmes and decide on their funding. They monitor the implementation of these programmes on the basis of reports from the head of the local PES. There is a good working relationship between the PES units and labour councils. The municipalities are also represented in the county labour councils and thus help to bring the PES close to as many citizens as possible. With the future strengthening of NGOs and local voluntary organizations, the PES local partnerships will be widened so as to involve local community representatives more closely in tackling employment problems. At the same time, the involvement of the social partners and municipalities will be reduced.

Ireland is the country which has had the most experience in joint initiatives between government and various kinds of social actors concerned with specific employment problems.[13] A series of national agreements have led to various forms of social partnerships. These are based on local communities and include representatives of weaker labour market actors such as people with disabilities, the long-term unemployed and women. The key idea on which these partnerships are based is that they should target an area small enough to constitute a real community known as an "area-based partnership". This makes it possible to address a broad number of issues that cut across the life of residents such as jobs, housing, transport, social services and so forth. These national and local partnerships have enabled the actors in these communities to define their most serious problems and to try and solve them together. Voluntary organizations in specific social fields may also participate in these partnerships.

The objective of this area-based model is to enable marginalized individuals to re-enter the labour market by developing suitable jobs for both the short- and the long-term unemployed. Local partnerships seek to find innovative solutions to meet needs that are otherwise addressed through welfare or simply neglected. The goal is to invest in human resources and training while strengthening the innovative capacities of local systems and individuals. With the active support of the European Commission, 39 area-based partnerships and 33 community groups have been set up in particularly disadvantaged areas. The partnership board of directors has equal representation from a range of actors. They come from various government sectors such as the following: education, health and welfare; from local authorities, trade unions and local employers; and from voluntary/community groups active in economic and social development. The latter provide assistance to those with disabilities and support for the long-term unemployed.

One of the innovations of these local partnerships was the establishment of a network of integrated local employment services (LES) under the auspices of the local partnership. The LES bring together the resources of state agencies and community-based organizations and receive the support of the social partners.They focus on the needs of individual unemployed and aim to ensure that the opportunities available to them are relevant to their needs and interests and also realistic in terms of the requirement of the labour market. The intention is to provide an intensive and coordinated service for those most in need which is based on a one-to-one approach between the unemployed client and the LES mediator. The LES are now active in 18 locations: 14 of these are in urban areas, 4 in rural areas.

In each partnership area, the LES implement through a number of local contact points which are used as gateways for all available services. These are likely to include community-based resource centres, centres for the unemployed, the Irish PES (called FÁS) offices, social welfare offices, partnership offices, and other special outreach offices as deemed necessary. While all of these offices maintain their core functions, they also act as a contact point through which the LES can be accessed and through which elements of the services are made available. Some of these contact points provide a more intensive service than others. For example, some provide additional specialist career path planning or provide a placement service for the long-term unemployed.

The LES in Ireland may be an example in which the advantages of local policy are successfully combined with the necessary procedures and systems of national policy. In this way, the national PES is developed with a local element targeted at particular types of clients. The Irish experience with area-based partnerships was adopted by Finland in 1998 which today has 34 operating partnerships.[14]

Relationships with PREAs

As indicated in Chapter 1, the PES began as a state job-broking organization in most countries, often with a monopoly in placement as required by Fee-Charging Employment Agencies Convention, 1933 (No. 34) and Fee-Charging Employment Agencies Convention (Revised), 1949 (No. 96). The main arguments for this arrangement were firstly, that there was a need for the protection of workers against exploitation such as when agencies supplied cheap foreign labour or when temporary workers were engaged by temporary work agencies (TWAs) for user enterprises. Secondly, the PES needed access to the full spectrum of vacancies if was to assist harder-to-place unemployed to counter the "creaming" effect of PREAs. However, a significant group of countries such as Australia, Ireland, Switzerland, the United Kingdom and the

United States rejected the monopoly and allowed PREAs to operate with varying degrees of regulation.

Over the last two decades, scepticism about the monopoly has spread to several other OECD countries. This has been due to several factors. Firstly, in a climate of economic liberalism, doubts about the ability of a public monopoly institution to service a rapidly changing and flexible labour market has increased. Secondly, the PES, like other public institutions, has become subject to public spending constraints thus restricting its activities and making it more difficult to defend a ban on PREAs. Thirdly, the PES monopoly has not prevented employers from using other channels of placement such as advertising and professional and informal contact networks. This made the ban on PREAs look anomalous.

Not surprisingly, the PES monopoly was formally removed in a large number of developed countries, including Portugal (1989), Denmark (1990), the Netherlands (1991), Sweden (1993), Germany (1994), Finland (1994) and Austria (1994). Among EU member States, only France, Greece and Luxembourg continue to prohibit private commercial placement agencies. However, all these countries now allow TWAs, which represented the first wave of liberalization in countries where the PES had previously had a monopoly.[15] Over the last two decades, there has also been a rapid growth of PREAs, especially TWAs.[16] Their co-existence with the PES has come about because in many countries these are strictly speaking not involved in placement activities.

These developments made Convention No. 96 look increasingly anachronistic. Following a general discussion among experts in Geneva in 1994, the ILO decided to revise this Convention in order to respond to the realities of the modern labour market and to provide better protection to workers engaged by TWAs to work in user enterprises. The end of the PES monopoly was internationally recognized *de jure* in June 1997 through the adoption of the Employment Agencies Convention (No. 181). Its scope is wider than that of Convention No. 96 in that it encompasses in addition to intermediaries in placement, other categories of PREAs such as labour-skill providers and also suppliers of direct services. The Convention recognizes that PREAs can contribute to the functioning of the labour market and it sets general parameters for the regulation, placement and employment of workers engaged by PREAs and in particular by TWAs. Furthermore it seeks to promote cooperation between the PES and PREAs for a better functioning of the labour market. In other words, Convention No. 181 tries to provide a modern and flexible framework for ending the PES monopoly without abandoning its core mandate to protect temporary workers. Up to December 1999, eight countries, namely Albania, Ethiopia, Finland, Japan, Morocco, the Netherlands, Panama and Spain, had ratified the Convention, which came into force in May 2000.

What have been the effects of deregulation in placement services? A comparative study in EU member States found that thus far, the impact has been small and in countries with a relatively high share of private placements, this has not been the result of recent changes in legislation.[17] In some countries such as Belgium (Flanders) and the Netherlands, TWAs remain the biggest group of PREAs but these had been already active before the deregulation of job-broking took place. Other factors such as population size and density, the role of the social partners and cultural factors have also played an important role in the growth of TWAs.

A second finding of the study was that the PES handles more jobseekers and vacancies than PREAs. Reliable evidence on relative shares of the placement market are lacking, but it seems likely that the PES will remain a bigger player than the PREAs, though other recruitment channels, in particular advertisements and informal channels, also command large market shares. It was also found that with the exception of TWAs, market segments in terms of sector or qualification levels are different for the PES than other types of PREAs. So far, competition only exists between the PES and the TWAs where market segments are shared and their activities overlap. PES and agencies which act as intermediaries between employers and jobseekers complement each other as the latter serve different clients than the PES. One final feature that the study noted was that deregulation in placement services has compelled the PES to become more sensitive to the needs of individual jobseekers and employers.

As we move into the twenty-first century, one of the most pressing concerns for the PES is the nature of the relationship it should have with PREAs.[18] Within a European framework, the European Commission[19] has identified three possible types of relationship: firstly, cooperation in the fields of information and basic matching services and in active brokage and adjustment; secondly, complementarity in particular labour market segments or in particular kinds of services; thirdly, competition in providing services to employers with the possibility of fee-charging by the PES.

All three approaches are being adopted. Cooperation or partnership is illustrated by arrangements that have been made in France and the United Kingdom which allow the PES to fill PREA vacancies. The same arrangement is evident in joint ventures such as that in the Netherlands between the PES and two major TWAs to deliver a wide range of services to employers. Cooperation can also take the form of contracting with PREAs to deliver certain services for government such as is the case in St. Gallen, Switzerland, where PREAs were commissioned to assist unemployed people.[20] Annex IV.26 describes further examples of innovation in partnership between the PES and TWAs. These partnerships aim at improving the services rendered to firms, increasing both the flexibility of the labour market and the employability of employees and jobseekers.

The idea of complementarity is illustrated by the example of Mexico, where 32 state employment systems have been set up to foster the exchange of information on openings and jobseekers. In general however, the PES may well decide to leave the professional and executive market largely to the private sector because it lacks the resources to provide a credible service. Competition exists naturally where the PES and PREAs are operating in similar segments of the market and this can be healthy in encouraging sensitivity to customer needs. However, PREAs complain of unfair competition where PES services are free or are subsidized. (On the issue of charging, see "Resources" in Chapter 3.)

In the future, the relationships between the PES and PREAs are likely to depend on the following factors:

- the employment policies being pursued by governments;
- the relative capacities of the PES and PREAs to deliver those policies in the market segments in which they operate most effectively;
- the strength of competition policies; and
- judgements about the extent of the market share needed by the PES to help disadvantaged groups.

The latter factor may be the most critical one. From a PES point of view, there are dangers in complementarity or market segmentation if it reduces the PES to operating in low-skilled and declining segments of the market. The PES remit to assist the disadvantaged will be difficult to achieve where the PES has a poor reputation and is caught in a downward spiral. To counter this risk, the PES in some countries has deliberately moved into expanding, flexible market segments. For example, the Belgian PES set up a public TWA (T-Service Interim) in 1980 which now has over 40 local agencies. (For a description of this service, see Annex IV.26A.) Despite PES initiatives like this, it can no longer be assumed that PREAs cannot play a role in relation to the disadvantaged simply because they are profit-making organizations. There are examples in Switzerland (St. Gallen) and in the New Deal in the United Kingdom where they have undertaken work to help unemployed people. (The New Deal example is described in Annex IV.26C.)

While it is difficult to predict how the future relationship between the PES and PREAs will develop, Convention No. 181 nevertheless encourages its members to formulate, establish and periodically review conditions to promote cooperation between the PES and PREAs. The first study comparing the way in which the PES and PREAs operate in France, the Netherlands and the United Kingdom, reached several interesting conclusions.[21] First among these was that the PES in the three countries has sought to strengthen its competitive position by seeking to innovate and introduce new ways of influencing the labour market. At the same time, public and private operators have progressively laid the foundation for an approach and a dynamism based more on ideas of complementarity, cooperation, partnership and subsidiarity rather than on the idea of competition. In relation to this point, it found that the PES in its new role as a service enterprise is a driving force in the process of cooperation. Finally, even though there is no truly concerted action by public and private operators in the labour market, the following factors suggest that this may develop:

- technology transfers between the PES and PREAs means that some services now share the same basis;
- funding arrangements;
- the creation of multidisciplinary teams or consortia to secure certain deals;
- unexpected new communications such as the advertising of job vacancies by temporary consortia in PES offices;
- interlinked efforts by the PES, consortia and voluntary groups to redeploy disadvantaged groups;
- a shared interest in professionalism and competence; and
- the appearance of an embryo code of conduct on aspects such as confidentiality, procedural ethics, information on workers and measures against discrimination.

Networking among public employment services

From the early days of the twentieth century, there has been a powerful flow of ideas and experience between countries about PES affairs, and since 1919 this process has been encouraged by the ILO. More recently, several networks have been developed to promote the exchange of information between the PES in various countries. In 1988–89, various PES directors felt a need to create an organization to network and exchange information. Accordingly, leaders in six countries (the United States, Canada, France, Sweden, the Netherlands and Germany) founded the World Association of Public Employment Services (WAPES) with ILO support. WAPES is organized for and by PES directors to encourage contacts and exchanges between member bodies and to promote cooperation between more and less developed bodies. Its services include: a world congress every two years; technical workshops; training stipends for developing countries; joint development with the ILO of the world's first automated database on the PES; a technical journal, *Public Employment Service*, published two or three times a year; a technical consultancy service;

and a twinning programme between local offices in developed and developing countries. WAPES is a non-profit organization, with a small budget and low membership fees. For its effectiveness, it relies on the goodwill of members. It now has 73 members, reflecting its growing importance in the eyes of the world PES community.

In the last few years, the Directorate-General of Employment, Industrial Relations and Social Affairs (DGV) of the European Commission has also begun to organize regular information exchange among its member countries in recognition of the central role that the PES plays in the implementation of employment policy. This networking has also promoted joint activity, such as the EU benchmarking project, information exchange and technical assistance to those countries of central Europe that are strengthening their economies and governmental institutions with a view to gaining EU membership.

A sub-national network that serves a similar purpose links together the state and territory employment services in the United States. This non-profit organization is the Interstate Conference of Employment Service Agencies (ICESA). Its mission is to strengthen the national workforce development network through information exchange, liaison and advocacy. It maintains an extensive information network of national and state level activities and a great deal of information on these activities is accessible on their web site. (See Annex VI.1 for web site addresses). The ICESA staffs a number of standing committees and workgroups on various topics of concern for state PES administrators and also operates the Centre for Employment Security Education and Research (CESER), which is the education and research arm of the organization.

These networks exemplify a different kind of partnership to those discussed elsewhere in this chapter but are nevertheless extremely worthwhile. They help to ensure that the PES in one country (or federal state) can learn from the experience of others. And there is much to be learned. The same problems occur in many countries and no one country can claim a monopoly on good practices.

Conclusion

This chapter has described one of the most profound changes currently affecting the PES. From once having been a self-sufficient organization, the PES now finds itself having to carry out much of its work in partnership or in contractual relationships with a wide range of other organizations. These organizations include the social partners, governmental agencies, voluntary/ community groups and associations, and private, profit-making agencies.

Partnership arrangements require highly developed skills in contracting, negotiation and communication on the part of senior PES managers.[22] But while this dimension of PES work is demanding and difficult, it is also potentially rewarding. By harnessing a wider range of skills than those available to it alone and working in an integrated way with other agencies, the PES is being given the opportunity to make major improvements in services to the public.

Notes

[1] European Commission: *The modernisation of public employment services in Europe – Three key elements* (Luxembourg, Office for the Official Publications of the European Communities, 1999), p. 27.

[2] H. Mosley, T. Keller and S. Speckesser: *The role of the social partners in the design and implementation of active measures*, Employment and Training Paper No. 27 (Geneva, ILO, 1998), p. 4.

[3] Namely, Austria, Belgium, Germany, Luxembourg, the Netherlands, Canada, France, Greece, Ireland and Portugal.

[4] ILO: *The public employment service in Norway* (Geneva, ILO, 1998; mimeographed), pp. 17–18.

[5] ILO: *The public employment service in the Netherlands* (Geneva, ILO, 1998; mimeographed), p. 50.

[6] In France, a framework agreement is planned and agreed between the ANPE and a number of large firms, e.g. Elf-Antar, Total, Domaxel Group, Mousquetaire Group, Promodes Group, McDonalds and Agepos/PME. See "ANPE's cooperation with firms", in European Employment Observatory Mutual Information System on Employment Policies (MISEP): *Policies, No. 44* (Berlin, European Commission, Winter 1993).

[7] ILO: *Les services publics de l'emploi: Le cas de la France* (Geneva, ILO, 1998; mimeographed).

[8] See "Delegation of ANPE services to partners", in European Employment Observatory Mutual Information System on Employment Policies (MISEP): *Policies, No. 57* (Berlin, European Commission, Spring 1997).

[9] OECD: *Decentralising employment policy: New trends and challenges – The Venice Conference* (Paris, OECD, 1999).

[10] R. Flores-Lima: "A new stage of decentralisation in Mexico: granting autonomy to the states", in OECD, op. cit., p. 67.

[11] A. Smith: "Local partnership in the UK: A key for effective welfare to work policies", in OECD, op. cit., pp. 111–114.

[12] L. Garzo: "Local management in economies in transition: The positive experience in Hungary", in OECD, op. cit., pp. 173-175.

[13] T. Crooks: "The contribution of local partnerships to employment services in Ireland", in OECD, op. cit., pp. 179–183.

[14] P. Saikkonen: "An introduction to local partnership and institutional flexibility", in OECD, op. cit., p. 152.

[15] H. Mosley: "Market share and market segment of employment services in the EU: Evidence from labour force surveys", in European Employment Observatory Mutual Information System on Employment Policies (MISEP): *Policies, No. 57* (Berlin, European Commission, Spring 1997), p. 26.

[16] According to a survey undertaken by the *Confédération Internationale des Entreprises de Travail Temporaire* (CIETT) in 1998, the number of TWA branches or outlets has at least doubled or tripled since the late 1980s in EU member States. See CIETT: *Temporary work businesses in the countries of the European Union* (Diemen, Netherlelands, Bakkenist Management Consultants, 1998), pp. 37–38.

[17] J. de Koning et al.: *Deregulation in placement services: a comparative study for eight EU countries*, Unpublished Report (Rotterdam, 1998), pp. 51–52.

[18] Walwei has examined the modes of existence between the PES and PREAs in the following publications: *Monopoly or coexistence: An international comparison of job placement*, Labour Market Research Topic No 5 (Berlin, Institute for Employment Research, 1993); idem: *Placement as public responsibility and as a private service*, Labour Market Research Topic No. 17 (Berlin, Institute for Employment Research, 1996); idem: *Job placement in Germany: Developments before and after deregulation*, Labour Market Research Topic No. 31 (Berlin, Institute for Employment Research, 1998); idem: "Improving job-matching through placement services" in G. Schmid, J. O'Reilly and K. Schömann (eds.): *International handbook of labour market policy and evaluation* (Cheltenham, Edward Elgar, 1996), pp. 402–430.

[19] *European Commission: PES-PREA's relationship in a European framework*, Issue Paper submitted at the Meeting of the Heads of Public Employment Services within the EEA, Baden, Austria, 16 Nov. 1998, sect. II, p. 4.

[20] OECD: *Labour market policies in Switzerland* (Paris, OECD, 1996), p 82. To prevent "creaming", PREAs are compensated on time-budget basis.

[21] M. Sansier and D. Boutonnat: *The relationship between public employment services and private employment agencies: Developing a cooperation framework*, Labour Administration Branch Document No. 51 (Geneva, ILO, 1997).

[22] For example in the United States, the ICESA has suggested 10 ways to build better partnerships: 1) identify the one-stop common values; 2) establish a joint vision; 3) define desired outcomes to be measured; 4) align all partner organizations with the vision; 5) create shared standards and definitions of success; 6) form cross-agency work teams; 7) cross-inform and cross-train; 8) develop shared customer process maps; 9) use common customer responses; 10) communicate the partnership. For more, see http//www.icesa.org.

CONCLUSIONS 10

To be the nation's leader in providing services to its customers and serving as a univer-
sal gateway to workforce development resources by professional empowered staff.[1]

Introduction

In this chapter we draw together the strands of the study and highlight the key
points. It consists of three sections. First, we draw general conclusions about
the PES responsiveness to its external environment and to its relations with
government. We summarize what is involved in an integrated service delivery,
in working in partnership and in the new kinds of service enterprise. Second,
we discuss the special considerations affecting the PES in developing countries.
Third, we consider the dilemmas facing the PES.

General conclusions

This study has drawn attention to the tremendous changes in the nature and role
of the PES in most countries during the twentieth century. In most countries,
the PES started out as a state job-broking organization, often with a monopoly
and often strongly linked to unemployment insurance and other regulatory
functions. By the end of the century, the PES in many developed countries had
become a key instrument of government employment policies, heavily involved
in programmes of labour market adjustment and had become an important
source for labour market information. On the other hand, the PES no longer had
a monopoly on job-broking but worked alongside a number of public and
private organizations engaged in the labour market, either in formal or informal
partnerships or under contractual arrangements.

   On the whole, the PES have been resourceful and responsive in meeting the
challenges of constant change in recent years and international organizations

such as the OECD and the EU have recognized the importance of the PES for achieving their policy goals. The PES in many countries has introduced modernization programmes and major innovations such as new counselling frameworks and new information systems; it has also introduced the Internet and modern telephone communications systems to job-broking.

But established institutions like the PES can take nothing for granted in a world where public sector bodies have been coming under increasing challenge. In the turbulence of the modern world, "institutions have to learn rapidly and to reinvent themselves".[2] Over the last decade, one major country, Australia, has privatized its PES while the PES in other countries such as the United States and Canada has faced severe resource constraints. It is important to consider how best the PES can position itself to cope with the challenges it faces.

Responsiveness to the external environment

First and foremost, the PES needs to be constantly ready to change and adapt its services in the light of changes in its external environment while also striking a balance between change and stability. Chapter 2 describes the unprecedented rate of change in the labour market. It is easy for the PES to get trapped in declining sectors of the market such as manufacturing and as a result be unable to meet the needs of growing numbers of displaced and unemployed workers. On the whole, private agencies have proved more flexible than the PES in their responses. The PES can learn from the abilities of these to detect changing trends and respond to them. Examples of positive PES responses include adapting services to cater for a growth in part-time, self-employed or temporary jobs, and developing new self-help instruments on the Internet. Unless the PES continues to adapt and change, it will simply become a monument to a past age. At the same time, a tension exists between the pressure for change in response to new and unexpected developments and the need for organizational stability to enable a process of continual improvement in quality to take place. PES managers need to strike the right balance between these two objectives.

Relations with government

Second, the PES has to recognize its position as an instrument of government employment policy, to win the confidence of government and to influence government employment policies. In most cases, virtually all PES resources come from government. Even where there is funding from insurance contributions as is the case in Germany, the goodwill of the government is essential to the continuance of the arrangement. It is therefore vital for the PES to maintain the confidence of government ministers and senior officials about the relevance of PES work to government policies and to promote the effectiveness of the PES as a delivery tool. This confidence needs to be earned in finance ministries and in labour ministries. The aim should be to win enough respect in senior government circles for PES expertise in labour market and programme delivery that the PES becomes a major contributor to both the development of employment policies and an agent for their delivery.

Many countries are introducing labour market adjustment programmes in order to tackle unemployment and social exclusion. The PES, with outlets in local communities and with a proximity to end users, is strategically well placed to contribute both to the design and to the delivery of these programmes. With regard to design, there has been a proliferation of programmes in many countries which have either been superimposed upon or have overlapped with existing programmes. This has not alone created artificial compartmentalization and confusion in the minds of the public, but also in the minds of those tasked with the delivery of programmes. As a result of this tendency, PES managers can become overloaded and find it difficult to reconcile the various conflicting demands placed upon them. The PES needs to work with policy-makers to make employment policies more simple and more coherent.

Another aspect of relations between the PES and governments is the question of resources. As pressures have grown to either contain or reduce public expenditure in many countries, PES resources have been squeezed. This can have a healthy effect in stimulating innovation and the use of information technology. But it can also damage services to disadvantaged and unemployed people, whose problems cannot simply be resolved by the use of self-help computer terminals. Cuts in staff-intensive services can be false economies, leading to extra benefit expenditure and an increase in social exclusion. It is important that there should be a serious dialogue between the PES and government on these issues, the dialogue being underpinned both by evaluation data and labour market information.

Integrated service delivery

Third, it is important that the four main functions or services identified in this study be integrated as much as possible. (See "Functions" in Chapter 3 and "Institutional integration" in Chapter 8, p. 122.) If government employment policies are to be effective, they need to be well coordinated and consistently focused on the individual. The OECD in particular has emphasized the need for an integrated approach between unemployment benefit authorities and those responsible for job-search assistance. Complete institutional integration is in some ways the ideal solution but may not be practical. Other forms of integration include the one-stop shop, where a variety of local institutions share common premises, regular meetings of local managers to discuss common problems, and integrated computer systems shared by staff whether these be concerned with job-broking, job-search assistance or benefits. An integrated approach should ultimately benefit the individual jobseeker, since it should make for more coherent and consistent efforts to help the individual back to work.

Fourth, the PES should work closely with a wide range of partners and where necessary, exercise a leadership role. (See Chapter 9.) PES directors in the EU have suggested that the PES needs a partnership strategy. In a sense, this is nothing new, particularly at the strategic level. The idea of associating the social partners with the running of the PES goes back to the Unemployment Convention, 1919 (No. 2) and has been the pattern in many countries. But despite this, there has been a tendency for the PES to become insular. The modern PES needs to be open to the outside world and willing to work closely with others such as private employment agencies or with providers and users of labour market information. More fundamentally, the trend towards partnership reflects the broadening role of the PES and a growing recognition that problems such as long-term unemployment and social exclusion are multi-faceted. Problems like these cannot be resolved if public bodies operate in watertight compartments; a concerted approach by a variety of agencies is therefore needed. Another strand is the constant pressure for greater efficiency from public bodies which makes it important to determine what work is most cost-effectively done by the PES and what can better be done by others, either as partners or under contract. The days of monopoly and insularity are over and a more open and collaborative approach is needed in the twenty-first century.

Through its central position in the labour market, the PES is well placed to exercise a leadership role in such partnerships. The PES should not seek to take the lead for its own sake, but rather it should do so where it has the proper competency and can thus offer others the best prospect for success.

A new kind of service enterprise

Fifth, the PES needs to become a new kind of service enterprise with a new profile for managers and staff and needs to strive for continual improvement in effectiveness and quality. The EU has defined a service enterprise as an organization that seeks to be centrally placed in the market and be sensitive to the changing needs of jobseekers and enterprises. This is a reminder that PES work is very different from that of most civil servant work: it is more like that of a business enterprise than a traditional civil service bureaucracy. At the same time, the constant pressures of PES work, particularly at times of high unemployment, can engender a mood of cynicism or pessimism among PES staff and even lead to negative attitudes towards clients. Senior management in the PES needs to pay constant attention to the culture of the organization, to foster a sense of empowerment and initiative, to celebrate achievement and to encourage outreach to the outside world. The demands placed on local managers and staff require them to have a wide range of skills. Priority should be given to building their capacity through appropriate education and training, including training in customer relations and in the use of information technology. Given the wide dispersion of PES staff, senior management also needs to pay close attention to internal communications, including measures to seek the views of staff through regular attitude surveys and focus groups.

The PES also needs to aim for continual improvement in effectiveness and quality. (See Chapter 8.) We deliberately use the term "effectiveness" here rather than "efficiency" since the ultimate test of PES success should be the outcomes achieved in the real world in relation to the resources deployed, rather than simply the ability to achieve economies or cut costs. The PES needs clear aims and objectives and these should be reflected in challenging but achievable performance measures. It needs to organize periodic surveys to test the attitudes of employers and jobseekers to PES services. It also needs to adopt a quality approach in which criticisms and complaints are seen as potential stimuli towards better performance. Harnessing information technology is but part of this quality approach. All major PES programmes and innovations need to be subjected to careful evaluation, the findings of which should be taken very seriously.

Special factors affecting the PES in developing countries

The conclusions so far reflect in the main the situation in developed countries, though some of them, such as the need for responsiveness to the external environment and government employment policy, are clearly relevant to developing countries. However, there are other considerations for developing countries which we discuss in this section.

In some ways, the greatest challenges of all are faced by the PES in developing countries where resources are often the most constrained and PES influence on government the most limited. The PES in developing countries may be so taken up with regulatory work that it cannot make a more positive contribution to the labour market. Often, it faces daunting labour market problems in terms of the levels of unemployment and under-employment. Although, we have not been able to research these problems in sufficient depth to be able to offer detailed policy prescriptions for the PES in developing countries, there are nonetheless certain points on which we can be clear.

- First, as in all countries, political commitment to the role of the PES is likely to be critical to its success. Without a willingness in senior political circles to provide adequate resources, little progress will be made.
- Second, it would be unwise to simply transpose onto developing countries PES services found useful in developed countries; the PES in developed countries is far from uniform and has developed services in response to particular problems which may well differ from those in developing countries. For instance, in some developed countries the PES has been profoundly influenced by the need to contain unemployment benefit expenditure, whereas in many developing countries, unemployment benefit systems do not exist. Even job-broking services may be less relevant in developing countries. Rather than just copying services from elsewhere, it is essential to analyse the labour market requirements of a developing country in the context of the overall approach to economic development being pursued in that country.
- Third, the starting point for such an analysis is likely to be a study of the relevant labour market information. If such information is not available, then a sensible preliminary step would be to carry out surveys, neither researching highly detailed nor precise information, but rather gathering enough information on which to build a broad picture of labour market problems and identifying whether PES services might in fact be of help in tackling these problems. At the same time, the PES should avoid taking on commitments to provide labour market information which are beyond its capabilities.
- Fourth, if a decision is taken to set up PES services to tackle some of the labour market problems identified, the next step should be to launch pilot schemes. It is vital that the staff recruited to carry out these schemes should be thoroughly trained and adequately paid.
- Fifth, while job-broking has been the core function of the PES in most developed countries, the relevance of this in a developing country needs to be carefully assessed. In a mainly rural economy or in one in which the informal economy dominates, a job-broking service is much less relevant. If, however, a developing country has reached the point where it has decided to introduce some form of unemployment benefit system, then job-broking facilities are likely to be essential for ensuring that job opportunities are

found as quickly as possible for benefit recipients. Again, the role of the PES relative to private employment agencies may need special attention whether this be to allow an unregulated growth of private agencies, to introduce regulation and/or to use the PES, perhaps in partnership with private agencies.

We recommend that further research be carried out on the role of the PES in developing countries as a basis for guiding the governments, social partners and labour officials in these countries.

Dilemmas facing the public employment service

Given the complex position of the PES in modern society, it is not surprising that there should be a number of dilemmas surrounding its role which sometimes raise fundamental issues about the values and goals of the PES itself. These dilemmas are not amenable to easy solutions and are likely to persist. It is important that those involved in steering the PES are aware of them and seek to minimize adverse effects.

First, there is the tension between a universal self-help service and enhanced personalized service. (See Chapter 4.) Modern technology, either through the Internet and other self-help mechanisms, offers unprecedented opportunities for a universal self-help service. But it is unrealistic to think that these facilities, however formidable their potential, can simply take the place of PES front-line services. There will continue to be a need for staff-intensive services to assist those who are more vulnerable in the labour market and perhaps even to assist those who are simply unfamiliar with job-search. The increased flexibility and insecurity of the modern labour market reinforces this view. Nonetheless, it is difficult to judge where best to strike the balance and already different approaches are being adopted in different countries.

Second, there is the tension between providing customer-oriented services and policing unemployment benefit. (See Chapter 7.) This is a long-standing dilemma for the service. In countries with unemployment benefit systems, the State expects the PES to ensure that benefit recipients move off welfare and back into work as quickly as possible, applying the threat of sanctions for cases of non-compliance. Although this is entirely understandable and is advocated by the OECD, it is not easily reconciled with a quality service seeking to satisfy the customer. The modern PES has adopted different approaches to policing ranging from distancing itself from it to engaging fully in it. There is no easy answer to the dilemma and again, a balance needs to be struck. The tactic of distancing the PES from benefit control is unrealistic, given the political importance of unemployment, given the day-to-day involvement of the PES with unemployed people and given the need to prevent people from sinking into longer and longer periods of unemployment. But PES senior management needs to be aware of the fact that policing duties can encourage negative attitudes among staff and alienate the public. Where necessary, it needs to be ready to make strenuous efforts to change the culture in the direction of better customer service.

Third, there is the future role of the PES in lifelong learning and in vocational guidance. (See Chapter 6.) Ever since the establishment of the PES, countries have differed in the extent to which the PES have been involved in training and vocational guidance. With the extraordinary rate of change in the modern labour market (see Chapter 2), education and training can no longer be seen as a one-off process completed in early life and the term "lifelong learning" neatly sums up the approach required these days. The PES has potentially an important role to play as the gateway to lifelong learning, helping people to review the direction of their careers, helping them determine what learning would benefit them and steering them to appropriate institutions or learning packages. Guidance of this kind is highly demanding. In part, it could be achieved through well-designed computer systems but highly trained counsellors are needed as well. This is an area for potentially important developments. We are unable to recommend just how the necessary assistance should be provided, but believe that governments would do well to consider seriously the claims of the PES to fulfil this role in relation to the claims of other organizations.

Finally, there are unresolved organizational issues, relating to private ownership and decentralization. PES managers in many countries are watching with fascination and trepidation the Australian experiment in privatizing the PES. We cannot prejudge the Australian Government's evaluation of this arrangement, but we would make two observations. Firstly, it is clear that the PES in many countries will have to adapt to a mixed economy in which there may remain a core employment service in the public sector, but in which the PES will have to share its role with a variety of private and public bodies. PES senior managers need to build up their expertise in order to successfully deal with this situation. Secondly, before embarking down the road that Australia has taken, governments would do well to weigh up not only the potential cost savings, but also the potential loss of experience that could be the price of ceasing to have a recognizable PES. Up till now, governments have taken it for granted that the PES, when asked to undertake an urgent new programme, has had the competence to deliver successfully because it has been able to draw on its corporate memory to correct any weakness. A switch to private ownership could mean that this corporate memory was no longer available as a national asset.

The other organizational trend which is affecting the PES in many countries is decentralization, driven in part by wider trends in government and in part by a wish to improve services by bringing decision making closer to end users. This trend has considerable attractions in terms of harnessing local energies, particularly in running labour market adjustment measures, but there are a number of constraints which affect the process. First, if employment policies vary significantly from place to place, this could lead to a loss of equality in the delivery of PES services and ultimately to labour market segmentation, with jobseekers in certain location receiving more favourable treatment than others. Second, job-broking requires standardized national systems and procedures for it to be effective, particularly in the age of mass communications. Some vacancies, however, especially those requiring scarce skills of strategic importance, need to be handled on a regional or national basis. Third, unemployment benefit rules need to be national for equality reasons. Fourth, labour market information needs uniform systems and definitions even where modes of delivery and presentation vary locally.

Decentralization policies need to take account of these considerations and need to be accompanied by arrangements for performance management, operational planning and review. This should help to maintain a degree of control from the centre and thus coherence in employment policies and in nationwide job-broking arrangements. Linked to the issue of decentralization is the trend towards local partnerships, which was discussed in Chapter 9. These partnerships have the advantage of combining the efforts of a wide range of local bodies in resolving problems linked to employment. But the leadership and coordination of local partnerships can present a difficult challenge for PES managers. For example, there is the question of how to balance diverging interests and aspirations at national, regional and local levels and the question of how to ensure that local partners have the necessary expertise in programme management, jobseeker counselling and advising employers. Moreover, there is the question of how best to monitor and evaluate the effectiveness of local partnerships and their use of public funds.

In conclusion, the PES may be likened to a ship navigating through an ocean of employment problems. It is riding out the tremendous waves of social and economic challenges that are battering it on all sides. Through recent reforms, the crew has become empowered, innovative and service-oriented and the ship has become more efficient, buoyant and capable of moving faster. But as the captain stares out from the bridge, he or she finds that the reforms that have been undertaken give little guidance as to what course or speed to take.

What is more, there is no safe haven to which he or she can turn. These are the tensions between the efforts for greater efficiency and the fundamental values and ethics of a public service. The PES "captain" feels isolated and is compelled to work with others in government and outside it to help set the right direction for the ship and to find the route that will be most beneficial.

Notes

[1] Vision agreed by PES leaders in the United States. See ILO: *The public employment service in the United States* (Geneva, ILO, 1998; mimeographed), p. 35.

[2] C. Leadbeater: *Living on thin air: The new economy* (Viking, London, 1999), p. 24.

ANNEXES

ANNEX I

GLOSSARY OF TERMS

Terms	Explanation
Active broking	A process of matching which involves a preselection by a PES officer of suitable candidates from the register for a vacancy or of suitable vacancies for a jobseeker.
Active labour market policies (ALMP)	According to the OECD, active measures seek to rapidly redeploy labour and develop new skills and employment opportunities for workers. They include labour exchange services (job-broking and job-search assistance), labour market information services, training and retraining programmes, assistance for small enterprise development and other job creation schemes.
Automated self-service broking	Direct and immediate matching of vacancies and job-seekers either on computer terminals or via the Internet without intervention from PES staff.
Benchmarking	A continuous, systematic process of measuring products, services and practices against organizations regarded to be superior with the aim of rectifying any performance gaps.
Closed file system	A system where vacancies are not advertised and are only available to PES staff who are supposed to preselect a number of candidates.
Contracting out	A situation where the delivery of a former public sector function is the subject of private sector competition, though it continues to be supported wholly or mainly from public funds.
Employment Counselling	An intervention or a sequence of interventions designed to help jobseekers or the unemployed to identify and resolve issues which must be faced when entering employment.

Terms	Explanation
Job-broking	A process through which the PES or PREAs arrange for jobseekers to find jobs and for employers to fill vacancies.
Job-search assistance	Services provided to advise and support jobseekers in seeking work, often in combination with job-broking services. These services can operate at different intensities and include provision of information, group activities like job clubs and individual employment counselling.
Kansmeter	A Dutch instrument for the administrative intake of job-seekers to assess their "distance" from the labour market and to tailor employment services to their needs.
Kiosks	User friendly computer terminals in PES offices, shopping malls or public places through which jobseekers can access labour market information.
Labour market adjustment programme (LMAP)	In this study, labour market adjustments are part of active labour market policies and are intended to increase the employability of jobseekers and of certain special groups. LMAP includes job-search assistance, training and retraining and job creation programmes.
Labour market information (LMI)	Any information concerning: the size and composition of the labour market; the direction of it or any part of its functions; its problems; the opportunities which may be available to it; and the employment-related intentions or aspirations of those who are part of it.
Labour market information system	Establishment of a framework to collect, analyse, report and disseminate labour market information.
Labour market penetration	Relative share of the PES in total recruitment activities in the labour market. Potential measures are either the percentage of total vacancies in the labour market or the percentage of total hirings made in the labour market achieved by the PES.
Lifelong learning	Need for the continual upgrading of knowledge and skills.
Local partners	Employers, trade unions, statutory agencies and voluntary community groups at the local level capable of taking concrete action.
Market testing	Situation similar to that of contracting out, except that the existing public sector deliverer competes against other bidders.

Terms	Explanation
One-stop shop	A variety of employment services delivered from the same premises to assist jobseekers.
Open file system	A system where vacancies are advertised and displayed with full information given about the job and the employer.
Passive labour market policies	Passive measures help to reduce the short-term costs of economic policies adjustment to individuals and communities by providing income support and maintenance programmes.
Placement	The recruitment of a worker into a job as a result of activities of intermediaries such as the PES.
Private employment agencies (PREAs)	In accordance with the Private Employment Agencies Convention, 1997 (No. 181), private employment agency means any natural or legal entity, independent of the public authorities, which provides one or more of the following labour market services: (a) services for matching offers and applications for employment; (b) services consisting of employing workers with a view to making them available to a third party; (c) other services relating to job-search.
Privatization	A situation where a former public sector function is moved permanently into the private sector to become self-financing.
Public employment service (PES)	A network of public offices that provides job-broking services and may provide labour market information, labour market adjustment programmes, and unemployment benefits.
Self-service broking	A system whereby vacancy details are displayed to enable jobseekers to select those that suit them best and either submit themselves directly to the employers (open system) or submit themselves via the PES or PREAs (semi-open system).
Semi-open file system	A system where vacancies are advertised and displayed without details of the employer's identity so that any submission has to be made to a PES officer.
Social partners	Organizations or associations of employers' and workers' representatives.

Terms	Explanation
Tiered service delivery	A way to organize PES services according to the level of intensity of service necessary to remove barriers to employment for jobseekers or to assist employers to fill vacancies.
Unemployment assistance	Benefits are paid to the unemployed based upon need regardless of work history and are normally financed by taxation. They are often not limited to a specific period of time.
Unemployment benefits	Payments made to the unemployed to reduce the costs of economic adjustment to individuals and communities. They may be financed from insurance or from taxation or from a combination of both. Unemployment benefits are divided into two broad categories: unemployment insurance and unemployment assistance.
Unemployment insurance	A system by which workers are entitled to compensation for lost income based upon past contributions. Benefits are financed by pay-related contributions and are paid out for a limited amount of time.
Vocational guidance	The process in which a training counsellor helps an individual to make a career choice by giving information about the labour market, discussing educational and training qualifications and by exploring their interests and abilities.
Voucher	A system of delivery which enables the client or customer to shop around among suppliers.
Worker profiling	A statistical methodology that identifies those unemployment insurance recipients who are most likely to exhaust their benefit entitlement and refers them to the required re-employment services.

ANNEX II
MAIN FUNCTIONS AND TASKS OF THE PES

Function 1 Job-broking	Function 2 Development of labour market information systems	Function 3 Administration of labour market adjustment programmes	Function 4 Administration of unemployment benefits
1. Vis-à-vis jobseekers • Registration of jobseekers	**1. As provider of labour market information** • Collecting, registering and providing administrative records on jobseekers, job vacancies and occupational classification • Conducting short-term qualitative surveys • Analysing regular employer and household surveys conducted by other agencies • Reporting and publishing the various activities of the national economy, related changes in the labour demand and supply needs, and making projections about their trends	**1. Job-search assistance** • Providing universal services to all jobseekers (resource rooms, information centres or the Internet) • Organizing group activities: job clubs; proactive and special mass lay-off services to retrenched workers • Providing intensive individual assistance: skill assessment; vocational counselling/guidance; preparation and negotiation of employability development plan and follow-up	**1. Management of unemployment benefit funds (including tax collection)** • Providing information on unemployment benefit claims and entitlements • Examining and certifying the right to unemployment benefit • Registration of the unemployed and verification of the unemployment situation and of job-search procedures and situation • Handling complaints and disputes concerning entitlements (calculation of benefit, expiry of entitlement) • Payment of unemployment benefits to those concerned

unction 2

Main functions and tasks of the PES (contd.)

Function 1 Job-broking	Function 2 Development of labour market information systems	Function 3 Administration of labour market adjustment programmes	Function 4 Administration of unemployment benefits
2. Vis-à-vis employers • Periodic visits to enterprises for contacts and marketing • Job canvassing • Registering and classifying job vacancies	**2. As user of labour market information** • Providing employment counselling to jobseekers • Determining priorities for training programmes for the unemployed and jobseekers • Advising employers on labour demand and supply changes and trends	**2. Training and education programmes** 2.1 Training and apprenticeship within enterprises: • Registration of apprenticeship applications and vacancies • Establishment of contacts • Placement of apprentices and follow-up activities 2.2 Special training and retraining programmes: • Determining training needs and objectives • Analysing and determining the content of the courses to be organized, their duration and organization • Contacting and selecting public or private training institutes • Entrusting the organization of the course to those that offer the best terms • Monitoring evaluating the effects of training on jobseeker employability	**2. Administration of other public social assistance funds** for the unemployed and those unfit for work (health, housing, family, childcare, etc. reasons)

3. Job-broking
- Under closed system: active matching by PES staff including pre-screening of jobseekers, appraisal and updating of job vacancies, and negotiations of job-matching alternatives with jobseekers and employers)
- Under semi-open system: displaying job vacancies, providing information on employment requests
- Under open system: computerized matching, self-help or self-service, the Internet

4. Providing job-search assistance if the above job-broking fails (see task 1 in function 3)

5. Other related tasks

3. Other related tasks

3. Job creation programmes
- Managing the funds of these special programmes
- Participating in the design, monitoring and evaluation of special employment programmes
- Assisting in screening workers and providing specialized training for workers to be recruited in job creation programmes
- Making contacts with firms, community authorities and other agencies

4. Other related tasks

3. Other related tasks

ANNEX III

PUBLIC EXPENDITURE IN LABOUR MARKET AS A PERCENTAGE OF GDP, 1997

Country	Public employment services and administration	Labour market training			Youth measures		
		Training for unemployed adults and those at risk	Training for employed adults	Subtotal	Measures for unemployed and disadvantaged youth	Support of apprenticeship and related forms of general youth training	Subtotal
Australia [1]	0.21	0.06	—	0.07	—	0.05	0.06
Austria	0.14	0.15	0.02	0.17	0.02	—	0.02
Belgium	0.19	0.17	0.12	0.29	—	0.01	0.01
Canada [2]	0.18	0.15	—	0.15	0.02	0.01	0.03
Czech Republic	0.08	0.01	—	0.01	0.01	—	0.01
Denmark	0.13	0.68	0.30	0.97	0.10	—	0.10
Finland	0.14	0.53	0.02	0.54	0.11	0.13	0.24
France	0.16	0.31	0.04	0.35	0.07	0.19	0.26
Germany	0.21	0.36	—	0.36	0.06	0.01	0.07
Greece	0.12	*No breakdown available*		0.06	0.02	0.07	0.10
Hungary	0.13	0.08	—	0.09	—	—	—
Ireland [3]	0.24	0.14	0.08	0.21	0.11	0.13	0.24
Italy [4]	0.04	—	0.01	0.01	0.04	0.38	0.42
Japan [5]	0.03	0.03	—	0.03	—	—	—
Korea	0.04	0.01	0.02	0.04	0.05	—	0.05
Luxembourg	0.03	0.01	—	0.01	0.09	0.05	0.14
Netherlands	0.40	0.32	0.03	0.35	0.06	0.04	0.11
New Zealand [6]	0.15	0.32	—	0.32	0.01	0.07	0.08
Norway	0.16	0.13	—	0.13	0.04	—	0.04
Poland [7]	0.02	0.02	—	0.02	0.03	0.06	0.10
Portugal	0.11	0.08	0.20	0.28	—	0.16	—
Spain	0.08	0.11	0.08	0.19	0.07	—	0.07
Sweden	0.30	0.43	0.01	0.43	0.02	—	0.02
Switzerland	0.15	0.23	—	0.23	—	—	—
United Kingdom [8]	0.16	0.06	0.01	0.07	—	0.12	0.12
United States [9]	0.06	0.04	—	0.04	0.03	—	0.03

[1] Fiscal year starts 1 July. [2] Fiscal year starts 1 April. [3] Figures are from 1996. [4] Figures are from 1996.
[5] Fiscal year starts 1 April. [6] Fiscal year starts 1 July. [7] Figures are from 1996.
[8] These figures do not include Northern Ireland. Fiscal year starts 1 April. [9] Fiscal year starts 1 October.

PROGRAMMES IN 26 OECD COUNTRIES

Subsidized employment				Measures for people with disabilities			Unemployment compensation	Total
Subsidies to regular employment in the private sector	Support of unemployed people starting enterprises	Direct job creation (public or non-profit)	Subtotal	Vocational rehabilitation	Work	Subtotal		
0.04	0.02	0.07	0.13	0.02	0.04	0.06	1.17	1.7
0.03	—	0.04	0.07	0.02	0.03	0.05	1.21	1.66
0.16	—	0.51	0.68	0.03	0.10	0.13	2.06	3.36
0.01	0.02	0.05	0.08	0.03	—	0.03	1.02	1.49
—	—	0.01	0.02	—	—	—	0.21	0.33
0.02	0.06	0.23	0.31	0.28	—	0.28	2.23	4.02
0.09	0.03	0.40	0.53	0.06	0.06	0.12	2.78	4.35
0.32	—	0.20	0.52	0.02	0.06	0.08	1.50	2.87
0.05	0.03	0.26	0.33	0.13	0.14	0.28	2.50	3.75
0.04	0.02	—	0.06	*No breakdown available*		0.01	0.50	0.85
0.08	—	0.15	0.23	—	—	—	0.46	0.91
0.24	0.02	0.63	0.88	0.08	—	0.08	2.29	3.94
0.56	—	0.04	0.61	—	—	—	0.68	1.76
0.02	—	—	0.02	—	—	—	0.43	0.51
—	—	—	—	0.01	0.01	0.02	0.02	0.17
0.07	—	—	0.07	—	0.04	0.04	0.42	0.71
0.06	—	0.20	0.26	—	0.53	0.53	3.63	5.28
0.09	0.01	0.04	0.15	0.02	0.02	0.03	1.47	2.20
0.04	0.01	0.02	0.07	0.36	0.22	0.57	0.70	1.67
0.08	0.02	0.07	0.16	—	0.01	0.01	1.77	2.08
0.01	0.02	0.06	0.09	0.02	0.01	0.03	0.72	1.23
0.11	0.03	0.06	0.20	—	0.02	0.02	1.88	2.44
0.20	0.08	0.42	0.70	0.04	0.59	0.62	2.16	4.23
0.01	—	0.22	0.23	0.15	—	0.15	1.41	2.17
—	—	—	—	—	0.02	0.02	0.82	1.19
—	—	0.01	0.01	0.04	—	0.04	0.25	0.43

Source: OECD: *Employment Outlook* (Paris, OECD, 1999), Statistical Annex, table H.

EXAMPLES OF PES INNOVATIONS AND GOOD PRACTICES

Annex IV.1 Canada: Setting up computerized kiosks

Starting year: 1995–1996

Problem to be solved

In the 1995 federal budget, Human Resources Development Canada (HRDC) committed to reduce its overall workforce by 5,000 full-time equivalents and its overall spending by $2.8 billion. At the same time, HRDC committed that by 1998, up to 97 per cent of Canadians could expect access to service within a 30-minute time limit, up from 94 per cent in 1995. Both of these forces were driven by the public demand for government services that were more accessible but cost less.

Objectives

To make HRDC's service delivery network more flexible and affordable while improving quality of service and reducing the number of HRDC centres from 450 to 300.

Approach

There are to date about 5,200 kiosks across Canada providing employees with ready access to labour market information (LMI) and other general information. While most are in HRDC or partner offices, 1000 are located in shopping centres, libraries and other public access locations. An additional 100 or so kiosks are located in isolated rural locations around the country. At the kiosks, clients have ready access to a range of services, from local, regional and national LMI to a listing of jobs available. They also have access to various self-help tools which can help a client to prepare a resumé or determine the skill sets required for different occupations.

The HRDC service-delivery network, which includes electronic dissemination tools such as kiosks and local/regional internet sites, is the most extensive of any federal department. The strategy over the next few years will be to move all the applications currently resident in the kiosk on to the Internet while using the kiosk itself as a touch-screen web browser. This means that the kiosk will provide an internet access point for citizens that is functional and public. Due to the demographics of some segments of end users, Canada foresees the need for a public-access web device for some time to come. As a result, HRDC's service delivery policy includes both the Internet and kiosks as part of its future direction. Neither one excludes the other at this point in time. Kiosks are still being used although some of them are based on internet technology.

Assessment

An evaluation of the kiosk network has not yet been conducted. Monitoring of the kiosk network reveals usage at a level over 20,000 accesses per day and growing. The work involved in expanding the use of kiosks is much greater than the numbers suggest because it has involved the replacement of many existing older kiosks as well as the addition of new ones. Projects are also under way to use kiosks for other purposes, for example allowing citizens to notify government bodies of changes in address. Though technology is a key factor in the delivery of service to PES clients and a significant amount of work is now automated, this does not mean that in-person service is decreasing. Kiosks are designed to expand access, not reduce it.

Sources: (1) ILO: *The public employment service in Canada* (Geneva, ILO, 1998; mimeographed).
(2) Notes from HRDC of Canada (Ottawa, February, 2000).

Annex IV.2 France: Computerized operational repertory of occupations and jobs (ROME)

Starting year: 1993

Problem to be solved

Faced with technological developments, changes in work organization and in the recruitment practices of firms, there is an urgent need for access to up-to-the-minute references and descriptions of the composition of occupations and skills.

Objectives

The aim of the new ROME is operational in nature. In particular it seeks to:

• redefine the occupations which translate the changes in the economic environment and which facilitate professional intervention;

- increase the quality of the dialogue developing between the various actors (ANPE, users, firms and so forth) concerning activity content and the skills and abilities required to exert them;
- determine with greater precision the skills, no matter how intangible, acquired by employees through work experience in order to facilitate their valorization;
- facilitate the identification of individual and collective training needs in order to enable the (re)integration of those who do not hold the skills and qualifications required in the labour market; and
- widen the range of career paths to which people confronted with occupational mobility have access.

Approach

ROME consists of four linked elements.

1. Alphabetical index of occupational terms

The alphabetical index of occupational terms constitutes a password into the ROME nomenclature and into the dictionary of occupations and activities. The occupations/activities are listed according to their current and most common titles. The index accords considerable space to new terms, thus reflecting occupational changes and the appearance of new functions and activities since the publication of the previous ROME. Due to its alphabetical structure, the index facilitates the identification and recovery of the title and the number of the relevant information sheet in ROME according to the occupational description formulated by the user. In brief, the index brings together the vast majority of occupational titles currently existing in France (around 10,000).

2. The ROME nomenclature

The new nomenclature is based on a tree-diagram. Its function is to identify, classify and process job offers and labour supply more efficiently. This procedure enables job offers and labour supply to be analysed more thoroughly, based on an approach which moves from the general to the specific. Entries to the nomenclature are made by occupational categories: 22 occupational categories (CP) corresponding to the first two digits of the ROME number. The occupational categories link social status with a distinct occupational area. Each category is divided into a number of areas corresponding to the different fields of knowledge and technical know-how and includes 61 occupational areas (DOM) in all. The occupational areas allow trans-sectoral occupations, of which large numbers have arisen in recent years, to be identified and processed. There are 466 occupations/jobs (E/M) corresponding to the two final digits of the ROME number. These are listed in the dictionary of occupations/jobs.

3. The ROME dictionary of occupations/jobs

Together with the ROME nomenclature, the ROME dictionary constitutes an exhaustive national reference guide to occupations and activities. For the ANPE it serves a triple purpose:

- it supports the qualitative analysis and the definition of the job offers profiles placed with local employment agencies;
- it represents an operational and up-to-the-minute documentary source of occupational and job content for placement staff and users; and
- it reinforces a common language between ANPE and its partners to increase the effectiveness of its labour market interventions.

The dictionary presents in two volumes, 466 information sheets on occupations/ jobs. The occupation/job forms the basic unit of the nomenclature. It employs the concept of aggregated jobs (*agrégation d'emploi*), which identify areas of similarity between related occupations in order to promote occupational mobility.

This wide-ranging approach enables occupations/jobs to be identified in a way which does not confine individuals within strictly defined or restrictive categories. Rigidly defined categories are largely incompatible with the way in which the labour market now operates and with the way job content is changing. The following are some examples:

- Within one occupation or job, secretaries are grouped, irrespective of their specialization, as specialized office secretaries (*secrétaire bureaucratique spéciale*).
- Home-helps (*l'intervenant à domicile*) is a generic title covering family-support, household-aid, health-care activities, and so forth.
- Information technician (*l'informacien d'étude*) groups together the jobs of programmers, analysts, application technicians and development technicians.

The subdivisions take account of the diversity of working situations which the occupation/job in question covers in the labour market. If they are carefully and flexibly combined, the profiles of job offers and demands can be characterized according to the type of enterprise organization and according to the experience and know-how of employees. The subdivisions, the number of which varies from job to job, allow the ANPE to identify and compare essential information in bringing together the profiles of job offers and jobseekers.

4. Mobility areas

Mobility areas are one of ROME's tools. Starting from a source occupation/ job they allow a series of related occupations/jobs to be determined to which the user is given access. They are developed on the basis of a comparison between occupations/jobs, and aim both to provide orientation support and a guide to possible re-orientation within the same sector, in neighbouring sectors, or in other sectors. These mobility areas are the result of intensive evaluation of research and on-the-ground experience. Starting from the principle that knowledge and skills are transferable, they reveal occupational similarities and point out new career paths which are accessible either directly or in stages.

Source: European Employment Observatory Mutual Information System on Employment Policies (MISEP): *Policies, No. 43F* (Berlin, European Commission, Autumn 1993).

Annex IV.3 Japan: Overall employment information system (OEIS)

Starting year: 1988

Objective

To extend placement services at PES offices and to upgrade and to strengthen their function of providing employment information, even in the worst unemployment situations.

Approach

The development of the OEIS began in 1982. After a trial operation in Tokyo and four prefectures, the operation was introduced on a nationwide basis in 1988. The system was updated in 1994–95 with improved functions. In 1997, new systems were introduced such as the "Talent Bank", a "University Graduates' Bank" and a "Part-time Workers' Bank".

The OEIS contributes to various placement services, including the reception of job orders and job-search registration, counselling, guidance, job-broking services and the provision of employment-related information. For instance, Talent Banks provide professional employment counselling and placement services for managerial, specialized or technical jobs; the University Graduates' Bank stores and retrieves information on graduate jobseekers; Part-time Workers' Banks (with satellites) provide guidance and placement services for part-time jobseekers.

Since the OEIS handles image data for decentralized processing, computers were installed at prefectural government offices and at PES offices so that computers at different levels could access the information. Nationwide data for job orders and jobseekers and the employment insurance total system (EITS) are stored in computers and are available for retrieval. For more prompt and accurate data input, handwritten letters and maps are recognized in addition to conventional keyboard input.

Impact on PES work

The OEIS enables the PES offices nationwide to share relevant information so that they can promptly respond to both the requirements of employers seeking workers and jobseekers who have different needs. Moreover, the retrieval function can reduce mismatches in occupations, working conditions and in other areas. The OEIS has simplified placement and extended services to a larger region. In the future, there will be a closer linkage with the EITS system.

Source: ILO: *The public employment service in Japan* (Geneva, ILO, 1998; mimeographed).

Annex IV.4 Mexico: National employment information service system

Objectives

Mexico's national employment service information system, *Sistema de Información del Servicio Nacional de Empleo* (SISNE), is an information processing system that enables the national employment service, *Servicio Nacional de Empleo* (SNE), to carry out the following actions:

- Support the provision of placement services for workers and the SNE's efficient execution of its programmes
- Generate and provide systematic information on the characteristics and situation of labour markets

Approach

SISNE operates at three interrelated levels: an operative unit subsystem; a state subsystem; and a national system. The point of departure for SISNE is at the level of the operative unit subsystem of the state employment service, *Servicios Estatales de Empleo* (SEE), which captures, links, processes and follows up information on the job supply and demand handled by the SEE. The information furnished by each operative unit is transmitted and incorporated into the state subsystem at the main offices of the SEE, which in turn sends it on to the national employment service for its incorporation into and processing in the National System. The operational structure of SISNE makes information on labour markets available at three different levels: local, state and national, thereby servicing the entire geographic coverage of the national employment service.

SISNE is not only a database for obtaining statistical series and reports on the labour markets, but is also the main tool employed by the SEE and operative units for putting jobseekers into contact with the openings registered by the SEE client companies. It also serves to speed up the selection process for sending candidates to registered openings by allowing SISNE to match a given company and/or occupation to the jobseeker that best fulfils the requirements of the job opening. The two basic types of information currently being processed by SISNE are: a) the information obtained from the capture and processing of the work applications, openings, dispatching of candidates and placements handled by the SEE offices; b) the information supplied by job openings published in the country's main newspapers.

SISNE has been developed using the Dataflex V.23b/DOS programming language, with a relational, multiple-user type architecture and uses a Netware/Novell V:311/DOS environment operating platform. Its design is based on information modules and subsystems, and operation of the system requires at least a PC–286 with a hard disk. It offers the following major elements in its user interface:

- Design based on options menus
- Validated capture and correction routines for all its procedures
- On-screen consultation
- Simple procedures for the consultation, printing and graphing of tabulated statistics;
- Processing of tabulated statistics
- Utilities for the maintenance, screening, incorporation and dispatch of information

To put SISNE into operation, the Secretariat of Labour and Social Welfare provided the SEE with information-processing equipment consisting of 48 file hosts, 204 computers, 152 printers and 100 modems. SISNE generates directories, catalogues and listings of supply and demand records. In addition, it generates a series of predesigned statistical tabulations in each of the modules and subsystems in which it operates. These statistical tabulations or reports not only offer information for those supplying jobs, but also provide information on the principal labour and socio-demographic characteristics of jobseekers including: occupation, type of job sought, wages, work experience, length of time unemployed and reasons for unemployment, age, sex, marital status and so forth. Jobseekers, for their part, are provided with information on the number and type of openings available, requirements set by the employers for filling those openings (experience, schooling, age, marital status), wages offered and so forth. Statistics are also tabulated on the number of jobseekers directed or dispatched to a job opening and on those successfully placed in jobs.

The follow-up and monitoring of this information makes it possible to pinpoint the most acute maladjustment in the job market and the fluctuations occurring between over-qualified and non-qualified applicants. In addition, it allows the identification of possible areas of intervention in which training programmes suitable to the needs of the productive apparatus might be established. The information generated by SISNE is passed on to the SEE client companies, training institutions and government offices and is also circulated among members of the SEE executive committees and the state employment systems. In addition, a considerable portion of this information is made public through an information bulletin that is prepared, published and distributed every three months by each SEE.

As of mid-1997, and as one of the actions taken to strengthen the SNE information services and SISNE itself, the SNE labour exchange and training consultation system, *Sistema de Consulta de Bolsa de Trabajo y Capacitación del SNE* (BOLTRANET), was established. BOLTRANET operates through the Secretariat of Labour intranet, with access restricted to the SEE. It allows online consultation of information on openings and training courses existing in or emanating from any SEE operative unit. At present, 76 operative units of the SEE in 30 states are included in BOLTRANET.

Future development

- Updating of SISNE and migration to an Informix database.
- Development and incorporation of an information module for the operation of a programme of training scholarships for the unemployed (*Programa de Becas de Capacitación para Desempleados* – PROBECAT).
- Incorporation of the national occupations catalogue (*Catálogo National de Ocupaciones* – CON).
- Link-up and communication via the Internet.
- Development of a means of interfacing with the normalization and certification of labour competence systems.

Source: F. D. Tejeda: *New technology and placement service*, Paper presented at WAPES workshop, Aske (Sweden), 26–27 May, 1998.

Annex IV.5 Slovenia: Use of internet technology

Starting year: 1996

Objectives

To bring the national employment office (NEO) and its information closer to those unemployed and jobseekers who are internet users and also to enable staff to take maximum advantage of the new technology as an important aid in their work.

Approach

The Slovenian NEO established its web site in 1996. It includes: job vacancies (updated weekly and searchable by region, profession, and other variables); a jobseekers' notice board; a register of talented students completing their studies; answers to questions of the unemployed; NEO statistical data; NEO publications; and general information on the work of the NEO. Jobseekers enter their personal details and the job they are looking for into the jobseekers' notice board run on a UNIX server. They can also emphasize their specific qualities and knowledge so that employers get a good idea of the kind of person they are dealing with. The NEO intends to upgrade this part of the service by enabling searches by various criteria and by introducing data security. Employers looking for employees will be able to e-mail candidates. Employers can also find suitable employees among talented students currently finishing their studies (holders of NEO scholarships who have posted their details on the Internet). It is also possible to subscribe to data on job vacancies through the use of an employment agent "intelligent agent". This system sends an e-mail to the user on the specific days in the week that a suitable job appears. The agent functions in both English and Slovene.

The NEO is also accessible to the public via a free phone line which people can use to ask various questions relating to the rights of the unemployed or the activities of the NEO. Some of the most common questions are also posted on the web site. Among the most visited of the NEO's web pages are those featuring leaflets and booklets detailing the rights of the unemployed and those offering opportunities for unemployed people registered with the NEO to take part in various NEO activities. Users can find publications ranging from employment policy measures (refunding of contributions to employers, educational programmes, public works, and so forth) to simple guidelines on the filling-in of job applications. Users are also informed via electronic mail of all important changes in the labour market.

The NEO also makes use of the intranet for internal communications. Its Windows NT server provides the following information to NEO employees: current events; calendar of important meetings; reports; the NEO in-house magazine; official documents; invitations for applications; and instructions.

Assessment

Slovenia is an example of where a recently established employment service has made great strides in automating its labour exchange function. Use of the Internet is widespread in Slovenia, and the homepage of the NEO is one of the 40 most visited sites in the country. Research indicates that in one year alone, three-quarters of all companies with internet access occasionally used the site to look for staff; a tenth of these were frequent visitors. The NEO has collaborated with the University of Ljubljana throughout this developmental process, and annual research into internet use by the University now includes questions on employment. The data generated by this will be incorporated into NEO planning.

Future development

The NEO intends to further develop its internet activities in the following directions:

- transfer of NEO pages to a Windows NT/IIS platform;
- provision of daily updated job vacancies for the whole of Slovenia;
- improvement of the jobseekers' notice board, of employee selection and of communication between employees and employers;
- improvement of user interfaces;
- development and introduction of new intelligent agents; and
- enabling of employers to announce job vacancies via the Internet.

The NEO will also carry out intensive development of the intranet and intend to use it alongside electronic mail as the organization's information backbone.

The Slovenian NEO web site address in English can be found at the following address: http://www.ess.gov.si/English/elementi-okvirjev/F-DirectorGreeting.htm.

Source: J. Glazer: *Use of the Internet in the work of the national employment office of Slovenia*, Paper presented at WAPES Workshop, Washington, DC, December 1998 or @ http://www.icesa.org/articles/template.cfm?results_art_filename=slov.htm.

Annex IV.6 Sweden: Customer self-service systems on the Internet

Starting year: 1995

Problem to be solved

In Sweden, as in many other countries, the ordinary citizen no longer regards the PES as mainly a government authority but as a service enterprise. This means that there must be new standards of availability and in particular, the service must be available at times convenient for customers rather than just for providers. Customers also want promptness in service delivery. When there is information to hand, the PES is expected to make it accessible quickly and not just when it suits the working situation of the PES. Customers also want to have more control over information, with less filtering by public officials. In short, the general public demands improved quality and a clear customer orientation from the PES. When these demands are not fulfilled, customers turn to private sector alternatives.

In order to meet the challenge of demand for improved services and higher quality (despite ever-increasing workloads), it is clear that the PES must find new ways of producing and delivering services and must systematically use all available new technologies. Self-service information can be offered in ways that are rational both for producers and customers, thus freeing up resources for services that still need to be staff delivered. The Swedish PES has chosen to achieve this by providing an open placement system delivered via the Internet which is available to all actors in the labour market.

Approach

The Swedish PES open information system can thus far be presented as a "service family" with three generations. Chronologically speaking these can be represented by: a) the Job Bank; b) the Jobseeker Bank; c) the Recruitment Assistant.

The Job Bank contains all open vacancies notified to the PES, in other words the same information that is contained on the PES internal computer system (AF-90). The Job Bank is updated daily from the AF-90. This system was very easy to adapt to an internet-based application and the implementation was quick and smooth. The Job Bank is a simple information retrieval system, where applicants can search for vacancies by occupation or by region/municipality. It has a very quick response time and is very easy to use, even for inexperienced web users. It was introduced in November 1995 and has become one of the most visited web sites in Sweden. The Job Bank currently (in September 1998) has 40,000 visitors per day and about 250,000 unique visitors each month, not including those jobseekers who access the Job Bank from PES customer workstations. The number of visitors during a month corresponds to about 6 per cent of the total workforce in Sweden.

As a result of the popularity of the Job Bank, the labour market board (AMS) has decided not to change its basic concepts of simplicity, promptness and user-friendliness. However, supplementary functionality is added intermittently. A jobseeker can apply for a job directly by using an e-mail function (for employers with e-mail addresses) and an employer can notify a vacancy to the PES via the Job Bank. It is also possible to include information about how many times an advertisement has been read and to link a company's homepage directly to the vacancy advertisement. The AMS is now developing a standard format for presenting a company to potential job applicants so that employers without homepages can display photos about the working environment and so forth.

The second generation in the internet service family is represented by the Jobseeker Bank. Here jobseekers can register information in a database – their qualifications, experience and so forth. They can choose to expose their identity or remain anonymous until they have been identified by a particular employer. Employers can, by creating a structured search profile (with specifics about education, vocational experience, skills and competencies), pick out the jobseekers that match their demands. The Jobseeker Bank is much more sophisticated than the Job Bank and is a matching system as advanced as that used by PES staff. It is a highly accurate search system, which enables employers to use very specific search criteria to find a special combination of skills from among a large number of potential applicants. The core of the search system is a set of around 1,200 vocational profiles, including a total of about 6,500 specific competencies or qualifications which are the main search elements in the matching system.

The Jobseeker Bank is open to all jobseekers who register with the system by giving their names and addresses. The registration is confirmed by mail, which includes a password and the search elements registered by the jobseeker. The Jobseeker Bank is also open to all employers registered with the PES internal system. For first-time visitors, registration can be done through the bank. Private employment agencies can also use the system. Employers receive confirmation in the same way as jobseekers. The jobseeker controls all information about himself or herself (what information should be exposed without special permission, anonymity and so forth) and can delete all information concerning himself or herself at any time. For reasons of personal confidentiality, no information about jobseekers is linked to or can be transferred to other systems. For the same reason, jobseekers do not give their social security number to the system. In the system, they are identified by the special ID created by the system itself. In September 1998, the Jobseeker Bank had about 60,000 jobseekers and 5,000 employers using the system and the numbers are increasing steadily. Every day, about 3,000 jobseekers and 200 employers use the service.

The third generation of the PES internet placement/recruitment service family is now under development. This generation, with the working name, "Recruitment Assistant", will offer further administrative services in the recruitment process. It will make it possible for employers and jobseekers to get into a customized dialogue once a preliminary selection of vacancies or applicants has been made from the Job Bank or the Jobseeker Bank. Employers will be able to create their own questionnaires to be filled in by interested applicants and make a second and more specific selection among candidates based on the results of this interaction. The Recruitment Assistant is planned to be introduced in the first half of 1999. Together with the Job Bank and the Jobseeker Bank, it will form a comprehensive and coherent set of placement/recruitment services available on the Internet. The introductory period for this PES open customer service, which will have more daily visitors than ordinary PES offices, will be less than four years: from mid-1995 to mid-1999.

To support users of the PES internet services, a toll-free helpdesk function has been established and those jobseekers who do not have access to the Internet can use the special customer workstations at the PES offices. All staff are expected to master the Internet service systems and a special computerized training programme has been developed to this end. The increasing use of self-service systems will gradually make it possible to relieve staff from information service duties and make it possible to devote more staff time to tasks where personal contact is necessary. In the long run, new ways of organizing the PES must be developed.

Assessment

The implementation of the Job Bank went very smoothly. The reason for this is that an application already existed which was very easy to adapt to a web format. The dramatic increase in the number of visitors has been largely met by upgrading hardware. The development and implementation of the Jobseeker Bank, however, has met with significant problems. These include the following:

*   The technical environment is new and changing very quickly. It is tempting for the developers to use state-of-the-art technology and as the PES cannot control the technical platforms of the users, there is a risk that many potential users have equipment which does not match the requirements of the application. During the trial period, there were many complaints from jobseekers who had trouble running the application.
*   The efficiency of the matching process is crucial for the Jobseeker Bank, which is intended to handle very large volumes of applicants while at the same time handling the specific demands from employers. To ensure that jobseekers and employers use the same terminology to express vocational qualifications, it was deemed necessary to wait for the development of a vocational profiling system to be used in the internal staff-operated matching system.
*   To be successful, the Jobseeker Bank needs to strike a balance between the volume of jobseekers and volume of employers using the system. It turned out that the number of jobseekers was growing much faster than that of employers. Much emphasis must therefore be placed on how to promote the services with employers.

The immediate success of the internet services can be measured by the number of jobseekers and employers using the systems. AMS has set up quantitative targets for the near future: 80,000 daily visitors to the Job Bank; 25,000 registered employers and 200,000 jobseekers visiting the Jobseeker Bank before the end of 1999. The quantitative targets must be complemented with measures focusing on end results Ultimately, this means how many jobseekers actually get a job and how many employers hire jobseekers with the help of the AMS internet services.

Source: Swedish Labour Market Board: *Customer internet self-service system* (Geneva, ILO, 1998; mimeographed).

Annex IV.7 United Kingdom: Employment Service Direct – A telephone jobs hotline

Starting year: 1999

Objectives

A jobs hotline has been launched by the United Kingdom employment service to help unemployed people find work. For the price of a local phone call, unemployed jobseekers are able to call and immediately be put in touch with employment service advisers who can inform them about a range of local employer vacancies and other vacancies throughout the United Kingdom.

Approach

Employment Service Direct advisers have access to a database of over 316,000 job vacancies and can put callers in touch with an employer or arrange a job interview. The hotline is open from 9.00 to 18.00 from Monday to Friday, and from 9.00 to 13.00 on Saturdays. There is also a telephonic text system for people with hearing difficulties. This jobs hotline facilitates job-hunting for people looking for work and is available to anyone who is unemployed, whether or not they are claiming benefit. In its first six months, this new service helped 30,000 jobseeker clients to find work. According to a survey, 98% of users found it easy to get through and found the advisers polite and helpful.

Source: European Employment Observatory Mutual Information System on Employment Policies (MISEP): *Policies, No. 65* (Berlin, European Commission, Spring 1999).

Annex IV.8 United States: America's Career Kit (ACK) – Internet employment services system

Starting year: 1993

Better quality and greater efficiency in employment services.

Approach

The system known as America's Career Kit (ACK) comprises three interlinked web sites: a) America's Job Bank, b) America's Career Infonet and c) America's Learning Exchange.

a) America's Job Bank

America's Job Bank (AJB) http://www.ajb.org, is a computerized network which helps employers and jobseekers find each other. It has become the most recognized national product of the employment services providing employers with the widest available distribution of their job openings, and jobseekers with the largest pool of active job opportunities available anywhere. The job openings and resumés found in AJB are available on computer systems in public libraries, colleges and universities, high schools, shopping malls, in transition offices on military bases worldwide and in other places of public access such as one-stop career centres. Most of the jobs listed in AJB are full-time and the majority are in the private sector. The job openings come from all over the country and represent all types of work: from professional and technical to blue-collar; from management to clerical and sales. Likewise, the resumés listed in AJB contain candidates with a wide range of skills and experience in all types of employment fields. There is no charge either to employers who list their job vacancies, or to jobseekers who utilize AJB to locate employment. The services provided by AJB and state employment service programmes are funded by unemployment insurance taxes paid by employers.

b) America's Career Infonet

America's Career InfoNet (ACINET), http://www.acinet.org/acinet, links to a comprehensive source of occupational information which allows people to find labour market information (LMI) such as which jobs are growing and which are declining, and what are the prevailing rates of pay. The following is a list of the types of information that are available:

- Career Exploration. This site navigation tool for ACK was created to help workers: a) identify their needs; b) learn how elements of ACK such as AJB, ACINet, and America's Learning Exchange (ALX) can help them meet their needs; and c) link them to appropriate features of AJB, ACINet, and ALX or link them to other appropriate resources. In particular, it helps workers explore options for work and learning; gain skills for getting a job or getting a better job; find financial assistance for education and training; find job-search resources and services to help getting a job; identify potential jobs and employers.
- General Outlook. This provides information on the employment outlook, prevailing wages, the education required for occupations plus economic and demographic information.
- Wages and Trends Occupation Search. This provides national data on specific occupational information such as wages and trends.
- Employer Search. This provides general information about possibilities. This search does not provide job listings, but it gives contact information for individual employers.

- State Profile Search. This provides demographic information, occupation rankings and information on resources at state level.
- Career Resource Library. This groups information under four main categories: occupational information; job-search aids; job and resumé banks; and relocation information.

c) America's Learning Exchange

America's Learning Exchange (ALX), http://www.alx.org/, is designed to allow people to find the training they need. It provides different categories of users with access to a marketplace of available training and providers, allows users to leave training specifications in a special marketplace where training vendors can bid to fulfil training needs, and allows employers to list courses they have developed and are willing to license or sell. ALX offers access to four specialized databases:

- Tools of the Trade: resources for workforce professionals.
- Environmental Career Center: jobs and information related to careers in environmental and hazardous waste.
- Federal Learning Exchange: education and training resources for the federal workforce.
- Network: shared curriculum and training for use by Community Colleges.

In addition to the universal access that the Internet provides for jobseekers and employers alike, this internet employment services system is also an integral component of the "bricks-and-mortar" one-stop centres. The average one-stop centre will have between 10 and 20 terminals connected to the Internet and can be used on a self-service basis. It has been found that self-service has freed up resources that can be devoted to people in need of personalized services; it is a way of allowing "self-selection" to take place. It also allows the PES to become more universal with internet access.

America's Job Bank is maintained by the AJB service center in Albany, New York. It is currently operated under a federal grant from the employment and training administration of the United States Department of Labor. It is governed by the PELEX Committee, a federal/state partnership workgroup formed in late 1997 to oversee the implementation and roll-out of the system. An intensive national informational campaign was launched in the autumn of 1999. It is designed to further establish AJB as a leading national brand through the use of a "Dream Job" theme. Awareness materials will appear in national magazines such as *Black Enterprise, Business Week, Fast Company, Popular Mechanics* and *Rolling Stone*. Other components of the marketing initiative include an aggressive outreach to college graduates, the creation of billboards/ signs and assistance with coordinated state marketing plans.

Evaluation

The use of AJB is growing tremendously. In September 1999, there were 253 million hits on this site, compared to 43.5 million hits for the month of September 1998. Between November 1–4 alone, there were 35 million hits, nearly equal to the total number of hits for the entire month of November 1998. The number of jobs posted on AJB increased from 960, 640 in April 1999, to 1,409,649 in November 1999 – an increase of more than 30 per cent. The number of jobseekers more than doubled during the same period, that is from 584,536 in April 1999 to 1,407,972 in November 1999. It also appears that more highly educated customers are using AJB: the percentage of college-educated jobseekers registering has increased from 26 per cent to 42 per cent since the summer of 1999. This increased use of AJB is attributed both to the extensive national marketing campaign as well as to increased marketing at the state level.

Sources: (1) J. W. Vollman: "Centralised information technology and decentralised employment service: A successful combination in the United States", in OECD: *Decentralising employment policy: New trends and challenges – The Venice Conference* (Paris, OECD, 1999), pp. 95–99.

Annex IV.9 France: *Fichier historique* – A history file of jobseekers registered at the ANPE

Starting year: 1993

Objectives

The history file, or *fichier historique* (FH) is a component of a statistical tool entitled *Amélioration des Études des Demandeurs d'Emploi* (AEDE) or "improvement in jobseeker studies". This tool has been designed to compile and analyse the jobseeker statistics of the French public employment service (ANPE). It responds in various ways to the needs of the ANPE (for example, regarding its network) and those of its partners, particularly the public authorities. It is also used to help design and implement employment policy measures. It is an analytical, evaluation and simulation tool, one that supports the intensification of ANPE partnerships with other organizations.

Approach

The FH covers in succession each event affecting jobseekers from initial registration with the ANPE: the jobseeker profile (personal details and qualifications); the job request (or previous requests); data on part-time working; information about the services and benefits provided by the ANPE; and information on corresponding training plans and periods. The FH is thus an exhaustive databank encompassing all the data relating to ANPE activities and to the labour market. Under the system, files are stored for at least three years. When jobseekers' requests for employment are cancelled, their files are stored in the FH for 37 months before being cancelled and archived. Provided that at least one event is recorded during this three-year period, the file is retained indefinitely. By means of longitudinal analyses, the FH enables the ANPE to gain greater knowledge of current and former jobseekers, and of the labour market in general. A more detailed knowledge of jobseekers enables the operational capacity of the partnership network to be increased, for instance by improving the quality of the services rendered to firms, and thus to jobseekers as well, by means of a better selection of candidates.

The FH enables the ANPE to refine its evaluation of the impact of the employment measures administered by it and of the benefits provided to participants and benefit recipients respectively. In this way it can orient the content of the services (financial support, practical training, vocational training) to the characteristics of jobseekers and to measure changes in the services provided by the ANPE. The FH also enables the impact of various action scenarios on vocational training or employment to be anticipated by developing simulation models. This enables priority groups or regions to be better targeted and measures to be defined and distributed more favourably. Operational concepts can be defined more precisely with the help of the FH. In addition to its technical features, the FH constitutes an important tool for the maintenance and intensification of ANPE partnerships.

Source: European Employment Observatory Mutual Information System on Employment Policies (MISEP): *Policies, No. 56* (Berlin, European Commission, Winter 1996).

Annex IV.10 The Netherlands: The *Kansmeter* – A new instrument for the administrative intake of jobseekers

Starting year: 1999

Background

In 1997, a new Act on the public employment service was enacted to improve the balance between the supply and the demand for labour, in particular by providing services for hard-to-place jobseekers and hard-to-fill vacancies. The emphasis was on delivering services to jobseekers in need of job-search assistance, especially the long-term unemployed, ethnic minorities and women re-entering the labour market.

Objectives

A new four-phase model classification and its new instrument for the administrative intake of jobseekers, the *Kansmeter*, were developed in order to obtain a realistic and unambiguous view of the chances of jobseekers in the labour market. The *Kansmeter* was introduced on 1 January 1999 and offers the jobseeker an idea of what is needed to obtain employment. At the same time, it offers the possibility to tailor services to the needs of jobseekers. It has been applied by employment offices and the centres for work and benefits, the latter being the space where the employment offices, municipalities and social security agencies cooperate.

Approach

The first step in the four-phase model assesses the chances and the shortest route to work or the so-called "distance from the labour market" for the jobseeker. If the chances of finding work are high, the jobseeker is assigned to Phase 1; if the chances are low in the short term but there is a possibility of improving these in a relative short period by training or work experience (in other words attain a sufficient level of employability), the jobseeker is assigned to Phases 2 or 3. Jobseekers deemed to be at a great remove from the labour market are assigned to Phase 4. Those in Phase 4 are unlikely to be able to participate in paid employment for the time being. Often these people suffer from problems which cannot be solved by the public employment service, for example people with social, psychological or psychiatric problems. They are often referred to the services of social welfare institutions.

The aim of phasing is to deliver the services which are most suitable to the individual situation of the jobseeker and by doing so, reduce the period of unemployment benefits. Each phase is related to a package of services and instruments. Phasing is not only an efficient way of assisting jobseekers to improve their employability, it also offers jobseekers the opportunity to get a better feeling for their possibilities in the labour market. Phasing also improves the transparency of jobseeker files and offers better opportunities for planning activities, for allocating resources and for monitoring and controlling operations.

The process of phasing begins with the administrative intake process using the *Kansmeter*. It gives the consultant and jobseekers alike an indication of the possibilities or (provisional) impossibilities in the labour market by classifying jobseekers in one of the four phases or in as a "phase yet to be determined". It is also an instrument for reviewing the situation of the jobseekers at a later stage. The *Kansmeter* contains a standardized questionnaire for the jobseeker which covers the following: work situation; reason for registration; impediments (health situation or other); work experience; and profession or occupation. There is also a section for job prospect assessment and an explanatory note for the officer registering the jobseeker. The officer assesses the responses in terms of the professional profile, the qualification profile and the job-search profile, and then determines a score. The core element of the *Kansmeter* is to calculate the realistic prospects of jobseekers in the labour market. The result is the sum of the statistical perspectives of the occupation sought and the extent of relevant education, work experience and personal skills of the jobseeker.

The outcome of this process is that the jobseeker is either assigned to one of the four phases or a development plan is drawn up of the services needed to meet his or her needs. The latter could include for instance, vocational training, job-search assistance, vocational guidance or re-integration plans for the hard-to-place unemployed. All the outcomes are registered. The *Kansmeter* will be integrated into the new information system to be implemented in 1999.

Phasing is not only a question of technique but also one of policy. To assess the chances of jobseekers requires professionalism, knowledge of the working of the labour market, an ability to observe and to interpret the data of jobseekers and also proficiency in interviewing techniques. Phasing also depends upon the relationship between services to be delivered and the relevance of these services to the improvement of employability in the labour market. The public employment service is considered to be a service organization and strives to deliver services which contribute to the improvement of the chances of those jobseekers who need help obtaining employment. It is being transformed from a "problem owner" into a "problem solver" and will be assessed by its performance in solving labour market problems.

Evaluation

Since the four-phase model was planned to be implemented in January 1999, no evaluation has yet been conducted.

Source: T. van Keulen: *Targeting services towards the needs of jobseekers,* Unpublished Paper presented at the WAPES Workshop, Washington, DC, 9–10 November, 1998.

Annex IV.11 France: New tools and services for job-search assistance

Starting year: 1998

Objectives

The aim of these new measures was to respond to the needs of as many jobseekers as possible by:

• developing instruments and services adapted to the expectations and needs of job-seekers;

- furthering internal implementation and suggestions;
- promoting the self-evaluation and self-determination of jobseekers; and
- ensuring a rapid response by means of tools placed at the disposal of jobseekers and by means of workshops that are open almost permanently.

Approach

1. Tools placed at the disposal of jobseekers in the free-access zone

Free-access zones are being enhanced by upgrading the availability of:

- Tools. These include Minitel, software for drawing up CVs, photocopiers, telephones and notice boards with job and training offers.
- Self-service information. This service is to be enriched by the following elements:
  - information leaflets about the labour market;
  - advice leaflets providing information about how to use a tool for a documentary source (Kompass, ROME, offers, telephones and so forth);
  - action guides which provide jobseekers capable of autonomous job-search activities with basic information;
  - "know-more dossiers" which are distributed by the staff of the free-access zone for use on the premises and which provide more detailed information on topics sketched out in the action guides such as interview techniques; drafting of CVs; writing of application letters; making speculative applications; making connections; finding information in the press; or looking for work in Europe

2. Types of service within the framework of intermittent support

Intermittent support is a service level in which it is particularly important for quality, quantity and speed of service provision to be combined. It is to be further developed in local employment offices by progressively implementing individual interviews, workshops and evaluations.

A. *Interviews*

There are three types of interviews. First, the vocational interview, which is held on registration, aims to define the job-search more precisely, in most cases to initiate a first concrete action and to determine, where appropriate, the date of the next contact. Second, the follow-up interview aims to renew the dialogue with jobseekers after a period which is determined by the local employment office. Third, the "contact-establishing" interview aims to ensure that jobseekers fit the criteria agreed with the employer. It also helps jobseekers to ensure that their applications are successfully completed.

B. Workshops

Modular individualized workshops (such as individualized job-search workshops) are open more or less permanently and offer support from an adviser. Workshops are used to perform all the following tasks:

- identifying one's strengths and job-search difficulties;
- identifying one's skills;
- targeting potential employers;
- drawing up a CV;
- making a speculative application;
- writing a letter in response to a job advertisement;
- looking for work using one's connections;
- preparing for a recruitment interview;
- looking for training in order to achieve one's career project;
- identifying personal strengths with respect to one's career project;
- looking for information on a given occupation;
- verifying the pertinence of one's career project;
- drawing up an action plan to implement one's career project;
- using job advertisements;
- organizing job-search activities;
- having telephone conversations with employers;
- choosing one's "look";
- familiarization with recruitment tests;
- being successful during the probation period; and
- setting up a company or becoming self-employed.

Access to the workshops is free and participation can be initiated by an adviser or on the jobseeker's own initiative. Individuals participating on their own initiative are to be offered the best possible conditions. The publicity work of the employment office, the organization of notice boards and even the names given to the workshops are important elements in the efforts to make jobseekers aware of the workshops and overcome their "distance" from them.

3. Guidance

Guidance by employment office staff aims to define an individual re-integration project, to ensure the success of job-search activities and where necessary, to follow up after recruitment. Guidance towards employment is characterized by the following features:

- having a named staff member as partner as this is indispensable for individual guidance;
- regular contacts (at least twice for month) between this staff member and the jobseeker;

- the voluntary participation of the jobseeker and the formalization of two-way commitments between the adviser and the jobseeker;
- a fixed duration (between three and six months); and
- a joint identification of the targets to be reached in the course of the guidance period.

Assessment

Surveys of customer satisfaction and auditing from external observers will be undertaken to assess the quality of services provided by the local PES offices. If these meet internal quality control standards, they will be awarded a national certificate of internal quality control. It is expected that 770 local offices will have received the national certificate of internal quality control by early 2000.

Sources: (1) European Employment Observatory Mutual Information System on Employment Policies (MISEP): *Policies, No. 62* (Berlin, European Commission, Summer 1998). (2) ILO: *Les services publics de l'emploi: Le cas de la France* (Geneva, ILO, 1998; mimeographed). Additional information, 1999.

Annex IV.12 United States: Integrated menu of employer services – The case of the Racine County Workforce Development Centre (WDC) in Wisconsin

Starting year: 1996

Objectives

The objectives were twofold: to renew the importance placed on employer services and to present employers with an integrated menu of services and a single point of contact.

Approach

Among a staff of 43 working in WDC, nine are assigned to the employer services team (EST). The team is split into five account managers and four representatives providing specific services linked to various partners in the WDC. The EST team systematically contacts the 4,000 registered employers in the county. During March 1998, the staff had contacted 2,700 and as a result, generated 1,200 active employer accounts. The procedure is to first send a letter, then call to make a brief presentation of the menu of services available from the WDC. The team invites employers to come to the WDC, or otherwise they mail materials to the employer. The team also produces a quarterly newsletter that is distributed to employers.

The WDC menu of services, which is developed in consultation with an employer advisory board, consists of various offerings. Overall, the state JobNet vacancy database is the most popular service for employers. The employer services staff do not generally provide placement or job-broking assistance directly to employers, but give them access to the database instead. Upon the request of an employer, they screen potential applicants using objective criteria, but this option is not commonly used.

The second most popular service is the use of the WDC for on site recruitment and interviews. Other popular services include business development support (information about various local, state and federal business incentive programmes) and provision of labour law information. The team also offers additional fee-charging services including an annual job fair, periodic mini-job fairs and assessment services such as the testing of job applicants. Fees are set to cover the cost of materials and staff time.

The team also makes employer referrals to other WDC services, including apprenticeships, short-term training for specific skill shortages and customized training for incumbent workers. They also make referrals to outside service providers who work partly on a fee-charging basis, for example in relation to customized job training.

Source: OECD: *The public employment service in the United States* (Paris, OECD, 1999).

Annex IV.13 United States: Successful state practices in job-broking – An assessment study

Starting year: 1996

Objectives

In the mid-1990s, a study of employment service job-broking was jointly designed and undertaken by the Center for Employment Security, Education and Research (CESER), the Ohio Bureau of Employment Services (OBES) and the United States Department of Labor. The purpose of this study was to help states tailor public labour exchanges to meet their own needs. The objectives of the study were the following: to describe the range of job-broking features currently being used by states; to identify the strengths and weaknesses of those features; and to establish criteria for evaluating the suitability of alternative features where additional information about alternatives could be obtained

It should be noted that this study was published in 1996, before the widespread implementation of America's Job Bank (AJB) which is described in Annex IV.8. Rather than using traditional job-broking procedures for closed vacancy systems,

United States PES staff are now much more likely to be redeployed to assist jobseekers in PES resource rooms or to use the Job Bank and other job-search assistance tools. The conclusions of the study, however, influenced the design of the self-service AJB and may be useful for other public employment services when assessing the merits of open and assisted job-broking systems.

Approach

The report discusses options, strengths/weaknesses, and assessment criteria in the six major areas of the job-broking process: 1) staff search of registrant pools and job orders; 2) jobseeker registration and service; 3) notifying jobseekers that they have been matched to a job order; 4) browsing of job orders by jobseekers; 5) developing and maintaining lists of job orders; and 6) obtaining feedback on job-broking operations.

For the above decision-making areas, the report includes the options available to state employment security agencies; the advantages and disadvantages of choosing each option; the set of criteria for evaluating the options; and the conclusions about particular choices. In addition, a profile is included for each state which identifies the specific processes used by that state. Each profile lists unique features or planned improvements/changes and also a contact person for additional information.

Key conclusions

1. Staff search techniques

Three major types of systems were examined:

- traditional systems that primarily search on occupational titles;
- skill-list systems that primarily search checklists containing details of job-related skills filled out by jobseekers; and
- free-form text systems that search a broad range of worker and job characteristics selected by well-trained staff.

Key conclusion: No one system is perfect. States are moving towards hybrid systems that combine the best features of skill lists and text search systems.

2. Jobseeker registration

Three types of registration procedures were examined:

- paper forms filled out by jobseekers that are later keyed in by staff;
- staff interviews and paperless information entry; and
- direct computer entry keyed in by jobseekers whether these be scanned forms or data transferred from computerized records.

Key conclusion: Both computerized self-registration and the use of machine-readable forms produce high quality information, particularly when used with skill lists. Such systems also save a lot of money because the cost of equipment is low and the savings in staff time enormous. However, old style paper forms and staff interviews are needed to supplement special situations such as aiding individuals with disabilities who cannot use automated equipment or when providing information for people who live in areas too remote for office visits.

3. Notifying jobseekers

Three alternative notification methods were examined:

- phone notification by staff;
- mail notification by staff; and
- automated phone notification with mail back-up.

Key conclusion: Inexpensive, automated telephone-notification systems are readily available, and are easily integrated into job-broking systems. They save huge amounts of staff time when replacing staff telephone-notification systems.

4. Browsing of job orders by jobseekers

There is little variation in the way computerized browsing systems work. Basically, they involve the following steps: first, computer screens present jobseekers with options concerning the types of job listings they want to view; second, additional screens display all listings with the attributes designated by the jobseeker in a compact form (often a single line); third, jobseekers select those jobs to which they would like to be referred and are either given contact information by staff after being screened, or contact information is provided with the listing.

Key conclusions: The study came up with three main conclusions. First, because there is substantial value in getting a good feel for the job market and jobseekers can view thousands of one-line job descriptions in a ten-minute session, an ideal system would allow jobseekers to narrow an initial search by general occupation and general location to produce a relatively long list of openings. Although not essential, it would be helpful in giving jobseekers the option to further narrow down searches to specific locations, industries, wage levels and openings received since their last search. Second, employers should be encouraged to try using unsuppressed listings, but satisfaction should be monitored and staff screening be offered as an option. Third, it is the view that highly effective browsing systems can be developed using either mainframe computers or PCs. Having a large number of terminals placed in local offices and remote sites is of great importance, and makes a far greater difference in labour exchange effectiveness than the type of computer used to support the terminal.

5. Developing and maintaining lists of job orders

The most common way orders are placed in every state is by telephone discussions with staff. Faxing orders is also common. In contrast to other major areas, there appears to be very little to be gained in modifying the way jobs are listed and filled. The most commonly discussed technical changes involve giving employers the option to directly enter job orders and second, allowing them to search applicant files. Direct entry of job openings by employers appears to save only a little staff time as usually, staff must still review the order to perform the match and then often contact the employer to improve the listing. Key issues with employers browsing registrant files are: a) respecting the privacy of registrants, in particular preventing employers from determining which of their own employees may be looking for work: b) suppressing information that would permit inappropriate discrimination; and c) maintaining existing ranking systems such as giving veterans preference. The cost of dealing with these problems would probably be high and once all the restrictions are applied, there might be too little information available for employers to isolate suitable candidates. One area where employer browsing has promise, however, is in recruiting workers for jobs that are hard to fill because of their technical complexity. Since most of those jobs offer high pay and relocation expenses, having a national Talent Bank of resumés available for employer searches makes sense.

Key conclusion: Implementation of the planned national Talent Bank could make it unnecessary for states to develop independent employer browsing systems.

6. Obtaining feedback

States vary tremendously in the collection and use of labour exchange information. Some states use unemployment insurance wage records to produce highly accurate placement statistics, to conduct surveys to assess customer satisfaction, or to set goals at the local office and individual staff level. But some states do only the minimum necessary to comply with federal reporting requirements. There is wide agreement, however, that federal reporting is unduly burdensome and fails to provide adequate feedback.

Key conclusion: Less burdensome feedback systems are needed. Periodic surveys would be more than adequate substitutes for the current ETA–9002 tracking system. In addition to eliminating the need to register every browser, surveys could measure the value of information provided by the employment service that does not lead to referrals. In addition, it could produce large savings by making it unnecessary to obtain and store a lot of information only used for federal reporting.

Summary conclusions

The features of an improved job-broking system that would both improve service quality and greatly reduce cost are:

- Computer-aided browsing in office lobbies that permits a search of a broad category of jobs and allows the option to narrow the search.
- Automated self-registration that includes the use of skill checklists and the drawing of information from computerized files.
- Machine-readable registration forms that include skill checklists
- Automated telephone notification systems.
- Requesting telephone numbers where notification messages can be left on answering machines or with individuals likely to be home during business hours.
- Computerized staff-matching systems.

In addition, computer-aided browsing and registration at a wide variety of remote sites would greatly improve service quality but would require an additional investment.

Source: Center for Employment Security, Education and Research (CESR): Unpublished Paper presented at the ICESA, 61st Annual Conference, Juneau, 22–25 September, 1997.

Annex IV.14 Sweden: Customer workstations – Self-service for jobseekers

Starting year: 1997

Objectives

Specially designed computer workstations intended for use by jobseekers have been installed at employment offices. From these customer workstations, an unaided jobseeker can carry out various tasks such as enrolling as a jobseeker and searching for job vacancies by using the labour market administration's self-service computer programmes. In addition, jobseekers can find out about various labour market policy programmes and so forth.

Approach

The following applications are available on the customer workstations:

- The Jobseeker Bank. This allows applicants to introduce themselves, their skills and experience, and then be matched against the requirements specified by employers reporting job vacancies.
- The Temporary Replacement Bank. This allows people looking for short-term jobs to introduce themselves to employers.
- The Vacancy Bank. This describes job vacancies.
- The Occupational Guide. This contains facts about 500 occupations, partly in multimedia form. It also contains a test on the basis of which applicants can be directed to jobs that match their interests and preferences. These self-service programmes (with the exception of the Occupational Guide) are also available via the Internet.

In addition, jobseekers can access job vacancies outside Sweden, for example in the Nordic countries, in EU member States, in the United States and in Canada. Customer workstations also provide an internet connection, but the degree of internet access is determined by the office manager using a flexible menu system.

A customer workstation is more than just a computer with special self-service programmes; it is an article of furniture with an in-built PC, display screen, keyboard and trackball and does not even look like a computer. In other words, jobseekers who are unfamiliar with computers will not be deterred by it. The number of workstations per employment office at present varies from one to twenty. A customer workstation can serve between about ten and fifteen people every day. One potential problem in this is that customers can sit at workstations for a very long periods. Those enrolling in the Jobseeker Bank for example, tend to take 45 minutes to do so.

The customer workstation system means that thanks to the unique system of software used, virtually all available information can be accessed on the Internet while at the same time, access to sensitive information can be restricted. Economically speaking, the customer workstation is definitely cheaper than a stand-alone computer with an internet connection because the customer workplace is connected with the labour market administration's internal network. The cost of a customer workstation is SEK 1,950 per month no matter how many hours it is used during the course of a day. Customer workstations have the effect of relieving placement officers of certain duties, thereby enabling them to concentrate on and improve the quality of tasks that require a more personalized service. The individual jobseeker has the advantage of being able to influence the information given and sought in connection with placement. (For a more detailed description of the design of the entire Swedish self-service system on the Internet, see Annex IV.6).

Source: European Employment Observatory Mutual Information System on Employment Policies (MISEP): *Policies, No. 61* (Berlin, European Commission, Spring 1998).

Annex IV.15 Denmark: Local labour market monitoring

Starting year: 1995

Objectives

The overall aim of labour market monitoring is to establish a basis for initiatives to ensure a flexible labour market in general and to counter negative trends in particular. The Danish national and public labour market monitoring system was established in the period 1975–79 and has been subject to continuous adaptation and refinement ever since.

Approach

Independent monitoring activities are conducted both at regional and national level in order to increase the current knowledge of developments in the labour market. However, national monitoring efforts are to a large extent based on regional monitoring activities and regional analyses. At the regional level, the PES collects information through contacts with a wide range of partners. For this it maintains a permanent contact with the following: enterprises; jobseekers; people applying for training; regional and local authorities; institutions for education and vocational training; trade associations; unemployment funds; and authorities in charge of industrial and political matters. On the basis of these contacts, it presents monitoring results in the form of analyses, forecasts and suggestions for interventions to the 14 regional labour market councils which are responsible for planning and coordinating policy initiatives concerning the labour market. The results obtained regionally are passed on to the national level, that is to the Directorate-General for employment, placement and vocational training. This level is in charge of professional support and the development of regional labour market monitoring. It presents labour market information to the national labour market council, enabling the latter to advise the Ministry of Labour in matters of planning for future labour market policy.

In cooperation with the regions, the national office has defined an overall monitoring plan which stipulates the framework and the frequency of the monitoring activities of the regions and also the products to be used in the monitoring. The national office is responsible for the overall development of concepts, methods, tools and for the coordination of the monitoring activities at the national level. The regions receive national guidelines for their monitoring work, and the national office organizes meetings with the regions on professional, technical and methodological subjects. The regions may undertake special analysis projects, either by themselves or on behalf of the regional labour market council.

Such surveys are normally based on questionnaires and administrative register data. The regions have considerable freedom to choose the methods of analysis and projections as part of an active and targeted labour market policy at the regional level. In their regular, ongoing monitoring of the labour market, regions use data from administrative registers such as data on enterprises and unemployed people in the regional labour exchange system. They also use data from the National Bureau of Statistics on such aspects as population, education and training activities, size and structure of the work force, employment, unemployment and enterprises.

Source: P. Buchholt: *Labour market monitoring in Denmark: Ensuring flexibility* (Copenhagen, Arbejdsmarkedsstyrelsens, 1998).

Annex IV.16 Canada: Local labour market information

Starting year: early 1990s

Objectives

In the late 1980s, a significant shift began in the economy, with an increased demand for workers with high technology and newly evolving skills and also for part-time workers. More traditional occupations, previously required for the exploitation of Canada's natural resources, began to take a secondary role. At this time, Human Resources Development Canada (HRDC) began to experiment with the use of labour market information (LMI) systems in an attempt to provide both workers and employers with up-to-date LMI. The aim was to provide LMI – local, regional and national – to all Canadians to help them find and retain work.

Approach

HRDC made a major investment in this function, with a total of 229 staff involved in the LMI core function at the present time, distributed as follows: 14 staff at the national level, 25 staff at the regional (province and territory) level, and 190 staff at the local level. The LMI service is a universal service with a wide range of clients. Its primary purpose, however, is to offer all Canadians access to information which helps them find and retain work; this includes information on all local labour markets. Most major local offices have a LMI analyst, a person with knowledge and training in labour market statistics. Using a combination of operational data and local economic and demographic information, the analyst produces a variety of reports. The reports are used by workers and jobseekers to measure their job expectations against the conditions in the local labour market, to help employers develop recruiting strategies, to help other service providers work with their clients and very importantly, to help the local office plan its labour market strategies.

The reports include: occupational profiles and forecasts; community profiles; human resource profiles; industrial/sectoral profiles; wage and salary data and conditions of employment; vacancy and employment opportunities; labour market reviews and trends; occupational demand (high opportunity) lists; potential employer lists; major project updates; information about training providers; job-search tools; and newsflashes.

The reports produced by the analyst are disseminated in a variety of ways. Hard copy versions are available in local offices and are distributed to media outlets and labour market partners such as educational institutions. The information is also presented at computer kiosks both in local offices and in external sites such as libraries, shopping malls and schools. Increasingly, local offices are making the information available on the Internet. A good example of this is the site maintained by HRDC in the Niagara area. This site, which is listed with other Canadian and United States labour market information web sites in Annex VI.2, gives a wide range of information on jobs available, wages and working conditions and trends in the labour market. It also provides links to other HRDC regional and national sites.

Source: ILO: *The public employment service in Canada* (Geneva, ILO, 1998; mimeographed).

Annex IV.17 Finland: Activation and improvement of individual employment service processes (or job-search assistance) as part of a comprehensive labour market policy reform

Starting year: 1998

Problem

In the early 1990s, Finland faced a deep recession with its unemployment rate reaching 17.5 per cent in 1994. In the first quarter of 1999, the seasonally adjusted unemployment rate was about 10.5 per cent, which is still higher than the EU average rate. While unemployment decreased in general, the structural problems of the Finnish labour market became more and more critical during the period of economic recovery. At the same time as the number of unemployed young people was being halved, the number of skilled people among the unemployed declined rapidly. In addition, the number of people with the least employability among the unemployed increased. This called for new labour market policy measures, namely active job-search and training and education for the hard-to-place unemployed. It also called for reform in employment services.

Objectives

The reforms had two aims:

- Create a better functioning of the labour market and provide a more comprehensible, aggregate labour-market policy system.
- Improve labour market dynamics through the prevention of exclusion from the labour market.

The first objective was to be achieved by improving the processes of the employment services and by reforming active labour market policy measures; the second one was to be achieved by active measures and by better focusing of the employment services. In addition, some totally new measures such as a measure designed to help recruitment in the small and medium enterprises (SMEs) were introduced.

Approach

The reform was specifically intended to shorten the duration of unemployment periods, to increase the job-search activity of unemployed jobseekers, and to focus the activities of jobseekers and the PES alike more effectively towards re-employment in the open labour market. The following elements of service process were created for all PES offices and were to be implemented according to local circumstances:

- Fixed-term interview. This is a one-hour service where the jobseeker's circumstances and aims are discussed and job-search plans drawn up. Use of labour market adjustment measures in improving the jobseeker's employability is also considered in the interview.
- Job-search plan. This corresponds to the individual action plan defined by the indicators of the EU employment guidelines. It is created on the PES officer's computer, printed, and then both the jobseeker and PES officer sign the plan. Part of the job-search plan is to chart the actual skills of the jobseeker, not just his or her formal educational qualifications.
- Skill-mapping. Some forms of skill-mapping have been created in cooperation with the social partners so as to better define and describe skills. The information is stored in a computerized information system.
- Job-search manual. This is used to support the jobseeker in his or her own job-search. It consists of PES brochures and a job-search notebook in which the jobseeker can make notes on job-search activities, for example details of what happened, how active the job-search is and how it is progressing.

- Job-search training. This is given either on a job club basis organized by PES officers themselves or is part of labour market adjustment training courses. The aim is to increase knowledge of the labour market, job vacancies and job-search methods and in addition to these, to practise writing applications and contacting employers.

About 160 specialists were recruited by the PES offices in the main population centres to reform the employment services process and supplement the 2,400 customer service staff working both in the 15 regional employment and economic development centres and the 178 local offices.

Assessment

Feedback was gathered from the PES offices in 1999, about one year after the start of the implementation of the service process reform. The findings revealed the following.

- About 45 per cent of the PES offices reported that they had implemented the reforms reasonably well and about 5 per cent reported poor implementation.
- The most successful part of reform was the implementation of job clubs which had the most effect and the most positive client feedback.
- PES offices reported they had the least success implementing the job-search manual.
- Changes had taken place in jobseeker services mainly but not in employer services.
- The service offered by the PES had become more consistent, sustained and systematic according to many PES offices.
- The workload of PES officers was said to have increased and the duties had turned out to be more diversified, demanding and responsible.
- The reform seems to have had a mainly positive impact on the quality of employment services and some PES offices even reported that the image of PES had improved because of it.

In addition, a statistical monitoring system was set up in 1998 to produce information on fixed-term interviews, job-search training, post-training, labour-market status, and placements that were combined with subsidies. Besides these, job-search plans are also being monitored. Five evaluation studies on labour market policy reform were launched at the beginning of 1999 and were to be completed by June 2000. These studies are focusing on: the functioning and effects of job-search training; measures to help recruitment; the effectiveness of new active measures; the effectiveness of changes in the employment service process at local level; and the effects on labour market dynamics.

Source: H. Raisanen, I. Nio, E. Heinonen, M. Tuomaala (1999): *Comprehensive labour market policy reform: Presentation of good practice – Activation and individual employment service*, Peer review programme, 3–4 June 1999 (Helsinki, Ministry of Labour, 1999).

Annex IV.18 France: The notion of guidance in the context of the extended range of ANPE services

Definition of guidance

The notion of "guidance" (*accompagnement*) has gradually established itself in French policy-making discourse as a response to the policy measures implemented to solve the problem of exclusion and prevent its occurrence. Yet its meaning varies depending on the usage made of it by the public bodies dealing directly with the public in the fields of employment, vocational training or social policy. In general terms, it refers to professional practices targeted at individuals facing difficulties, the solution of which requires more than one-off support.

In contrast to one-off support, guidance requires profound and lasting intervention, in particular in order to enable the client to diagnose his or her own strengths and weaknesses and to provide him or her with advice and support. This requires time and a permanent adviser for each client within the public service in question. The diversity of the problems encountered, which often occur in combination (loss of employment and housing, lack of qualifications and resources, health problems, relationship or social difficulties), and the need to combine benefits and measures for which various public bodies often are responsible, all make it necessary to create partnerships organized at a level that is "close" to the individual in need of support.

Given that the most effective responses are those that the client identifies and implements him or herself, it is important that the guidance is based on a certain dynamism and commitment on the part of the client. In other words, guidance is generally characterized by its extended duration, the presence of a unique, readily available adviser, reciprocal efforts on the part of the service and the individual, and the organization of a partnership at a level close to the individual client.

Approach

Within the new range of services offered by the ANPE, guidance represents a service level that is clearly conceived as "guidance towards employment". If it emerges that a client's problems are not directly linked to employment and the labour market, the client is transferred to other authorities. For instance, people facing serious social difficulties can turn to a number of other organizations or programmes: the departmental office offering individual social guidance (*Accompagnement Social Individual* – ASI); benefit from services provided within the framework of the local occupational integration programmes (*Programmes locaux d'insertion professionnelle* – PLI); or they may be transferred to the "access to employment pathways" (*Trajets d'Acces à l'Emploi* – TRACE), judicial youth protection services or another public authority providing support and social integration. If in the course of counselling a clearly defined vocational training programme is identified, the client is put in touch with the association for adult vocational training (*Association pour la Formation Professionnelle des Adultes* – AFPA), which then assumes responsibility for providing guidance. Those individuals whose capabilities are sufficient to gain access to employment on their own initiative or with the help of one-off support, do not come under the "guidance" level, but are instead offered various services or one-off support from the new range of ANPE services.

The ANPE offers guidance within the framework of the "New Start" defined by the European Commission, in application of the decisions taken at the Luxembourg Summit,[1] for the following target groups:

• Young people aged under 26 and entering their sixth month of unemployment.
• Adults entering their twelfth month of unemployment.
• Jobseekers registered for more than 24 months.
• Unemployed young people and recipients of minimum social benefit (*Revenu Minimum d'Insertion* – RMI) registered as unemployed for more than 12 months.

The ANPE commits that the guidance will last three months (where appropriate, extended further for three months), that jobseekers will be assigned a single adviser offering guidance throughout the guidance period, and that jobseekers will benefit from three advisory interviews and individual or collective services in agreement with the adviser. At the end of the guidance period, a report is drawn up jointly by the client and the adviser. The client commits to actively look for work, to take part in defined projects, to perform the activities agreed with the adviser and to attend the recruitment interviews and various meetings that they agree upon.

Guidance for jobseekers can be performed by three different institutions: the local employment office, a partner of the local employment office to which the ANPE has delegated guidance responsibilities, or a service organization working at the behest of the employment office.

Forms of guidance

The ANPE offers two forms of guidance: a) direct access to employment and b) the "employment project" or guidance in employment. The aims of these are successful job-search and defining an employment access project respectively.

1. Direct access to employment

This form of guidance is offered particularly to those lacking an appropriate job-search methodology, perseverance or the ability to present their skills in the right light. It is also offered to those who are penalized by the selectivity of the labour market (people over 50, young people lacking recognized qualifications or those lacking the contacts necessary for making a successful job-search). The institution offering guidance is committed to the following:

- help the clients to define actions to be taken;
- organize the process of learning job-search methods;
- organize, where appropriate, activities to define career targets;
- suggest job offers, work experience and contacts with employers;
- perform follow-up observation of contacts between employers and participants; and
- intervene in favour of clients with employers recruiting labour.

The results are measured against four criteria.

- The proportion of participants that have found at least one job and their statistical distribution in terms of the duration of employment (whether they are recruited under a permanent contract or a fixed-term contract of six months or longer, or are at work 78 or more hours per month).
- The proportion of participants who have had at least one job interview, even if they have not gained access to employment.
- The drop-out rate in the course of the process.
- The situation of those jobseekers not placed by the end of the guidance period three months after the end of the measure.

In those cases where the aim is to define an individual employment project, the elaboration of a career project will be offered to people wishing or obliged to change profession and to those (particularly young people) lacking a professional orientation who consequently cannot (or can no longer) decide the forms of employment towards which they should orient their search activities. Evidence of a successful project is accepted by a job interview for work that corresponds to the project, participation in a training measure or participation in a measure to assist business start-ups.

The institution offering guidance commits first, to assist the participant in defining the various stages of his or her project and second, to offer the participant evaluation and validation activities appropriate to his or her needs. The latter has a dual purpose: to help overcome the difficulties arising out of implementing the various phases of the project and to analyse the project together with the participant with a view to the labour market situation.

2. Guidance in employment

Three different forms of guidance in employment can be offered. Firstly, there is the "individual follow-up". In this system a commitment to monitor the client after recruitment, either inside or outside the enterprise can be entered into from the start of the guidance process. Whether or not this is done depends on the conditions agreed with the enterprise offering employment. The adviser enters into such a commitment in the name of the organization responsible for providing guidance. The adviser holds at least one interview per month with the client and contacts him or her (usually by telephone) at least every two weeks. The conclusions drawn from each interview and the actions to be taken before the next meeting are noted. The adviser also conducts a concluding interview. Results are assessed in terms of the project definition either at the completion of the first phase or on termination.

The second form guidance can take is participation in a job-search circle which is chaired by the adviser. The adviser conducts three individual interviews with each jobseeker and is responsible for the collective functioning of the circle. At the first meeting, the commitments mentioned above are formally entered into.

The third form guidance can take is participation in a mutual-aid club with the support of an adviser. In this situation, the adviser holds at least three interviews. In addition to the existing clubs for young graduates, additional jobseeker clubs are set up (in accordance with the action plan agreed at the Luxembourg Summit) for those participating in New Start. These clubs can be open to all jobseekers or can be restricted to young people or to managers. At the end of the guidance period, an interview is held in which, irrespective of the outcome, a record is made of the progress achieved by the client. The measure can be terminated at any time once the goal has been achieved. Achievement can entail any of the following: placement; placement with follow-up guidance at the workplace; or the conclusion of the first phase of a precisely defined employment project.

If the client fails to honour commitments at any stage, guidance can be terminated before the normal termination date. This is only done after the client has received notice of imminent termination. In the course of the guidance process, the two parties (three if an external service provider was involved) may agree to end the measure, even if the goal has not been attained. Normally this occurs in cases where the client has achieved an adequate degree of independence.

Source: European Employment Observatory Mutual Information System on Employment Policies (MISEP): *Policies, No. 63* (Berlin, European Commission, Autumn 1998).

Annex IV.19 United Kingdom: The New Deal

Starting year: 1997

Context

Rapid economic change and a serious recession in the early 1990s left large numbers of people, including many young people, unemployed for long periods and left them lacking the skills and qualities being sought by employers. Moreover, unemployment was being linked to family poverty. One in five of families with adults of working age had none of these in work.

Objectives

The New Deal is a welfare-to-work strategy designed to help people to move from unemployment into work. While it was in opposition, the Labour Party planned to secure substantial funds through "windfall" taxes on privatized utilities in order to pay for major New Deal programmes. These programmes were sometimes also called "welfare-to-work" programmes, the assumption being that the best route out of poverty and benefit dependency is through paid work.

Approach

When the Blair Government came to power in May 1997, David Blunkett, the Secretary of State for Education and Employment, immediately started to implement the New Deal programmes. The PES was given the central role of running the initiatives but unlike in the past, was expected to work closely with other bodies, particularly local ones, to ensure that the help offered matched the needs of local unemployed people and employers. This has led to a range of contractual relationships and in some areas to the private sector taking the lead in delivery. Despite this, the PES continues to play a major role in delivery.

The first initiative aimed to help those aged 18–24 who had been claiming jobseeker's allowance (unemployment benefit) for six months. Through this initiative, young people enter a "Gateway" period of up to 4 months in which they are helped either to find or prepare for a job, with the option of additional help and training. Each young person has a personal adviser, generally from the PES, who is his or her contact throughout the duration of the programme. If they are unable to find a job during the Gateway period, then the person is expected to take up one of the following options: subsidized employment with an employer; full-time education and training; work with the voluntary sector; or work with an "Environment Task Force".

Those interested in self-employment can pursue this through the "employment option". Training of at least one day a week is offered on each of the options. At the end of the option, individuals move into the "follow-through period" if they have not found permanent work. Here they receive additional support from their personal adviser. The programme is compulsory in the sense that young people do not have the option of remaining on benefit.

The programme was piloted in January 1998 in ten "pathfinder" areas. It became national in April 1998 and by November 1999, 391,500 young people had entered the programme. Over 58,000 employers (including 360 national employers) had signed up to support the programme. By November 1999, more than 178,980 young people had found jobs through the programme (157,640 in subsidized jobs and 21,340 in unsubsidized jobs); 63,200 had entered full-time education and training; 25,400 had started on the voluntary sector option; and 24,300 were in the Environment Task Force.

There are also New Deal programmes for the partners of the unemployed, lone parents and people with disabilities. In addition, there is a scheme for people aged 25 and over. This was initially intended for those who had been unemployed for 2 years or more but also included 28 pilot schemes for those who had been either 12 months or 18 months or more unemployed. Between June 1998 and November 1999, 32,850 of these individuals had started in jobs (25,990 subsidized, the remainder unsubsidized).

Outcomes

The cost of these programmes over the lifetime of the Parliament is estimated to be £3.365 billion. The United Kingdom Government has consistently said that its estimates of expenditure on individual welfare-to-work programmes will be amended from time to time in light of labour market developments and changing priorities. Employability is one of the main aims of all these programmes and evaluation is being undertaken to establish what has been achieved for people in this way. Work is already being undertaken on the first stage of the evaluation which is looking at those aged 18–24 who have been through the New Deal but it is not expected that a report will be available until late in 2000. In particular, the PES is keen to assess how many of the people who have taken advantage of the help on offer find a job and are able to sustain this employment by either being in employment for at least 13 weeks or not returning to benefit.

Source: ILO: *The public employment service in the United Kingdom* (Geneva, ILO, 1998; mimeographed). Additional information, March 2000.

Annex IV.20 United States: The Welfare Reform – Temporary Assistance for Needy Families (TANF) programme

Starting year: 1996

Objectives

The Aid to Families with Dependent Children (AFDC) programme introduced in 1935 was a cash-based assistance programme targeted mainly at single parents. It was based on the notion that single mothers whose husbands had died or were subject to disabilities should be allowed to stay at home and care for their children. However, working patterns have changed considerably since 1935 when welfare legislation was first passed. In addition, rising AFDC caseloads, large increases in public assistance outlays and a concern about work disincentives within the AFDC prompted a re-examination of the role of income support.

The Welfare Reform lays a strong emphasis on work and is based on the following four principles:

- It should provide short-term support and help people move into paid work.
- Parents should have individual action plans.
- Parents should receive child care and health care support to ease the transition.
- Programme administrators should focus more on outcomes and less on payment accuracy and programme procedures.

Approach

In August 1996, the Personal Responsibility and Work Opportunity Reconciliation Act created the Temporary Assistance for Needy Families (TANF) programme which replaced three federal/state match-grant programmes: AFDC; Job Opportunities and Basic Skills (JOBS); and Emergency Assistance (ES). Based on a "work-first" philosophy, programme activities are concentrated on job-search assistance. Under TANF, federal cash assistance is limited to 60 months over a lifetime and able-bodied adults are required to work or participate in an approved activity after a maximum of two years of benefit assistance. In addition, there is no entitlement to cash assistance but states have considerable flexibility to design their own welfare programmes (subject to some federal participation requirements) and to implement policies and provisions that promote self-sufficiency and personal responsibility. Accordingly, TANF has shifted a large element of the social safety net away from federal government towards state control. The federal government sets a number of requirements as part of the grant and states which do not meet the requirements can be penalized. Alternatively, they may be rewarded if they meet or surpass them.

Given the decentralized nature of the programme, states have taken different programme implementation approaches. Examples of state initiatives include:

- engaging communities and private sector to help meet the challenges of making the transition from welfare to work; this means finding ways not only to help welfare recipients find jobs, but also to help them keep jobs;
- care and transportation;
- promoting personal responsibility plans or contracts and community involvement;
- providing employer incentives; and
- shifting resources to prevention activities and support for working families.

The role of the PES was not specified in the legislation so it has tended to assume different roles in different states. In general, the PES role built on the following institutional strengths:

- an infrastructure of 1,800 local offices under the control of states, with formal agreements to provide services to welfare recipients in approximately 35 states;
- availability of extensive labour market information;
- strong partnership with the Job Training Partnership Act (JTPA) system;
- employer involvement through job service employer committees;
- experience in using profiling to prioritize jobseekers for services;
- a three-tiered service delivery system of a) self-help, b) basic intervention and c) more intensive service for those not "job-ready".

On the other hand, the new legislation has presented the following challenges for the PES:

- an increased demand for services;
- the need to provide universal services while meeting the needs of hard-to-serve clients;
- the need to expand employer outreach;
- the need to integrate many automated information systems;
- the need to develop capacity to administer work opportunities tax credit; and
- the need to re-orient staff attitudes about programme objectives.

Assessment

Initial results for the TANF programme were reported in the *First Annual Report to Congress* in 1998. While the results from the programme cannot readily be separated from the impact of a strong economy, the results are nonetheless impressive:

- Employment among the parents at risk of welfare recipiency is increasing dramatically. Between 1992 and 1996, the proportion of previous year AFDC recipients who were employed by the following March increased from 19 percent to 25 per cent. In 1997, this had jumped dramatically to almost 32 per cent.
- The proportion of low-income, single mothers caring for children under 18 who were employed has increased significantly. Employment among this population has increased from 44 per cent in 1992 to 54 percent in 1997.
- The proportion of people working in the period following welfare receipt is higher than in the past. Approximately 50 to 60 per cent of individuals leaving the welfare rolls are working in the period following welfare receipt, comparable to or slightly higher than the 45 to 50 per cent previously.
- Welfare caseloads have dramatically declined. Between August 1996 and March 1998, there was a 27 per cent decrease in the number of families and recipients on the rolls. The percentage of the United States population receiving assistance in March 1998 is the lowest since 1969.
- Evaluations of specific state programmes suggest that increased employment of welfare recipients is a result of the implementation of welfare policy changes. The increases in employment are frequently in the range of 8 to 15 percentage points. Although the approaches being evaluated are not truly representative of the nation, they are quite typical of state TANF policies.
- Early data indicate that although states are reducing spending on welfare programmes in the aggregate, some states are actually spending more per family given the reduction in caseloads. Thirteen states spent more per family in 1997 than in 1994, in recognition of the fact that a work-based system can require up-front investments.
- Early information suggests that as case loads drop, the proportion of long-stay families on state welfare caseloads is increasing. State welfare evaluations show that while some state welfare policies have strong effects on the employment of families with strong barriers to employment, others mostly have effects on those who are the easiest to employ.

Sources: (1) OECD: *The public employment service in the United States* (Paris, OECD, 1999). (2) United States Department of Health and Human Services: *TANF: First annual report to Congress* (Washington, DC, United States Department of Health and Human Services, 1998). (3) Interstate Conference of Employment Security Agencies (ICESA) and National Governors Association: *Notes on a dialogue on the welfare-work connection* (Cleveland, ICESA, 1997). (4) http://www.nga.org/Welfare/WelfareDocs/bul-970818.htm (5) http://www.doleta.gov/

Annex IV.21 United States: Unemployment insurance administration – Telephone claims service

Starting year: 1991

Objectives

To reduce the operating costs of unemployment insurance administration and to improve services to customers while maintaining the integrity of the unemployment insurance system.

Approach

The telephone claims service for unemployment insurance claimants in the United States is one of a number of technological initiatives in the unemployment insurance system. For several years, states have been moving from weekly or biweekly filing of certifications for benefits in person or by mail to filing by telephone using interactive voice response systems. In general, the individual punches in his or her social security number and answers a series of yes/no questions using a touch-tone telephone. If an answer raises a question about whether or not the individual is eligible, he or she is instructed what to do to have the issue resolved. If no issue is raised, the cheque is automatically issued. Most cheques are mailed, but a few states offer the option of transferring funds electronically to bank accounts. This has had the dramatic effect of eliminating or drastically reducing local staff levels involved in taking unemployment insurance claims in the employment service.

Telephone claims eliminate the time and cost involved in travelling to a local office to file a claim. They also buffer management from variances in the volume of claims filing. For example, a large lay-off in one community might swamp the local office. However, when claims are handled in one or several telephone claims centres, the claims generated by one community can be handled by state-wide staff. Translation services for non-English speakers can also be provided more readily in a telephone claims system. Some states have also linked interactive voice-response claims systems to their Job Bank systems. As a result, when unemployment insurance claimants call to file claim certifications, they may be told by the voice-response system to call or visit an employment service representative for a referral to a job opening.

Assessment

Telephone claims in Colorado, the first state in the United States to pilot this system, have reduced the time it previously took to file a claim (two to four hours) to the current figure of eleven minutes. Customer service research shows a high level of satisfaction by unemployed workers who have filed by telephone. Ninety-two per cent of customers were generally satisfied with the service, and 91 per cent rated the service better than what they receive from other government agencies.

Source: ILO: *The United States public employment service country study* (Geneva, ILO, 1998; mimeographed).

Annex IV.22 France: *Espaces Cadres* – Placement centres for managerial and technical staff

Starting year: 1995

Problem

For many years, the French employment service (ANPE) had neglected managerial and technical staff as a target group and employers seeking such personnel were obliged to resort to the services of specialized private recruitment agencies. In 1995, the ANPE took action to address this issue. This was important in view of the rapid and pronounced increase in the number of unemployed managerial and technical staff: by the end of 1994 the number of these had reached 191,691 – a rise of 84 per cent in 4 years.

Objectives

The objective of the programme is to provide, in cooperation with partner organizations, a specialized placement service for managerial and technical staff in a dedicated location.

Approach

Basic PES services are to be provided by the general employment offices, whereas the *Espaces Cadres* are to offer supplementary services only. The *Espaces Cadres* are to contain four different rooms (spaces) and each is meant to fulfil a different task:

- A room staffed by 3 advisers in which jobseekers are to be provided with immediate access to all services: access to employment and training offers, to general information on job-search, short interviews and so forth.
- An office in which jobseekers can be received in a personal way.
- A room for technical processing.
- A fourth room serves as a conference room in which informative group presentations, meetings, recruitment interviews and so forth can be held. This room also offers a suitable framework in which to welcome visiting partners.

In conjunction with the general employment offices, the centres are to establish contacts with employers with a view to the recruitment of management and technical staff by means of special action plans. In this regard, the ANPE is to intervene in four main areas: first, firms that are not yet clients of the ANPE are to be convinced of the quality and benefits of the service offered; second, the confidence of firms that are already clients in the ANPE is to be maintained; third, firms that are already clients with regard to low-skill job offers are to be convinced of the benefits of registering their job offers for managerial and technical staff; fourth, the ANPE is to promote job-creation (in permanent and fixed-term contracts, including part-time and job-sharing employment opportunities) in small and medium-sized firms.

The centres are to provide the following services for managerial and technical staff and also for young graduates

- services oriented specifically to the needs of these jobseekers' including jobseeker clubs and the skill profile cheque book;
- comprehensive labour market information on the regional, national and European demand for these positions;
- a job-search circle;
- the specialized daily and weekly press;
- offers of vocational training;
- ANPE job offers relevant to this category (Minitel, notices, specialized information);
- company files and dossiers;
- information on services provided by the association for the employment of managerial staff, engineers and technicians (APES), a partner organization of the ANPE;
- interviews providing diagnosis, counselling and job-search assistance; and
- meetings with firms, the ANPE partner organizations and employed and unemployed jobseekers and so forth.

The ANPE relies on partner organizations to assist it in pushing ahead with its measures and to help it fulfil its role as the focal point of the efforts being made to support unemployed executives and potential employers. These partners include: the various professional associations for management and technical staff; the national association of executives in enterprises (ANCE); the association of former pupils of the *grandes écoles* (elite universities); the job placement services of the *grandes écoles* and other universities; and the vocational training association and the *Association pour L'Emploi des Cadres* (APEC). The aim of these partnerships is to contribute to a mutual enrichment of the actions of all sides and to promote readily comprehensible and coordinated services. The ANPE informs its users about the services being implemented by its partners and provides services in cooperation with them. It offers them the opportunity to work on its premises and to serve their clients with the instruments and know-how of the Agency.

Source: European Employment Observatory Mutual Information System on Employment Policies (MISEP): *Policies, No. 50* (Berlin, European Commission, Summer 1995).

Annex IV.23 Hong Kong, China: The Employment Information and Promotion Programme (EIPP)

Starting year: 1998

Objectives

To enhance employment services to employers in order to achieve better placement results in the middle of an economic setback.

Description of the programme

Traditionally, employers notified the local employment service (LES) of job vacancies on their own initiative. At a time when the number of vacancies available in the labour market was actually decreasing, it was no longer viable for the employment service to rely on employers supplying vacancies on their own. There was a need for the PES to put in place more proactive measures so that there would be more systematic canvassing of vacancies through networking with major employers, employers' associations, industry and trades. To achieve this, the Labour Department launched an Employment Information and Promotion Programme (EIPP). This programme combines an employer-centred approach in service delivery with a new marketing strategy. The aims of the programme are as follows:

* canvass more vacancies for jobseekers registering with the LES;
* maintain close business ties with employer associations and major employers;
* deliver proactive and premier customer service to employers lodging vacancies with the LES with a view to addressing their manpower needs in the longer run;
* provide accurate market information and professional advice to both employers and jobseekers making use of the service of the LES;
* provide detailed and immediate analysis of the characteristics of jobseekers and vacancies in the job market;
* develop new strategies in the provision of employment services on the basis of job market analysis; and

- maintain a close working relationship with the Employees' Retraining Board, in particular to enhance the flow of vacancy information with a view to achieving the ultimate objective of improving the utilization of manpower resources through retraining and skill upgrading.

The EIPP also oversees the promotional work for the entire PES. It is responsible for the following:

- Centralized vacancy canvassing and matching of job applicants for major employers. The team canvasses vacancies from major employers with branches across the territory and carries out centralized matching. If suitable job applicants are identified, the team coordinates the referral of applicants of different branch offices with the employers concerned.
- Retraining-linked placement service. If no suitable job applicant is identified for major employers, the team goes back to the employers concerned with a proposal about the possibility of organizing tailor-made courses, or invites them to participate in an on-the-job training programme.
- Industry-based labour market information. This programme is building up an information bank on the manpower needs of various industry sectors, in particular the manpower requirement trends. The team launching the programme provides the information to map out long-term retraining programmes for local workers. It also launches special campaigns and recruitment drives to source potential jobseekers to meet manpower needs.
- Collection of feedback on service requirements. The team collects views from employers and jobseekers on service requirements and performance satisfaction levels. These allow the various divisions rendering employment services to review their work flow and to formulate business re-engineering plans to provide clients with quality employment services.

The full computerization of the LES is a major step forward enabling the employment service to capture more swiftly and accurately details of vacancies and jobseekers available in the job market. However, to make this data really useful in understanding the prevailing market situation, there is a need for a more detailed analysis of the characteristics of these vacancies and also of the profiles of jobseekers. The result of the analysis should shed light on areas where employment services should be targeted and placement activities can then be focused more on industries and occupations where vacancies exist. Where there is massive retrenchment, special efforts can be made through the contact networks to canvass vacancies from employers of specific trades in order to provide timely employment placement for retrenched workers.

Assessment

In June 1998, in the midst of a rapidly rising unemployment rate, this new programme was announced by the Financial Secretary of Hong Kong, China as one of the four new initiatives to help improve the PES. The EIPP was launched by a team comprising fourteen staff, nine of whom were new. As it is a relatively new programme, its effects will have to be evaluated at a later stage. In mid-1999, however, focus group discussions were introduced to improve communications with major end users of the PES and to seek their advice on the future development of the PES. The results have been encouraging for the PES.

Source: ILO: *The public employment service in Hong Kong, China* (Geneva, ILO, 1998; mimeographed).

Annex IV.24 Sweden: The Idea Bank

Starting year: late 1990s

Objectives

To pool hints, good ideas and working methods within the Swedish national labour market administration (AMS) in order to improve services vis-à-vis customers and to make the results universally available.

Approach

The task of the Idea Bank is to canvass and disseminate information on the work the AMS has already carried out in developing and improving working methods and services to customers. It is based on individual members entering the ideas and project methods which they wish to communicate to colleagues within the AMS. In this way the good work done by a working group can be made available in the Idea Bank. The same goes for the various activities in which the AMS is involved, but for which it does not have primary responsibility. Through the Idea Bank, hints and ideas can be retrieved concerning actions taken by others in similar situations. The search for hints and ideas is guided by the following questions:

*   Whom do I want to help? (i.e. which target group)
*   What can I do? (i.e. in which policy programme)
*   Whom can I collaborate with? (i.e. with which partner)

Hints and ideas can be retrieved by means of fixed search words such as "target group", "policy programme", "field", "partner", "ID", "date", "locality" or "county" or they can be retrieved by free-text searches.

Assessment

As of May 1999, the database of the Idea Bank contained roughly 1,100 descriptions. The aim is for it to contain thousands of descriptions of methods, ideas and projects.

Source: Swedish National Labour Market Administration (AMS): *The Idea Bank: A best practices database of the Swedish national labour market administration,* Report produced by AMS International Secretariat, ISEKen, 1999:6 @ www2.ams.se/ams/rapport_eng/index.html.

Annex IV.25 Canada: The PES comprehensive staff development commitment

Starting year: early 1990s

Objectives:

In the early 1990s, the Canadian PES started to experience the combined effects of staff reductions and increasing workloads. One way of coping with this was to increase the levels of new and emerging technologies. Staff faced a steep learning curve with the introduction of these changes. The organization decided to assist staff in meeting the many challenges facing the PES.

Approach

Canada quickly concluded that the PES must become a "learning organization" led by its executive level managers. The desire was to create and practise the principles of empowering employees at all levels of the organization. Several quality training initiatives were designed to encourage a move away from a command and control environment towards an organization where staff are free to contribute fully while accepting responsibility for client service results. Communications processes and the need for dialogue were central themes of the training as they sought to instil the notion of empowerment and accountability throughout the PES. It is important to note that Canada's process of training focused on two features: leadership training to impress upon managers the commitment to the new culture; a train-the-trainer (peers training co-workers) process which would greatly expedite the training across a vast geographic region spanning six time zones.

Canada has taken staff training and development a step further and initiated a competency-based training programme for employment counsellors. Competency-based training defines the specific knowledge and skills to be acquired through training, provides extensive practice in acquiring and demonstrating these skills, and provides feedback to both trainers and trainees about how well the skills have been demonstrated. Competency-based training on the Canadian model is centred on training the individual to meet measurable and observable learning objectives, with opportunities to practise what has been learned either on the job or through simulated exercises. The trainee must achieve a pre-established standard. Ninety per cent of trainees master the course work.

The Canadian PES intends to continue these ground-breaking training efforts by using technology, especially by making the training available on the Internet. This will enable field staff to access tools and will provide a series of tests both for refresher training and for training new recruits.

Source: ILO: *The public employment service in Canada* (Geneva, ILO, 1998; mimeographed).

Annex IV.26 Relations with PREAs: Some examples of innovation

A. Belgium. Cooperation between the *Office Communautaire et Régional de la Formation Professionnelle et de l'Emploi* (FOREM) and temporary work businesses (TWBs)

A public temporary work agency (called T–Service Intérim) was created in 1980 in order to introduce a regulatory element in the market. It became self-supporting within (FOREM) in 1994.

The agency cooperates with TWBs in the following ways:

- Job offers.
- Access to information, for example "job banks".
- Participation in the *Espaces Resources-Emploi*. This is an information forum and a common working forum for all partners in the labour market with a view to promoting labour market transparency.
- Pricing.
- Projects on integration through temporary work, in which the *Antennes d'Insertion par le Travail Intérimaire* (AITI) of FOREM collaborate with public and private TWBs to place school drop-outs (under 25), long-term unemployed and people whose sole source of income is the *Minimex* (social benefits) in temporary work. Common criteria for candidates to be placed in temporary work are defined between the AITI and the TWB before missions are entrusted to the TWB. This enhances the candidate profile from the point of view of enterprises and ensures a return of information to the AITI.

Source: J. P. Méan: *Relations entre service public d'emploi et agences d'emploi privées: Analyse de la situation et perspectives pour la région Wallonne et éléments-clés d'une stratégie pour les SPE dans le marché mixte européen,* Unpublished Paper submitted at the European Union meeting of Heads of Public Employment Services, Baden (Austria), 16 November, 1998.

B. France. Partnership agreement between the ANPE and two employer organizations covering temporary employment agencies

Objectives

- To improve the services rendered to firms.
- To increase the flexibility of the labour market, and prevent long-term unemployment by improving jobseeker chances of labour market integration.
- To collaborate on the basis of mutual respect for the specific characteristics of each organization.

Expected service exchanges

In general, the temporary employment agencies belonging to the *Syndicat des Professionnels du Travail Temporaire* (PROMATT) and the *Union Nationale des Enterprises de Travail Temporaire* (UNETT) are to intensify their collaboration with the public employment service. In particular they are to disseminate, with the help of local employment offices, their job offers more widely by making them available to all the users of the agency. In turn, they benefit from ANPE services that assist them in the search for and preselection of applicants. The temporary employment agencies and the local employment offices are also to exchange information pertaining to the regular labour market, the temporary employment market and employment measures, so as to tailor their respective services better to the needs of job-seekers. In particular, they are to make use of the opportunities offered by temporary employment to facilitate the process of integration or re-integration of specific groups such as young people, the long-term unemployed and people with disabilities.

On the basis of this agreement, the ANPE wishes to achieve three goals: first, to develop an active partnership at the local level with the temporary employment agencies; second, to increase the range of labour market solutions offered to jobseekers by making available to them job offers passed on by the temporary employment agencies; and third, to widen the range of re-integration opportunities offered to jobseekers.

Expected outcome

Additional employment opportunities can be offered, as in future it will be possible for jobseekers to view both the job offers provided by the ANPE and the offers provided by the temporary employment agencies in one and the same place.

Implementation arrangements

PROMATT and UNETT are to inform their members of this agreement and members are to be urged to make their job offers available to the relevant local employment office on the basis of location or occupational sector. At the local level, the ANPE commits itself to offering a personalized and privileged service to temporary employment agencies belonging to PROMATT and UNETT. This is to be based on cooperation between the directors of the local employment offices and the directors of the branches of the temporary employment agencies. Specifically, this service will mean that the local employment office will disseminate and process temporary job offers. Job offers will be made available by the ANPE in one of two ways:

- Displayed and made known to jobseekers, who may then present themselves to the agency. These publicly displayed offers will give the name and address of the temporary employment agency in question. They will be clearly identifiable as temporary job offers and will contain job descriptions and requirements so as to help jobseekers determine which offers apply to them.
- Processed in such a way that the local employment office can present suitable candidates to the agency.

Source: European Employment Observatory Mutual Information System on Employment Policies (MISEP): *Policies, No. 51* (Berlin, European Commission, Autumn 1995).

C. United Kingdom. Partnership between the PES and temporary work agencies under the New Deal

Background information on relations between the PES and PREAs

Before 1994, the PES and PREAs exchanged information about their services but vacancies were not generally exchanged. After 1994, the PES entered into a new agreement with the Federation of PREAs and agreed to display vacancies where a contract existed between agency/business and client.

Partnership under the New Deal

The Government asked the private sector to lead the New Deal delivery in 10 out of 140 areas of the country for young people, and in 10 out of 28 pilot areas for older people. The Government also decided that it wanted to see private sector employers, including PREAs, involved in all New Deal delivery partnerships.

Achievements in 1998

- When the PREA, Reed, won the bid to deliver the New Deal programme to 18–24-year-olds in Hackney and City districts, the PES established joint working groups with them and PES and Reed advisers worked closely to place clients in employment.

- When the PREA, Manpower, won the bid to deliver the New Deal programme to 18–24-year-olds in the Bridgend and Glamorgan Valleys, they established a joint management team with the PES and Manpower's stated aim was to add value to the efforts of the PES.

Source: United Kingdom Employment Service: *Relationships between public employment services and private employment agencies in the United Kingdom*, Unpublished Paper presented at the European Union Meeting of Heads of Public Employment Services, Baden (Austria), 16 November, 1998.

Note

[1] These guidelines can be found in the European Commission: *Employment policies in the EU and in member States: Joint report* (Luxembourg, Office for the Official Publications of the European Communities, 1998).

INVOLVEMENT OF THE PES IN TRAINING AND EDUCATION PROGRAMMES: SOME EXAMPLES

Introduction

Chapter 6 described training and education programmes as one the major instruments of labour market adjustment in developed countries, but pointed out that these programmes were not necessarily seen as one of the core functions of the PES. This annex sets out examples of the kinds of programmes that have been introduced in recent years and discusses the extent to which the PES has been involved in their funding and administration.

Different types of training and education programmes

The long-standing distinction between training and education is less relevant in the modern world. On the one hand, good literacy and numeracy-based education may be vital to employability. In this connection, it is interesting to note that in the New Deal scheme for unemployed young people in the United Kingdom, education programmes that have included basic literacy and numeracy courses have proved to be one of the most popular options. On the other hand, many learning programmes that focus on languages and information technology can be seen either as training or as education.

It is often difficult to define precisely the boundary between training and retraining programmes as part of labour market policy on the one hand and a country's broader universal education and training system on the other. Indeed, in certain countries such as the United Kingdom and Canada, this problem has been tackled by establishing a government department whose remit combines education, training and employment. In particular, the dividing line between vocational training for adults and active training measures targeted specifically at the adult unemployed is blurred. In fact, the most common role for the PES in the area of training and retraining is in the selection of people to be trained and in the selection of appropriate training courses. This is logically connected to the job-search assistance activities of the PES.

One way to define the boundaries is to distinguish between training for unemployed workers and training for employed adults as suggested by the OECD.[1] The PES often has the responsibility for organizing training for unemployed workers. In countries such as Belgium, Italy, Greece, Ireland, Poland, Spain, Sweden and Switzerland, however, the PES also participates in the training for currently employed workers by granting subsidies to firms that provide training for their own workers and/or jobseekers they hire.[2] In Spain for example, the training of the currently employed and the unemployed is run as a part of the same national vocational training plan, but each is treated differently. Training of employees is managed on a tripartite basis by employers, trade unions and the central government, while training of the unemployed is the responsibility of the Spanish public employment service. However, the Spanish public employment service also funds some training of current employees. The Polish PES also funds some training for both the currently employed and for the unemployed. In addition, a number of countries offer services to workers who are dislocated or laid off as a result of plant closures or mass lay-offs.[3] In these programmes, services including retraining may be provided while the worker that is about to be laid off is still in employment.

It is notable that even though some countries such as Greece, Ireland, Portugal and Spain still allocate considerable resources to training for the employed, many OECD countries have phased out this type of assistance on the grounds that subsidies do little to encourage firms to increase the volume of training, but lead instead to an increase in its reporting, with high "deadweight".[4]

Training for the unemployed and long-term unemployed

In some countries such as Finland, rules are flexible with regard to training for unemployed workers and workers may avail of training before actual unemployment occurs. This applies only to people threatened by unemployment. In addition, no distinct procedures have been developed that make participation more or less obligatory for the long-term unemployed. In many other countries such as Canada,[5] France, Germany, Portugal, Sweden and Switzerland, training is no longer a right for the unemployed and is linked to unemployment benefits. In Sweden, training allowances are paid for participation in regular education, but the use of this option has gradually become more restrictive.

In countries such as Austria, Belgium, Germany, Greece, Ireland,[6] Portugal, Sweden and the United Kingdom, vocational training modules leading to vocational qualifications in a number of fields are offered to long-term and low-skilled unemployed people. These courses are designed to meet the needs of local industry and last between three to ten months. They can be organized for groups or individuals and usually lead to a certified qualification. Since 1994, Germany and Sweden have introduced relatively short courses with a narrower occupational focus for the long-term unemployed. They are mostly designed to suit people from different backgrounds and are flexible with regard to entry requirements, timing and content. The courses usually do not lead to nationally standardized exams or certificates. Hence their labour market value depends to a great extent on the reputation each training provider enjoys among local employers.

In Norway, jobseekers of 19 and over can receive vocational education for up to ten months. The types and lengths of courses are adjusted to labour market circumstances and short work-related courses are given priority. The PES in Norway also provides on-the-job training in public and private enterprises for the long-term unemployed. In Denmark, packages lasting 13 weeks or more (up to one year) are introduced for the long-term unemployed combining general education or training, ordinary vocational modules, and general preparation for entry or re-entry into the labour market. In France, Greece and Ireland, training schemes whereby employers provide training to the unemployed (in particular the hard-to-place) are funded and run by the PES. In Ireland, this is done through a job training scheme. The training is full-time, certified and can last from 13 to 52 weeks depending on the type offered. In Greece, under Act 2434/96, firms are under an obligation to hire one-third of the trainees following training funded by both the Greek Manpower Employment Organization (OAED) and European Social Fund (ESF). This should ensure that firms strive to enhance the employability of the trainees. In France, the "Five-Year Law" of December 1993 set up job integration and training schemes (*Stages d'Insertion et de Formation à l'Emploi,* or SIFE). These are divided into collective schemes aimed at the long-term unemployed most in need, and individual schemes aimed at the short-term unemployed designed to prevent them from getting locked into long-term unemployment.

Lifelong learning

In certain developed countries, lifelong learning of employees and citizens has been promoted and developed. Canada offers language training, academic upgrading and skills development courses under its "employability improvement" programme. In Denmark, the labour market training centres (*Arbedjdsmarkedsuddannelse,* or AMU) offer about 1,800 training modules, grouped in trade clusters, to improve the lot of the unskilled and semi-skilled in the labour market. Nowadays, it also offers some courses for further training of skilled workers. In the Netherlands too, lifelong learning of employees has become an important issue since 1996 and a national programme has been launched to enable all citizens to maintain their knowledge and skills up to date and to enhance the employability of the labour force (workers and unemployed). In Japan, ability development grants and grants for self-enlightenment are given to employers who let their workers take training for re-employment, lifelong vocational training and education.

Training for special groups

Besides the training and education programmes for unemployed and employed adults, labour market adjustment programmes also include training programmes for special groups, such as the young and people with disabilities. In view of high youth unemployment since the 1980s, there are youth programmes in many countries.[7] These may be initial vocational training programmes or industrial apprenticeship contracts or alternating training programmes that combine training and apprenticeship stages.

The role of the PES in administering these youth training and apprenticeship programmes varies from country to country. In countries such as Greece, Ireland and Portugal where the PES regulates and runs the initial vocational training and apprenticeship system for young people through its vocational training centres, it tends to overlap with the Ministry of Education, which also offers its own technical and vocational education courses as part of the regular school system. In countries such as Austria, France, Italy and Norway where the PES provides support to apprenticeship or/and alternating training contracts, its role is limited to selecting candidates for apprenticeships and broking between training applicants and employers who offer apprenticeship slots. In France, an effort is currently being made to strengthen support for young people by setting up *Espaces Jeunes* under tripartite agreements between central government, the regions and the ANPE. *Espaces Jeunes* offer a full range of services to young people which are currently provided by the ANPE, by local agencies and by the social services of local authorities. Excluded from their remit is the management of the jobseekers' register, the control of job-search and the elimination from benefit.

Funding and administering training programmes

As was shown in Annex III, developed countries allocate considerable resources to labour market training (both for the unemployed and employed adults). There are several ways of funding and administering these labour market training programmes. Public resources for training of the unemployed may be allocated either through the PES in countries such as Belgium, Poland, Portugal and Spain or through the Social Security agencies as in Argentina, the Netherlands and Switzerland. Poland and Canada have introduced training or "skills loans" as a new way of financing the training of the unemployed. This system places much greater responsibility for the choice of training on the unemployed but it also increases the workload of vocational counsellors who provide vocational testing and assistance.

In some countries, job training systems are administered separately from the PES. For instance, in Hong Kong, China, the provision of training for labour market adjustment and for skills upgrading are provided by the Employees' Retraining Board and the Vocational Training Council respectively; both of these take their leads from the

Education and Manpower Bureau. In Japan, a special body under the Ministry of Labour, called the Employment Promotion Corporation, runs skill development centres which provide retraining and upgrading courses. In France, the training market is highly fragmented with a rise in the number of private firms offering training. The public training institute, AFPA (*Association Nationale pour la Formation Professionnelle des Adultes*), which is distinct from the ANPE, is the biggest provider of low-skilled training. In the United Kingdom, the job training system is at present administered by Training and Education Councils (TEC) but the Government is now proposing, in cooperation with about 50 local Councils, a new system built around a national learning and skills council. However, the main training programme for unemployed adults (work-based learning for adults) will be transferred to the PES from 2001.[8] In the United States, private industry councils administer the bulk of training programmes for disadvantaged people.

Only in a few countries such as Belgium, Greece, Ireland and Portugal does the PES run training centres which offer the greater part of training courses directly to the unemployed and which also provide facilities for most of the programmes. In a number of developed countries such as Austria, Denmark, Finland, France, Germany, Japan, Norway, Sweden and Switzerland, the PES do not run these centres nor provide training courses themselves but arrange for them to be provided to the unemployed through local private and public organizations. PES offices usually advertise courses and provide initial screening of applicants. It is notable that Canada, in accordance with the 1996 EI Act, has phased out training purchases at the national level as this responsibility has been decentralized to the provincial or territorial level. Organized training courses are also in the process of being replaced by skill loans and grants. This system is based upon research which claims that training is more successful when a client contributes financially. In the Netherlands and Spain, the PES itself delivers training programmes through vocational training centres, but can also purchase training from external providers.

Outsourcing of training programmes

The previous paragraph makes it clear that the current trend is away from direct delivery in PES training centres towards the outsourcing of training to other public or private sector organizations. This frees the PES from the temptation to be influenced by a supplier role in determining what training should be provided. It also means that the PES relationship with training providers is indirect: financial, administrative and contractual, rather than operational. It involves preparing public tenders and purchasing training services from other public and private sector agencies. The training contractor may also provide additional counselling services and may be required to accept a negotiated responsibility for placement of a portion of the trainees in jobs.

When purchasing training courses for the unemployed, the PES applies different procedures in different countries.[9]

- In Denmark, training offer procedures have led to the development of a range of training provisions, with many local variations. In each region, the labour market council was complemented by a "Training Offer Committee" (UTB) whose function was to invite local education and training institutions to propose courses and thereafter to purchase those courses it found useful.
- In Finland, training courses and places on them are generally purchased by 13 regional PES offices, with 43 labour market training centres as principal suppliers providing about 60 per cent of the total labour market training volume in Finland. These centres were previously part of the state administration but they are being progressively switched over to a commercial basis. The purchasing procedure gives the PES considerable freedom to decide on the content of courses and to insist, in consultation with trainers, that particular unemployed workers should be accepted. Curricula can be developed and changed at short notice.
- In Austria and Germany, the PES buys most of its training needs in the market place, sometimes selecting modules or sometimes whole courses. In principle, the PES is only concerned with the planning of its training requirements and should not have any responsibility for managing the provision of training services. But in practice, these functions may be blurred because the PES effectively controls a few training centres and is expanding some of these by further investment - even though they are owned by other bodies. Moreover, the local markets for adult training are dominated by a few big providers such as employer and worker organizations, which compete little with each other because they tend to focus on different market segments.
- In Sweden, the PES annually purchases a large number of courses, most of which are specially designed for a specific target group. It purchases courses in accordance with the EU's general principles for public procurement, which require equal treatment for all providers. A nationwide network of labour market training centres (called AMU) was created in the 1960s and 1970s under the joint administration of education and PES agencies, but separated from these in the 1980s. Since 1993, the AMU group is a publicly owned company financed entirely by course fees, and is in competition with other training providers. From 1990 to 1995, the AMU share of PES sponsored training dropped from 75 per cent to 36 per cent. It still provides two-thirds of the courses in manufacturing jobs, but in most other sectors, the bulk of training is now given by specialized, private training enterprises. Thus increased competition among training providers has played a crucial role in bringing down average training costs and has been coupled with gradual improvements in the procurement skills of PES staff and their awareness of the importance of efficient procurement.

- In Switzerland, those that organize training courses (e.g. trade unions and employers' organizations, institutions created jointly by social partners, cantons and communes and other public or private institutions) may be reimbursed from the federal unemployment insurance fund for the cost of organizing training courses. At least two weeks before retraining or upgrading courses are due to begin, the organizers must submit a subsidy application to the cantonal labour office which then forwards it to a federal office of economic development and employment (OFDE) after examination.

- In Norway, the PES defines the type of courses it wants and purchases these from external institutions (public and private). Previously, the PES organized labour market training centres which gave training courses. Lately, these centres have been handed over (free of charge) to the counties, which are responsible for providing secondary education. The PES has an agreement with the counties on purchasing some courses from the centres. The outsourcing of the provision of courses gives the PES flexibility in the composition of courses and they are not constrained by the skills of trainers nor the capacity of the centres.

- In the Netherlands, the vocational training centres are organized as business units within the PES. For the time being, institutions in the Netherlands are obliged to buy their services from the PES, but from the year 2000, they can buy re-integration services, including training, from other service providers as well.

- In Poland, training programmes are purchased from other training providers through public tender and the PES has developed cooperation with training institutions. For instance, the PES has developed methodology to help training providers with the preparation of training curricula. It has also drawn up a preliminary catalogue of professions most desired in the labour market to be used as a guide by training institutions. Furthermore, it has established a ranking of training units cooperating with PES local offices.

Notes

[1] This distinction is made by the OECD in various country studies on public employment services.

[2] See the various country studies on the public employment service published by the ILO and the OECD.

[3] Mass lay-off programmes are discussed in Chapter 6.

[4] See OECD: *The public employment service in Greece, Ireland and Portugal* (Paris, OECD, 1998).

[5] In Canada this is called "unemployment insurance sponsored training to assist the unemployed".

[6] Ireland also has a general training scheme (called the Vocational Training Opportunities Scheme or VTOS) for the long-term unemployed aged over 21 which provides courses of up to two years. It is run by the Department of Education and offers courses at different levels (basic to advanced), leading to a recognized qualification.

[7] The youth training and employment programmes are not dealt with at length here as they are covered by other ILO publications, namely ILO: *Employing youth: Promoting employment-intensive growth*, Report for the Interregional Symposium on Strategies to Combat Youth Unemployment and Marginalization, 13-14 Dec. 1999 (Geneva, ILO, 1999). See also various country studies on sub-Saharan Africa, Asia and Latin America. Other publications of interest include N. O'Higgins: *Youth unemployment and employment policy: A global perspective* (Geneva, ILO, 2001);

J. Gaude: *L'insertion des jeunes et les politiques d'emploi-formation*, Employment and Training Paper No. 1 (Geneva, ILO, 1997); D. Cross: *Youth unemployment and youth labour market policies in Germany and Canada*, Employment and Training Paper No. 37 (Geneva, ILO, 1998).

[8] United Kingdom Department for Education and Employment: *Learning to succeed*, White Paper (London, Stationery Office, June 1999).

[9] See the various OECD and ILO country studies on the employment service.

ANNEX VI

LIST OF WEB SITE ADDRESSES

The following lists of web site addresses are believed to be up to date at the time of publication but they may be subject to change in the future. Most of these web sites have English sites. If they do not have English sites, the languages used in the sites are specified.

Annex VI.1

A. National public employment services

Country	Department	Web site address
Argentine	Ministerio de Trabajo Empleo y Formación de Recursos Humanos	http://www.trabajo.gov.ar/home.htm *(In Spanish)*
Australia	Job Network	http://www.jobnetwork.gov.au/
Austria	Arbeitsmarktservice Österreich *Public Employment Service Austria*	http://www.ams.or.at *(In German)*
Bahrain	Ministry of Labour and Social Affairs	http://bah-molsa.com/
Belgium	FOREM (Community and Regional Vocational Training and Employment Office)	http://www.hotjob.be/

Country	Department	Web site address
Belgium	Vlaamse Dienst voor Arbeidsbemiddeling en Beroepsopleiding (VDAB) *The Public Employment Service for Flanders*	http://www.vdab.be/ *(In Dutch)*
	Office Régional Bruxellois de l'Emploi (ORBEM/BGDA) *The Public Employment Service for Brussels*	http://www.orbem.be/ *(In Dutch & French)*
Brazil	Ministério do Trabalho e Emprego	http://www.mtb.gov.br/ *(In Portuguese)*
Canada	Human Resources Development Canada (HRDC)	http://www.hrdc-drhc.gc.ca
Denmark	Arbejdsmarkedsstyrelsen (AMS) *Labour Market Authority*	http://www.ams.dk/
	Arbejdsformidlingen (AF) *Public Employment Service*	http://www.af.dk/ *(In Danish)*
Dominican Republic	Secretaría de Estado de Trabajo	http://www.set.gov.do *(In Spanish)*
Finland	Työministeriö *Ministry of Labour*	http://www.mol.fi/
France	Agence Nationale Pour l'Emploi (ANPE)	http://www.anpe.fr *(In French)*
Germany	Bundesanstalt für Arbeit *Federal Employment Service*	http://www.arbeitsamt.de/ *(In German)*
	Bundesministerium für Arbeit und Sozialordnung (BMA) *Federal Ministry of Labour and Social Affairs*	http//www.bma.de/

Country	Department	Web site address
Greece	Greek Manpower Employment Organization	http://www.oaed.gr/
	National Labour Institute	http://www.eie.org.gr/
Hong Kong, China	Employment Services	http://www.info.gov.hk/labour/service/
Iceland	Vinnumálastofnun	http://www.vinnumalastofnun.is/ *(In Icelandic)*
Ireland	Foras Áiseanna Saothair (FÁS) *Training and Employment Authority*	http://www.fas.ie/
Italy	Ministero del Lavoro e della Previdenza Sociale *Ministry of Labour and Social Welfare*	http://www.minlavoro.it/ *(In Italian)*
Japan	Ministry of Labour	http://www.mol.go.jp/
Lithuania	Socialinës Apsaugos ir Darbo Ministerija *Ministry of Social Security and Labour*	http://www.socmin.lt/
Luxembourg	Ministère du Travail et de l'Emploi *Ministry of Labour and Employment*	http://www.mt.etat.lu/ *(Mostly in French. Some German pages also)*
	L'Administration de l'Emploi (ADEM)	http://www.etat.lu/ADEM/ (In French)
Mexico	Secretaría del Trabajo y Previsión Social	http://www.stps.gob.mx/ *(In Spanish)*
Morocco	Office de la Formation Professionnelle et de la Promotion du Travail	http://www.ofppt.org.ma/ *(In French)*
Netherlands	WERKSITE (Arbeidsvoorziening Nederland) *Dutch Employment Service*	http://werk.net

Country	Department	Web site address
New Zealand	Work and Income NZ	http://www.winz.govt.nz/
Norway	Aetat arbeidsdirektoratet *Norwegian Directorate of Labour*	http://www.aetat.no/
Panama	Ministerio de Trabajo y Bienestar Social	http://www.mitrabs.gob.pa/ *(In Spanish)*
Portugal	Ministério do Trabalho e da Solidariedade (MTS)	http://www.mts.gov.pt *(In Portuguese)*
	Instituto do Emprego e Formação Profissional (IEFP)	http://www.iefp.pt/ *(In Portuguese)*
Singapore	Employment Service Department, Ministry of Manpower	http://www.gov.sg/mom/es/es.html
Slovenia	Zavod Republike Slovenije za zaposlovanje *Employment Service of Slovenia*	http://www.ess.gov.si/
Spain	Institute Nacional de Empleo (INEM) *National Institute of Employment*	http://www.inem.es/ *(In Spanish)*
Sweden	Arbetsförmedlingen *Swedish Employment Service*	http://www.ams.se/
Switzerland	SECO *State Secretariat For Economic Affairs*	http://www.seco- admin.ch/
Thailand	Department of Employment, Ministry of Labour and Social Welfare	http://www.doe.go.th/ *(In Thai)*
United Kingdom	Employment Service (ES)	http://www.employmentservice.gov.uk/
United States	US Department of Labor Employment and Training Administration	http://www.doleta.gov/

B. International organizations

Organization	Internet address
Confédération Internationale des Entreprises de Travail Temporaire (CIETT) *International Confederation of Temporary Work Businesses*	http://www.ciett.org
European Commission, Employment and Social Affairs	http://europa.eu.int/comm/dg05/index_en.htm
European Employment Observatory	http://www.ias-berlin.de/
International Labour Office (ILO)	http://www.ilo.org/
World Association of Public Employment Services (WAPES)	http://members.aon.at/wapes/en_home.htm

Annex VI.2 Selected specialized PES web sites

Organization	Internet address

1. On PES role and mission

1999 EU National Employment Action Plans	http://europa.eu.int/comm/dg05 /empl&esf/naps99/naps_en.htm

2. On job-brokerage/labour exchange

Canada Electronic Labour Exchange	http://www.ele-spe.org
America's Job Bank	http://www.ajb.dni.us/
Swedish Job Bank *(In Swedish)*	http://platsbanken.amv.se/
Irish Electronic Bank	http://www.fas.ie/defaultv.htm

3. On labour market information

US State of Washington LMI   http://www.wa.gov/esd/lmea/
web site

US State of Minnesota LMI   http://www.des.state.mn.us/lmi/index.htm
web site

US State of Wisconsin LMI   http://www.dwd.state.wi.us/dwelmi/
web site

US State of Utah LMI   http://wi.dws.state.ut.us/
web site

US and State Occupational Projections   http://udesc.state.ut.us/BLS

Canadian National LMI   http://www.hrdc-drhc.gc.ca/common
web site   /lmi.shtml

Canadian National Directory   http://www.workinfonet.ca/cwn/english
of LMI web sites   /main.html

4. On labour market adjustment programmes

Canadian Job-Search   http://www.hdrc-drhc.gc.ce/Job Futures
/Career Information

Canadian Job-Search   http://www.worksearch.gc.ca
Resources

Canadian Human Resource   http://www.hroe.org/index.cfm?lang=e
Office for Employers

America's Career InfoNet   http://www.acinet.org/acinet/

US National Career Resource   http//www.acinet.org/acinet
Information   /resource/#occup

Irish Job Creation   http://www.fas.ie/defaultc.htm
Programmes

Irish Business Start-up   http://www.fas.ie/
Training

5. On unemployment benefits administration

Unemployment Insurance
Telephone Claims web site

http://www.dwd.state.wi.us/UIBEN/
apply.htm

6. On management and partnership innovations

US Labor Exchange
Performance Measures

http://www.wdsc.org/transition/measure/
lepmfrn.htm

US Workforce
Development Staff Skills
and Training Project

http://www.icesa.org/subject.cfm?results
_sub_is=33

Slovenian PES web site

http://www.ess.gov.si/
(Click UK flag for English version)

7. Other

Access to Labour Department
web sites for all US State
Employment Service Agencies

http://www.icesa.org/sections/links/
index.cfm

BIBLIOGRAPHY

Almén, C. *Tiers of service: The service delivery system in the Swedish public employment service*, Paper presented at the WAPES Service Delivery Workshop, Washington, DC, 1998.

—. *New technology in the Swedish public employment service: Development of customer service self-service systems on the Internet.* Unpublished Report, Solana, September 1998.

Auer, P.; Kruppe, T. "Monitoring of labour market policy in EU member states", in G. Schmid et al.: *International handbook of labour market policy and evaluation.* Cheltenham, Edward Elgar, 1996, pp. 899–923.

—; Fortuny, M. *Ageing of the labour force in OECD countries: Economic and social consequences*, ILO Employment Paper 2000/2, Geneva, ILO, 2000.

Bayliss, V. *Redefining work.* London, Royal Society of Arts, 1998.

Bentley, T.; Gurumurth, R. *Destination unknown: Engaging with the problems of marginalized youth.* London, Demos, 1999.

Beveridge, W. "Public labour exchanges in Germany", in *Economic Journal*, Vol. XIII, 1908.

Brinkmann, C. *Controlling and evaluation of employment promotion and the employment services in Germany*, Labour Market Research Topic No. 36. Nuremberg, Institute for Employment Research, 1999.

Buchholt, P. *Labour market monitoring in Denmark: Ensuring flexibility.* Copenhagen, Arbejdsmarkedsstyrelsens, 1998.

Buchinger, E. *Achieving ISO 9001 certification in a public employment service*, Labour Administration Branch Document No. 49–3, Geneva, ILO, 1997.

Churchill, R. S. *Young Statesman: Winston S. Churchill 1901–14.* London, Minerva, 1991.

Confédération Internationale des Entreprises de Travail Temporaire (CIETT). *Temporary work businesses in the countries of the European Union.* Brussels, CIETT, 1998.

Crooks, T. "The contribution of local partnerships to employment services in Ireland", in OECD: *Decentralising employment policy: New trends and challenges – The Venice Conference*. Paris, 1999, pp. 177–183.

Cross, D. *Youth unemployment and youth labour market policies in Germany and Canada*, Employment and Training Paper No. 37, Geneva, ILO, 1998.

Dar, A.; Gill, I. S. "Evaluating retraining programs in OECD countries: Lessons learned", in *The World Bank Research Observer*, Vol. 13, No. 1, 1998, pp. 79–101.

Encyclopaedia Britannica 11th Edition, 29 Vols., Cambridge, Cambridge University Press, 1911.

European Commission: *The way forward: The European employment strategy – Contributions to and outcome of the Dublin European Council, 13 and 14 December 1996*. Luxembourg, Office for the Official Publications of the European Communities, 1997.

—. *Employment policies in the EU and in member States: Joint report*. Luxembourg, Office for the Official Publications of the European Communities, 1998.

—. *Employment Rates Report 1998*: *Employment performance in the European Union*. Luxembourg, Office for the Official Publications of the European Communities, 1998.

—. *PES-PREAs relationship in a European framework*, Issue Paper submitted at the Meeting of the Heads of Public Employment Services within the EEA, Baden (Austria), 16 November, 1998.

—. *The modernisation of public employment services in Europe: Three key elements*. Luxembourg, Office for the Official Publications of the European Communities, 1999.

—. Directorate General V (DGV). *Common indicators for monitoring the employment guidelines*. Luxembourg, Office for the Official Publications of the European Communities, 1999.

—. European Employment Observatory Mutual Information System on Employment Policies (MISEP). *Policies, No. 43F*. Berlin, Autumn 1993.

—. *Policies, No. 44*. Berlin, Winter 1993.

—. *Policies, No. 50*. Berlin, Summer 1995.

—. *Policies, No. 51*. Berlin, Autumn 1995.

—. *Policies, No. 56*. Berlin, Winter 1996.

—. *Policies, No. 57*. Berlin, Spring 1997.

—. *Policies, No. 60F*. Berlin, Winter 1998.

—. *Policies, No. 61*. Berlin, Spring 1998.

—. *Policies, No. 62*. Berlin, Summer 1998.

—. *Policies, No. 63*. Berlin, Autumn 1998.

—. *Policies, No. 64*. Berlin, Winter 1998.

—. *Policies, No. 65*. Berlin, Spring 1999.

Fay, R. G. *Making the public employment service more effective through the introduction of labour market signals*, Labour Market and Social Policy Occasional Paper No. 25, Paris, OECD, 1997.

Finn, D. *Working nation: Welfare reform and the Australian job compact for the long term unemployed*. London, Unemployment Unit, 1997.

Flores-Lima, R. "A new stage of decentralisation in Mexico: Granting autonomy to the states", in OECD: *Decentralising employment policy: New trends and challenges – The Venice Conference*. Paris, OECD, 1999, pp. 67–70.

Fraser, D. *Managing the Papua New Guinean labour market for the 21st century*, SEAPAT Working Party Paper No. 2, ILO, Manila, 1998.

Fretwell, D.; Goldberg, S. *Developing effective employment services*, World Bank Discussion Paper, Washington, DC, 1994.

Garzo, L. "Local management in economies in transition: The positive experience in Hungary", in OECD: *Decentralising employment policy: New trends and challenges – The Venice Conference*. Paris, OECD, 1999, pp. 173–175.

Gaude, J. *L'insertion des jeunes et les politiques d'emploi- formation*, Employment and Training Paper No. 1, Geneva, ILO, 1997.

Glazer, J. *Use of the Internet in the work of the national employment office of Slovenia*, Paper presented at WAPES Workshop, Washington, DC, December 1998 @ http://www.icesa.org/articles/template.cfm?results_art_filename=slov.htm.

International Labour Office (ILO). *Labour market information: Present issues and tasks for the future*. Geneva, 1980.

—. *World Employment Report 1996/97: National policies in a global context*. Geneva, 1997.

—. *World Employment Report 1998/99: Employability in the global economy – How training matters*. Geneva, 1998.

—. *The public employment service in Argentina*. Geneva, 1998; mimeographed.

—. *The public employment service in Canada*. Geneva, 1998; mimeographed.

—. *Les services publics de l'emploi: Le cas de la France*. Geneva, 1998; mimeographed.

—. *The public employment service in Hong Kong, China*. Geneva, 1998; mimeographed.

—. *The public employment service in Japan*. Geneva, 1998; mimeographed.

—. *The public employment service in the Netherlands*. Geneva, 1998; mimeographed.

—. *The public employment service in Norway.* Geneva, 1998; mimeographed.

—. *The public employment service in Poland.* Geneva, 1998; mimeographed.

—. *The organization and functions of the public employment service in Spain.* Geneva, 1998; mimeographed.

—. *Les services publics de l'emploi: Tunisie.* Geneva, 1998; mimeographed.

—. *The public employment service in the United Kingdom.* Geneva, 1998; mimeographed.

—. *The public employment service in the United States.* Geneva, 1998; mimeographed.

—. *The United States public employment service country study.* Geneva, 1998; mimeographed.

—. *Additional information to the ILO country studies.* Geneva, 1999; mimeographed.

—. *Decent Work*, Report of the Director-General, International Labour Conference, 87th Session, 1999. Geneva,1999.

—. *Employing youth: Promoting employment-intensive growth*, Report for the Interregional Symposium on Strategies to Combat Youth Unemployment and Marginalization, Geneva, 13–14 December, 1999.

—. *Worker retrenchment: Prevention and re-employment measures.* Geneva, Forthcoming.

—. *Atlas* @ http://ilo.org/english/dialogue/govlab/admitra/atlas/france/.

Interstate Conference of Employment Security Agencies (ICESA) and National Governors Association. *Notes on a dialogue on the welfare-work connection,* Cleveland, ICESA, 1997.

Interview. "Information technology as an asset in competition", An interview with Göte Bernhardsson, Director-General of AMS Sweden in *Public Employment Service*, Vol. 2, 1997, p. 20.

Jensen, M. *The EFQM-model in the Danish public employment service,* Unpublished Paper presented at the European Union Quality Networking Conference, Lahti (Finland), November 1999.

Kasserly, C. *Employment counselling, career guidance and occupational information provided through a public employment service,* Labour Administration Branch Document No. 40–2, Geneva, ILO, 1994.

Keskinen, A.; Millonen, I. *Staff development challenges in the Finnish labour administration,* Unpublished Paper presented at the WAPES-PES Staff Training Seminar, Greece, October 1999.

van Keulen, T. *Targeting services towards the needs of jobseekers,* Unpublished Paper presented at the WAPES Workshop, Washington, DC, 9–10 November, 1998.

de Koning, J.; et al. *Deregulation in placement services: A comparative study for eight European Union countries*. Unpublished Report, Rotterdam, 1998.

Kosonen, P. "Activation, incitations au travail et workfare dans quatre pays scandinaves", in *Travail et Emploi*, No. 79, 1999, pp. 1–15.

Lazerus, S. et al. *The public employment service in a one-stop world*, Policy Issues Monograph, Baltimore (Maryland), The Johns Hopkins University, 1998.

Leadbeater, C. *Living on thin air: The new economy*. London, Viking, 1999.

Leonello, T. "Benchmarking labour market performances and policies", in MISEP: *Policies, No. 61*. Berlin, European Commission, 1998.

Martin, J. P. *What works among active labour market policies: Evidence from OECD countries' experiences*, Labour Market and Social Policy Occasional Paper No. 35, Paris, OECD, 1998.

Méan, J. P. *Relations entre service public d'emploi et agences d'emploi privées: Analyse de la situation et perspectives pour la région Wallonne et éléments-clés d'une stratégie pour les SPE dans le marché mixte européen*, Unpublished Paper submitted at the European Union meeting of Heads of Public Employment Services, Baden (Austria), 16 November, 1998.

Mosley, H.; Degen, C. *The reorganization of labour market policy: Further training for the unemployed in the United Kingdom*, Berlin, Social Science Research Centre, 1994.

—. "Market share and market segment of employment services in the European Union: Evidence from labour force surveys", in MISEP: *Policies, No. 57*. Berlin, European Commission, Spring 1997.

—; Keller, T.; Speckesser, S. *The role of the social partners in the design and implementation of actives measures*, Employment and Training Paper No. 27. Geneva, ILO, 1998.

National Economic Research Associates (NERA). *Right to work assessment: An independent inquiry requested by the Prime Minister*. London, NERA, 1996.

Nesporova, E. et al., *Evaluation of labour market policies in transition countries*. Geneva, ILO, 2000.

Norton Grubb, W.; Ryan, P. *The roles of evaluation for vocational education and training*. Geneva, ILO, 1999.

Norway Labour Market Services. *More education? Vocational guidance*. Oslo, Directorate of Labour, 1999 and @ http://www.you.nls.no.

O'Leary, C.; Wandner, S. *Unemployment insurance in the United States: Analysis of policy issues*. Kalamazoo (Michigan), W. E. Upjohn Institute for Employment Research, 1997.

Organisation for Economic Co-operation and Development (OECD). *Manpower policy in the United Kingdom*. Paris, 1970.

—. *Employment Outlook 1991*. Paris, 1991.

—. *Jobs study: Facts, analysis, strategies*. Paris, 1994.

—. *Labour market policies in Switzerland*. Paris, 1996.

—. *Labour market policies: New challenges – Enhancing the effectiveness of active labour market policies: A streamlined public employment service,* Unclassified Paper presented at the Meeting of the Employment, Labour and Social Affairs Committee at Ministerial Level, Paris, 14–15 October, 1997.

—. *The public employment service: Belgium*. Paris, 1997.

—. *Employment Outlook 1998*. Paris, 1998.

—. *The public employment service in Greece, Ireland and Portugal*. Paris, 1998.

—. *Economic outlook survey by country*. Paris, 1998 and 1999.

—. *Local management for more effective employment policies*, Paris, 1998.

—. *Employment Outlook 1999*. Paris, 1999.

—. *Interventions in the unemployment spell managed by the public employment service*, Employment, Labour and Social Affairs (ELSA) Committee Discussion Paper, Paris, 1999.

—. *The public employment service in the United States*. Paris, 1999.

—. *Decentralising employment policy: New trends and challenges – The Venice Conference*. Paris, 1999.

—. Working Party on Employment. *Measures to assist workers displaced by structural change*. Paris, 1986.

O'Higgins, N. *Youth unemployment and employment policy: A global perspective*. Geneva, ILO, 2001.

Price, D. *Office of hope: A history of the public employment service in Great Britain, 1910–97*. London, The Policy Studies Institute, 2000.

Rama, M. "Public sector downsizing: An introduction", in *World Bank Economic Review*, Vol. 13, No. 1, 1999, pp. 1–22.

Raisanen, H. et al. *Comprehensive labour market policy reform: Presentation of good practice – Activation and individual employment service*, Peer Review Programme, 3–4 June, 1999, Helsinki, Ministry of Labour, 1999.

Reich, R. *The work of nations*. London, Simon and Schuster, 1991.

Ricca, S. *Les services de l'emploi: Leur nature, leur mandat et leurs fonctions*. Geneva, ILO, 1982.

—. "The changing role of public employment services", in *International Labour Review*, Vol. 127, No. 1, 1988, pp. 19–34.

—. *Introduction to public employment services: A workers' education manual*. Geneva, ILO, 1994.

Richter, L. *Present and potential role of employment services in developing countries.* Geneva, ILO, 1975.

—. *Upgrading labour market information in developing countries: Problems, progress and prospects.* Geneva, ILO, 1989.

Saikkonen, P. "An introduction to local partnership and institutional flexibility", in OECD: *Decentralising employment policy: New trends and challenges – The Venice Conference.* Paris, OECD, 1999, pp. 149–154.

Samorodov, A. *Ageing and labour markets for older workers,* ILO Employment and Training Paper No. 33, Geneva, ILO, 1999.

Sansier, M.; Boutonnat, D. *The relationship between public employment services and private employment agencies: Developing a cooperation framework,* Labour Administration Branch Document No. 51, Geneva, ILO, 1997.

Schmid, G. et al. *International handbook of labour market policy and evaluation.* Cheltenham (UK), Edward Elgar, 1996.

—; Reissert, B.; Bruche, G. *Unemployment insurance and active labor market policy.* Detroit, Wayne State University Press, 1992.

Schultz, G.; Klemmer, B. *Public employment services in English-speaking Africa: Proposals for reorganization.* Harare, ILO, 1998.

Siraut, M. *Comparing customer satisfaction: Case study on employers,* Unpublished Paper presented at WAPES Benchmarking Seminar, Oslo, December 1999.

Smith, A. "Local partnership in the United Kingdom: A key for effective welfare to work policies", in OECD: *Decentralising employment policy: New trends and challenges – The Venice Conference.* Paris, OECD, 1999, pp. 109–114.

Swedish Labour Market Board. *Customer internet self-service system,* Geneva, ILO, 1998; mimeographed.

—. *The Idea Bank: A best practices database of the Swedish national labour market administration,* Report produced by AMS International Secretariat, ISEKen 1999:6 @ www2.ams.se/ams/rapport_eng/index.html.

—. *The public employment service in the 21st century: A discussion process within the Swedish labour market administration,* ISEKen 1999:7 @ www2.ams.se/ams/rapport_eng/index.html.

Tejeda, F. D. *New technology and placement service,* Paper presented at WAPES workshop, Aske (Sweden), 26–27 May, 1998.

Tixier Essec, M. "Les outils de recrutement en Europe – Évolution de leurs spécifités", in *Humanisme et Entreprise,* No. 231, 1998, pp. 65–83.

Tuijnman, A. C.; Schöman, K. "Life-long learning and skill formation", in G. Schmid et al: *International handbook of labour market policy and evaluation.* Cheltenham, Edward Elgar, 1996, pp. 462–488.

United Kingdom Department for Education and Employment. *Learning to succeed.* White Paper, London, The Stationery Office, June 1999.

United Kingdom House of Commons Education and Employment Committee. *The performance and future role of the employment service.* Report and Proceedings of the Education and Employment Committee, Vol. 1, London, The Stationery Office, 1999.

—. *Active labour market policies and their delivery: Lessons from Australia.* London, The Stationery Office, 1999.

United Kingdom Employment Service. *Relationships between public employment services and private employment agencies in the United Kingdom,* Unpublished Paper presented at the European Union Meeting of Heads of Public Employment Services, Baden (Austria), 16 November, 1998.

—. *The way ahead: Towards 2000.* London, 1999.

United Nations. *Human Development Report, 10th edition.* New York, Cambridge University Press, 1999.

United States Department of Health and Human Services. TANF: *First annual report to Congress.* Washington, DC, United States Department of Health and Human Services, 1998.

United States Department of Labor. *Workforce development performance measures initiative: Menu of voluntary system measures,* Washington, DC, 1998.

—. Employment and Training Administration. *Labor exchange performance measures: Notice and requests for comments,* Washington, DC, 1998.

Vollman, J. W. "Centralised information technology and decentralised employment service: A successful combination in the United States", in OECD: *Decentralising employment policy: New trends and challenges – The Venice Conference.* Paris, OECD, 1999, pp. 95–99.

Walwei, U. *Monopoly or coexistence: An international comparison of job placement,* Labour Market Research Topic No. 5, Berlin, Institute for Employment Research, 1993.

—. *Placement as a public responsibility and as a private service,* Labour Market Research Topic No. 17, Berlin, Institute for Employment Research, 1996.

—. *Performance evaluation of public employment services,* Labour Administration Branch Document No. 47, Geneva, ILO, 1996.

—. "Improving job-matching through placement services", in G. Schmid et al.: *International handbook of labour market policy and evaluation.* Cheltenham, Edward Elgar, 1996, pp. 402–430.

—. *Job placement in Germany: Developments before and after deregulation,* Labour Market Research Topic No. 31, Berlin, Institute for Employment Research, 1998.

White, M.; et al. *The impact of public job placing programmes.* London, Policy Studies Institute, 1997.

World Bank. *World Development Report 1998/1999: Knowledge for development.* Washington, DC, Oxford University Press, 1999.

Books on employment

World Employment Report 1998–99
Employability in the global economy :
How training matters

The *World Employment Report 1998–99* reviews the global employment situation and examines how countries in different circumstances and stages of development can develop the best training strategy and flexible and responsive training systems to address these far-reaching changes. The report presents a close analysis of training systems worldwide and an examination of training strategies for increasing national competitiveness, improving the efficiency of enterprises and promoting employment growth. It critically examines policies and targeted programmes for improving women's employment opportunities and enhancing the skills and employablility of informal sector workers and members of vunerable groups (especially at-risk youth, long-term unemployed, older displaced workers and workers with disabilities). The report suggests specific policy reforms for making training more efficient and effective. Given the rapid and continuous pace of change in the demand for new skill, the report concludes that training and lifelong learning need to be given the higher priority. The best results from enhancing the education and skill levels of the workforce are achieved in an overall growth-promoting environment and when trainng decisions are taken in close consultations between government, employers and workers.

The *World Employment Report 1998–99* is the third in a series of ILO reports which offer an international perspective on current employment issues.

ISBN 92-2-110827-9

1998   271 pp., softcover
45 Sw.frs; US$34.95; £19.95

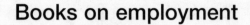

Key Indicators of the Labour Market
1999 (KILM)

This valuable, wide-ranging reference tool meets the ever-increasing demand for timely, accurate and accessible information on the rapidly changing world of work. *Key Indicators of the Labour Market* (KILM) provides the general reader, as well as the expert, with concise explanations and analysis of the data on the world`s labour markets.

Harvesting vast information from international data repositories as well as regional and national statistical sources, this important reference offers data on a broad range of countries for the years 1980 and 1990, and all available subsequent years. The volume employs an expanded, up-to-date range of 18 key labour market indicators allowing researchers to compare and contrast between countries and within regions across time. Using statistical data on the labour force, employment, unemployment, underemployment, educational attainment of the workforce, wages and compensation, productivity and labour costs, and poverty and income distribution as market indicators, the volume enables readers to access the most current information available.

In the process, KILM includes rich and varied overviews of topics such as employment to population ratios, hours of work, youth unemployment, wages in manufacturing, and labour productivity and costs. By highlighting multiple labour market indicators, this comprehensive resource sheds light on equity and other job concerns as well.

KILM is available in two formats – standard print version and CD-ROM. The CD-ROM`s interactive design allows users to customize their searches by any combination of indicator, country, year, data inputs, and more. Its easy-to-use format makes searching for relevant information quick and simple.

The CD-ROM version includes the *Key Indicators of the Labour Market, Country Profiles, 1999 Edition*, a quick reference for users.

ISBN 92-2-110834-1 CD-ROM   92-2-110833-1 book

1999   600 pp, A4, softcover
Price for either the CD-ROM or the book: Sw.fr 140, US$99.95, £59.95
Price for the set (CD-ROM + book): Sw.fr. 250, US$180, £110

Books on employment

The roles of evaluation for vocational education and training :
Plain talk on the field of dreams

W. Norton Grubb and Paul Ryan

The authors of this book work from the premise that some plain talk is needed about the subject of evaluation in vocational education and training. After providing substantive background on the conceptual issues, the book focuses on the why and how of evaluation before presenting and judging the results of available evaluations. The discussion takes in the use and abuse of available evaluation results in policy-making and the implications for evaluation of recent trends and issues in VET such as decentralization, the declining role for the State, the shift towards work-based learning and the continued concern for meeting equity concerns through vocational education and training.

ISBN 92-2-110855-4

1999   179 pages, softcover
30 Swiss francs, US$18.95, £12.95

Affirmative action in the employment of ethnic minorities and persons with disabilities

Jane Hodges-Aeberhard and Carl Raskin

Using the insights of eight national case studies, this book examines current trends in the implementation of affirmative action in employment for ethnic minorities and persons with disabilities. It analyses how legislative enactment, general policy measures and voluntary programmes have been tailored to particular national circumstances, and describes the policy implications of the successes and pitfalls of the activities highlighted in the case studies.

"The book is a useful resource for those involved with affirmative action, legislators world-wide, and all people interested in making this world a better place to live for everyone including the marginalized. The aims of the International Labour Organization should be given support and promoted."

International Third World Studies Journal and Review,
Volume 9, 1997

ISBN 92-2-109521-5

1997   120 pages
20 Swiss francs; US$ 18; £10.95